Robert Sabbag

SIMON & SCHUSTER
New York   London   Toronto
Sydney   Tokyo   Singapore

TOO TOUGH TO DIE

★ ★ ★

**Down and
Dangerous with
the U.S. Marshals**

SIMON & SCHUSTER
SIMON & SCHUSTER BUILDING
ROCKEFELLER CENTER
1230 AVENUE OF THE AMERICAS
NEW YORK, NEW YORK 10020

DESIGNED BY NINA D'AMARIO/LEVAVI & LEVAVI
MANUFACTURED IN THE UNITED STATES OF AMERICA

1 2 3 4 5 6 7 8 9 10

LIBRARY OF CONGRESS CATALOGING IN PUBLICATION DATA
SABBAG, ROBERT.
TOO TOUGH TO DIE: DOWN AND DANGEROUS WITH THE U.S. MARSHALS/
ROBERT SABBAG.
P. CM.
INCLUDES INDEX.
1. UNITED STATES. MARSHALS SERVICE—HISTORY.   2. UNITED STATES
MARSHALS—HISTORY.   3. POLICE—UNITED STATES—
HISTORY.   I. TITLE.
HV8144.M37S23   1992
91-47154
CIP
363.2'82'0973—DC20
ISBN: 0-671-66094-2

For my father and mother,
George and Evelyn Sabbag

CONTENTS

"He's a parole violator. He's considered armed and very dangerous. He's also wanted for a murder in Philadelphia. The call is going to be placed into the apartment from down there at seven o'clock. Alex, you're going to have an open phone line with Philly. You're going to be in radio contact with us. Once this fellow in Philly tells you it's on, the guy's in there, BOOM, we're going to move. . . .

"Toni, you're going to be in the backyard with Timmy and Billy. Billy's going to have the shotgun, okay? Joey, you're going to be in the front with Brian. Going through the front is going to be Dave, me, I'm going to be carrying the sledge, Mikey, Tony, Tony's going to have a shotgun, and Ted. Backing us up is going to be Joey and Brian. We're just going to roll right up on it, okay? . . .

"Raid jackets, everybody, because we don't want any confusion about who we are. Alex, when you call us and you tell us it's on, you immediately call the precinct and tell the precinct that there's a police action taking place on that block—you don't have to give them the address, because we don't want any patrol cars rolling around. You don't give the cops the address, you just call them up and say I want to talk to the desk officer, I'm a U.S. marshal, etc. . . . .

"We are going to give the guy a chance to come out. Okay? The guy's a bad guy, without a doubt, but right now, unless Dave changes his mind, we're going to try and give him an opportunity to come out. After the phone call is made and we believe he's in there, we're going to surround the place and probably call in on a cellular phone, say the place is surrounded and you have exactly thirty seconds to come out. He don't come out, BOOM, we go in. . . .

"It's a two-story brick building, attached houses, with easy access to the back. He's on the first floor, this guy. If this guy starts coming out the back, I'll tell you right now, take cover.

Take some kind of cover with this guy. Definitely. Any way you can. This is a very bad guy. And he knows he's facing a lot of time. He's supposed to be an enforcer for this black Mafia down in Philadelphia. And besides the parole time he owes, he also is facing a murder charge down there. He's supposed to have a TEC-9 machine gun. And this guy could be wearing a vest—the raid in Philly turned up machine guns, ammo, and bulletproof vests. Remember what you learned at the academy, two in the chest, one in the head. . . ."

—Briefing for a 6:00 A.M. hit,
Brooklyn, New York, August 10, 1988

★ ★ ★ ★

Born American

1.★

Authentic Life

Henry McCarty murdered his first man with a knife. He took the life of a neighbor in New York City in a Saturday-night street fight at the age of sixteen. When he was gunned down by a federal agent at the age of twenty-one, he had shot people to death under four known aliases and put some 2,000 miles between his miserable reputation and Manhattan's Lower East Side. When he shotgunned the federal officer who would be his last homicide victim, he had traveled as far as Lincoln County, New Mexico, and the alias he was going by, the name picked up by the local press and moved by wire service to newspapers back home, was Billy the Kid.

Short and slight, with brown hair, blue eyes, almost comical buckteeth, and the overall visual attributes of the stereotypical village idiot, Billy the Kid, in the years of his juvenile delinquency, was virtually ignored on the Rio Pecos, just one more borderline sociopath in a territory where they blossomed like weeds. Virtually unknown outside New Mexico and parts of the Texas Panhandle, he attained notoriety about the time he attained what may quaintly be referred to as his majority. By then, as one of a squalid and rather indolent band of cattle, horse, and mule thieves, he had begun to invite the attention of some of the nation's wealthier ranchers.

Billy the Kid's was to be a uniquely American destiny: more than one cold-blooded murder having accrued to his credit, it would be his depredations against private property, finally, that earned him the kind of attention that doomed him.

In the fall of 1880 he was being pursued, with varying degrees of enthusiasm, by lawmen of diverse jurisdictions: among others, cattle detectives in the private employ of the Canadian River Cattlemen's Association and the Panhandle Stock Association of Texas; territorial authorities in New Mexico's Lincoln and San Miguel counties; and quite probably, though not actively, the New York City Police Department.

The man who brought him to justice was the only peace officer among them whose authority was recognized across jurisdictional lines. Pat F. Garrett, the newly elected sheriff of Lincoln County, was the man carrying the federal paper on Billy; he was deputy U.S. marshal.

Garrett entered the field against the rustlers in November, and from that moment on, in more ways than one, Billy the Kid was history.

"There was snow on the ground, it was desperately cold, and Brazil's beard was full of icicles. . . . 'Get your guns, boys,' said I, 'none but the men we want are riding this time of night.' . . . We were after the gang, and would sleep on their trail until we took them in, dead or alive. . . ."

Garrett, thirty, a cowhand for six years, a buffalo hunter for two, author of the foregoing in April 1882, cut an imposing figure on several fronts: a good rider and roper and an excellent shot, he was over six feet, four inches tall. Alabama born, reared in Louisiana, striking out for Texas in 1869, he appeared in the valley of the Rio Pecos at the close of what had become known as the Lincoln County War, the violent economic and political power struggle there in which Billy the Kid, one of numerous cowhands whose guns were for hire, had been an obscure but enthusiastic participant. Campaigning on a reform ticket, backed by cattlemen John Chisum and J. C. Lea and by future governor George Curry, Garrett was elected sheriff in November 1880. Perceived as something of a flashy dresser, with a mustache of the long, drooping variety, associated at the time with Western peace officers in particular—with gunmen, in general, on both sides of the law—he was nevertheless a manifestly practical man.

When late in December, at Stinking Springs, San Miguel County, his thirteen-man posse had secretly surrounded the abandoned stone house in which Billy and four gang members had taken refuge for the night, Garrett, that he might impress upon the outlaws the merits of peaceful surrender, instructed his deputies to kill the first man out the door.

"Our victim was Charlie Bowdre."

Bowdre went down at dawn, with a feed bag in his hand and seven rifle rounds in his chest. Garrett, almost leisurely then, put a single round—Winchester .44-40—into one of the mounts that the fugitive had emerged from the building to feed:

"Just as the horse was fairly in the opening, I shot him and he fell dead, partially barricading the outlet."

It is here—with a dead horse in the doorway, a slaughtered man in the snow, and no exit from the cramped quarters but that which led, over the larger carcass of the two, into the gunsights of the posse—that Garrett's narrative achieves the zenith of the ruthlessly matter-of-fact:

"I now," he writes, "opened a conversation with the besieged."

Billy the Kid was arrested by Garrett on a U.S. warrant for the April 4, 1878, murder of Andrew "Buckshot" Roberts on the Mescalero Apache Indian Reservation (property over which the federal government still holds jurisdiction). It was a crime Billy the Kid did not commit. His March 1881 trial at Mesilla, New Mexico, was moved, on a technicality, to the territorial side of the district court, where he was acquitted. In the same session he was tried for a homicide he did commit, and for which Garrett, as sheriff, carried a second arrest warrant, the April 1, 1878, ambush of then Lincoln County sheriff William Brady. He was sentenced by District Judge Warren Bristol to be hanged May 13.

Billy the Kid arrived at what was serving as the county lockup in Lincoln with a reputation as an ungracious guest. He had been known, more than once, in the abbreviated course of his criminal career, to have obtained release from jail on a "leg warrant." Judged a serious escape risk, he was outfitted by Garrett in special-order handcuffs—they weighed fifteen pounds— ankle irons, and chains. He was guarded during the entirety of his stay by two experienced lawmen, Deputy Sheriff J. W. Bell, a former Texas Ranger, and Robert Olinger, a bloodthirsty, 240-

pound redhead who held the commission of a deputy U.S. marshal (and who probably had murdered as many men as his prisoner).

As Garrett explains it:

"On the bloody 28th of April, I was at White Oaks. I left Lincoln on the day previous to meet engagements to receive taxes. . . . I do not hold myself guiltless. . . . I realize how all inadequate my precautions were. Yet in self-defense . . . I must say that my instructions as to caution and the routine of duty were not heeded and followed."

Billy the Kid, as a guest of Lincoln County, did not stick around a week. He left town on horseback, carrying several weapons, among them the handcuffs he wore. As a kind of bread-and-butter note addressed to his host, the lad—depicted nearly unanimously by his biographers as "good humored, obliging, and generally polite" with an "engaging and guileless grin," and cited for his "agreeable and winning ways"—left behind the bodies of Garrett's two deputies. Bell, who by all accounts had been especially kind to him, he let bleed to death from the wound of a single, large-caliber revolver round. He took Olinger out with a shotgun.

Olinger had been absent when the prisoner, as he was being escorted up an interior stairway, turned on Bell with the cuffs. Where the Kid secured the weapon with which he then shot the deputy is open to debate, but Bell certainly was carrying one and Garrett's office was replete with them. It was there that he found the side-by-side that he used on Olinger—a ten-gauge Whitney, owned by the redhead himself. With Bell down, he waited, taking a position overlooking the street in a second-floor room of the county house. When Olinger returned, he casually stepped to the window and, taking aim from above, opened him up with both barrels.

What he did not do is disappear.

"For about two and a half months," Pat Garrett reports, "the Kid led a fugitive life, hovering, spite of danger, around the scenes of his past two years of lawless adventure."

Billy the Kid's possession of limited horizons, of a latent instinct for self-destruction, his lack of imagination, and finally (though he was not uneducated) his baseline stupidity, characteristics intimately shared by career criminals throughout history, are attributes undisguised in the common criminal today.

Among characteristics shared by Garrett and the modern deputy marshal is a talent for ruthlessly exploiting those deficiencies, a brutal aptitude for capitalizing on the predictability of human behavior.

Fatal to the typical fugitive, and indispensable to the fugitive hunter, is that seductive yet hallucinatory sense of well-being that springs from maintaining a proximity to home. That a wanted man, traditionally, fails to break entangling alliances is the flip side of every federal agent's favorite coin (the more conspicuous face of which is illuminated in the proposition that "pussy will get you every time").

The consensus, not only among historians but among his adversaries themselves—the lawmen, politicians, and officers of the court who, almost reluctantly, had brought him to justice— is that Billy the Kid, had he exhibited the foresight, or merely the good manners, simply to leave the territory, probably never would have been arrested in the first place.

"He had," Garrett concedes, "many friends who were true to him, harbored him, kept him supplied with territorial newspapers, and with valuable information concerning his safety."

Garrett knew more about the fugitive's whereabouts than he admitted at the time, or, for that matter, ever was to admit.

"I was constantly, but quietly, at work," is all he would say, "seeking sure information and maturing my plans of action."

What Garrett was doing, the formality of his statement notwithstanding, was getting ready flat-out to smoke the son of a bitch.

Garrett, in exploiting the manifold deficiencies of a delusional Billy the Kid, did it in classic fashion, and he did it the way federal agents routinely do it today.

He used informants.

Pat Garrett, coming off the south plains of Texas, had first ridden into New Mexico's Pecos Valley in 1878. He had first made the acquaintance of Billy the Kid in the barrooms around Fort Sumner. (That the two were friends is a dramatic device, embraced, understandably, by modern screenwriters and unsupported by the facts.) On January 14, 1880, a year before he arrested the Kid, Garrett married the town's Apolinaria Gutierrez.

Not only did Garrett have many loyal friends in the area, he had family there as well.

Billy the Kid had been a fixture in Fort Sumner before his arrest—having bunked around for about a year, staging cattle raids along the Canadian River from there, he had been captured at Stinking Springs only thirteen miles northeast—and when he continued to haunt the vicinity after his escape, he was under-estimating Pat Garrett's determination to a degree that could be expressed in logarithms.

Setting out from Roswell under cover of darkness, Garrett, with two men—Thomas K. McKinney, one of his territorial dep-uties, and John W. Poe, a cattle agent employed by the stockmen of the Canadian, who had distinguished himself as a lawman in the Texas Panhandle—started up the Rio Pecos on the night of July 10. Crossing Salt Creek, which flowed out of the Capitan Mountains, the horsemen hit range grass as high as three feet. North of Bosque Grande, where the river widened, the country grew rough, the vegetation increasingly sparse. Picketing their horses by day, sleeping on the trail in their saddle blankets, they covered a total of eighty-one miles.

"We rode mostly in the night, followed no roads . . . and ar-rived at the mouth of Tayban Arroyo, five miles south of Fort Sumner, one hour after dark on the night of July 13th."

Among Garrett's informants was a rancher named Manuel Bra-zil, who had been active in the initial arrest. He was to have rendezvoused with Garrett below Fort Sumner, where Taiban Creek emptied into the Pecos River, but failed to appear that night, presumably out of fear of reprisal.

Brazil is the only informant Garrett gives up in print. How many Garrett utilized is unknown to this day, but almost cer-tainly in complicity were three other Fort Sumner residents: Barney Mason, a local cowboy and a member of the original posse; Sabal (or Sabinal) Gutierrez, a relative of Garrett's by marriage; and Mason's employer, Pete Maxwell, a local rancher and businessman, the largest individual employer in the area, owner of many of the cattle and sheep camps at which the outlaw was known to be staying.

On the morning of the 14th, Garrett dispatched Poe, who was unknown in town, to make discreet inquiries in and around Fort Sumner. He and McKinney lay low. The three met at moonrise four miles north at La Punta de la Glorietta. From there they set out for Pete Maxwell's property, arriving shortly before midnight.

"We unsaddled . . . and, on foot, entered an orchard, which runs . . . down to a row of old buildings, some of them occupied by Mexicans, not more than sixty yards from Pete Maxwell's house. We approached these houses cautiously, and when within earshot, heard the sound of voices conversing in Spanish. We concealed ourselves quickly and listened. . . . Soon a man arose from the ground. . . ."

Later, Garrett says, he would learn that the man, who went unrecognized by him at the time, was Billy the Kid. The man was in shirt-sleeves, wearing a broad-brimmed hat, a dark vest, and pants. (If the man was Billy the Kid—if Garrett saw anyone that night—he also was wearing a beard.) Garrett says he watched the man get to his feet, go to a fence, jump it, and walk south, across the old Fort Sumner parade ground, in the direction of a long row of occupied adobe rooms that had once served as the quartermaster's storehouse.

Garrett circled west, behind a row of what formerly had been officers' quarters. One of the larger houses in the line, a long adobe with porches on three sides and separated from the parade ground by a picket fence, was occupied by the Maxwell family.

(The remains of the fort, including several square miles of land and a collection of buildings built by the U.S. government, had been abandoned by the army in the wake of the Bosque Redondo experiment, the federal effort in 1864 to "impound and civilize" several thousand Navajos and Mescaleros on a reservation established on the Rio Pecos. The property had been purchased by the late Lucien B. Maxwell after losing his vast estate on the Cimarron. His son Pete was now head of the family.)

Garrett left Poe and McKinney sitting on the south porch, and entered the young rancher's bedroom.

When Billy the Kid returned that night to the room he was sharing with Celsa Gutierrez, Sabal's wife, he removed his gunbelt, his boots, and his hat. He lay on the bed, picked up a newspaper, and asked for something to eat.

Celsa Gutierrez, offering to prepare the young outlaw some beef, if he were willing to fetch it, directed him to a yearling, freshly slaughtered, that hung from a rafter on the north porch of Pete Maxwell's house. Bootless, hatless, leaving behind his double-action Colt, he departed the room carrying a butcher knife.

He died hungry.

Approaching Maxwell's, walking parallel to the fence, he was startled by the presence of Poe and McKinney, loitering there in the shadows. Neither knew who he was. Nor could he identify them. Assuming they were Mexican, as were most of the two hundred to three hundred residents of Fort Sumner—the lawmen assumed the same of him—he spoke to the two deputies in Spanish, a language in which Billy the Kid, who could both read and write English, was fluent.

"*Quien es?*" he asked. "*Quien es?*"

Backing through Maxwell's bedroom doorway, away from the strangers, into the dark, he said, "Pete, who are those men outside?"

Garrett's second shot struck a metal washbasin. He put his first into Billy the Kid's heart.

2.★

New York State
of Mind

The invention of linoleum, credited to an Englishman named Walton, postdates Billy the Kid's nativity by approximately a year. For well over a century the tool designed to shape it has been in reliable service in the city of his birth. Cheaper than a twelve-inch cheese knife, the lethal instrument which sounded the overture to the eventual horse opera that was Billy the Kid's life (Billy, his first homicide behind him, discovered firearms never to look back, though he did die with a blade in his hand), the everyday linoleum knife, available at sundry outlets in the city of New York, recommends itself for that purpose to which edged implements today are most commonly turned in the Kid's hometown.

Armed assault.

Arcing down at the tip like the curling end of a broad mustache, the short, butt-handled tool is a masterpiece of mechanical advantage, its cutting edge on the concave side making it perfect for trimming the sheets in which linoleum is mass-produced and, alternately, eviscerating the average pedestrian.

It was at this particular intersection of technology and crime, an intersection he would cross in January 1988 in the New York borough of Queens, that a man by the name of Klein, an architect by profession, encountered the phenomenon that is Garnett Leacock.

Leacock, in the course of stealing Mr. Klein's two-door Toyota, had succeeded in securing the ignition key, readily surrendered by its helpless owner, when he decided—why not, for the hell of it—that he was going to cut off Mr. Klein's testicles. Klein, sixty-four, had already been disabled, his jacket pulled down over his shoulders, and was pleading for his life, when Leacock gave him the news.

When Mr. Klein, minus the blood he had lost, was admitted to the hospital that night, the crotch of his trousers had been cut away; his manhood was intact, but his thigh and groin muscles had been badly sliced, and it took five surgeons four and a half hours to stitch together his face.

Leacock disappeared with the car, and with the linoleum knife he had so casually used to change Mr. Klein's outlook forever.

An indiscriminate predator, with a special taste for women—his appetite for rape was gluttonous—Garnett Leacock scoured New York betraying no discernible rhythm, no semblance of reason, no rhyme. When his path crossed that of a Brooklyn woman by the name of Geraldine Doody, it was as close as Leacock would ever come in his pathological life to poetry.

"At first I thought he was just your usual guy with a long record, who'd escaped from jail and could be considered armed and dangerous, but, you know, we get that all the time," she said.

The people who get that all the time, along with Gerri Doody, are the deputy U.S. marshals in the Eastern District of New York.

Gerri Doody caught the Leacock warrant in August 1987. After circulating Leacock's picture to precinct houses in the city, she found victim after victim ID'ing him to local police out of the photo spreads. With that kind of intelligence coming in, Leacock, a federal escapee, made the Marshals Service's 15 Most Wanted list early the following March. By then he had become an obsession; his reign of terror had sparked the attention of every deputy in the district, but, as case officer, Gerri Doody—the ultimate instrument, as she perceived it, of poetic justice—had come to look at him the way Rome had eventually come to look upon Carthage.

Garnett Leacock, a native of Trinidad, British West Indies, a resident of Queens, New York, went to jail for the first time, charged with twenty-eight felonies, in 1967. He was eighteen years old. He had been out approximately a year when he was first rearrested, admitting in 1970 to 110 armed street robberies. (Ask Mr. Klein what that means.) It was a record. Not the robberies, but the year. His seven months as a federal fugitive in 1987 and 1988 was, after that, the longest Leacock ever managed to stay out of prison. By then he was pushing forty.

Over the intervening years, his access to what is commonly referred to as legitimate employment was limited.

While his job résumé bespeaks a man of undeniable industry —rape, robbery, aggravated burglary, assault, sexual abuse, and grand larceny—Leacock has long been stigmatized by the fact that his highest personal recommendation has issued from the police, his finest quality as an individual being that, to their knowledge, he has never murdered anyone.

The rape that put him in Attica in 1973, the one he was actually convicted of, though he was strongly suspected in several, was that of a Great Neck, Long Island, woman whose family he and two accomplices, one a convicted murderer, had terrorized for hours in one of a series of house-to-house break-ins that night, pistol-whipping her husband and threatening her child with death in the course of the protracted assault.

Sentenced to twenty-five years, he served thirteen, in various upstate prisons, marrying an outreach worker in a local college program during the period of his incarceration. He was paroled in August 1986. His wife, Deborah, thirteen years his junior, who had gone on to become an air force sergeant, was stationed in Rome, New York, living in government quarters, when, upon his release, Leacock moved in with her and the young son she and Leacock had conceived during a conjugal prison visit. Ninety days later Leacock was arrested for the rape there of a sixteen-year-old girl.

Because it occurred on Griffiss Air Force Base, the rape was a federal crime. Convicted in U.S. District Court—serving as his own attorney, he was allowed to cross-examine his victim—Leacock was awaiting sentencing, housed by the federal government in the Madison County Jail, when with the help of his wife he escaped. Because she cooperated in his recapture, seventeen hours later, no charges were filed against her. Three weeks after that, again with her assistance, Leacock escaped from the Montgomery County Jail, the facility to which he had been shipped when Madison County refused the government's request to take him back.

Leacock was sentenced, in absentia, to twenty-seven years in federal prison; his wife, who copped to one of seven felonies in abetting his escape, was sentenced to five years, federal time, as an accessory to rape after the fact. She was shipped off immediately to a penitentiary in Kentucky—there, no doubt, to develop a more genuine appreciation of the Tammy Wynette tune "Stand by Your Man"—and Leacock went to ground in New York.

Gerri Doody, born and raised on Baltic Street in what was then called downtown Brooklyn and is now called Cobble Hill, had come to work for the United States marshal for New York's Eastern District in 1971. Probably for the very reason that so many of her friends were police officers—Brooklyn breeds cops the way Beverly Hills breeds blonds—she harbored, at the age of twenty-four, no desire to enter law enforcement. She came to work on the civil desk, employed by the feds as a clerk. Because there were no female deputies in the district at the time, she was called upon now and then—in those circumstances where a woman's presence was essential to the assignment—to accompany deputies working arrest warrants. Also, side by side with the agency's sworn personnel, she regularly traveled the country escorting female prisoners.

Partaking of the work of the typical federal officer, Gerri Doody discovered that she enjoyed it. With only two years of college, and facing the requirement of a bachelor's degree or sufficient qualifying experience, she would log a total of 2,080 field-hours before she became eligible for a position. In May 1980, with nine years on the civil desk and after thirteen weeks at the Federal Law Enforcement Training Center at Glynco, Georgia, where she learned to drive fast, shoot straight, and fight, she was sworn and deputized.

"I was the old broad at Glynco. The kids, I call them kids, were in their early twenties. I was thirty-three."

For the next seven years, as one of some forty criminal investigators answering to chief deputy Mike Pizzi, she shouldered the manifold duties of routine district operations in Brooklyn.

She was permanently assigned to warrants in the spring of 1987.

In August, Leacock busted out.

. . .

The U.S. Courthouse for New York's Eastern District is located on Cadman Plaza East, in the stately shadow of the Brooklyn Bridge. The office of the U.S. marshal occupies Room 172, just beyond and to the left of that international sign of the times, the armed-security setup. On the afternoon of March 8, 1988, Gerri Doody walked to the nurse's station in the building's first-floor lobby to inquire about medication which had recently been prescribed for her father, who was hospitalized with cancer.

The Leacock investigation had hit a low. It had been almost seven months now, and the informants were not coming through. They were not putting "heart and soul" into it, in the words of warrants supervisor Dave O'Flaherty. A month earlier he had decided to shake them.

". . . with money," he would later explain.

Which is not as simple as it sounds.

What an informant wants to hear, if not entirely to believe, is that he is squealing for some greater good, the good of society, for instance. The agent's job is to convince the informant that the payment is nothing more than a by-product, a return on all the heartache, the simple aggravation; to assure him that he, the agent, understands that the informant is no Judas Iscariot and would never betray someone for cash. The fact that there exist many citizens who are sincerely insulted by the offer of money —you lose them forever right there—makes the proposition that much more sensitive.

The Leacock informants posed a special problem.

When Leacock fled Montgomery County, he sought familiar territory, as fugitives can be trusted to do (as Pat Garrett will readily tell you) in Leacock's case Queens, New York. It was why the escape warrant, which originated in the Northern District, where the crime had been committed, was kicked from Utica to Brooklyn. (The Eastern District of New York encompasses Brooklyn, Queens, Staten Island, and Nassau and Suffolk Counties.) The people with whom Leacock made subsequent contact were people he had known since his youth, people who had not seen him in well over thirteen years—the period of his incarceration—and who knew nothing of his case upstate. The majority were law-abiding, hard-working citizens against whom Gerri Doody and her fellow deputies could exert little traditional leverage. They were not the usual street scum to whom criminals like Leacock could be expected to gravitate; they were not susceptible to the wide variety of emoluments and intimidation, both legal and material, that one could bring, for example, to the questioning of the typical ex-convict, the garden-variety recidivist with whom a fugitive might characteristically associate. The threat of an aiding-and-abetting charge, the only legitimate fulcrum upon which leverage could be gained, carried very little weight. The effort to win their confidence was a long and tedious one.

There were several informants upon whom the deputies had been putting pressure, knowing Leacock, of no fixed address, could not survive on the street by himself (one in particular whom they had been working for months, the development of a relationship with whom and the ultimate winning of whose trust required exhaustive work on Gerri Doody's part), and through extensive interviews and the use of telephone traps they had isolated Leacock's recent movements to the vicinity of the Albany housing projects, at the corner of Bergen Street and Albany Avenue, in the Bedford-Stuyvesant section of Brooklyn.

Conducting interviews in the Albany projects, according to warrants inspector Victor Oboyski, was not without its share of excitement.

"There was shooting and crack dealing going on all the time. A couple of times, there were shootings going on while we were there. Right inside the building. One day they tried to kill a guy, they shot at him, they missed, and when the ambulance guys showed up—he was standing there, he was fine—he just hopped on the ambulance gurney. 'Get me the hell out of here,' he said. Just to be taken out of the area. 'I can't *walk* out of here,' he told them, 'these bastards are going to kill me.' The ambulance guys took him out."

To help snare Garnett Leacock, once made to understand the kind of animal he was, New York Telephone, which in the typical case might trap a twenty-block area, trapped the entire borough of Brooklyn. Given the number of the cooperating party's telephone and the time a call was received, the telephone company, searching its computer, could within five to thirty minutes trace the phone from which the call had been made. A deputy, taking the informant's call, would notify New York Telephone, mobilize a team—if the call came in at night, that meant reaching everyone at home—and wait for the company to report back with the appropriate location. Inevitably, however, Leacock's calls were coming from public telephones.

"And," as Dave O'Flaherty knew, "you can't have ten people respond to a pay phone on Nostrand Avenue."

Instead, with few exceptions, every deputy in the district put in his share of cold nights on surveillance, waiting for Leacock to go into or come out of the projects.

Having escaped twice in three weeks from jails upstate, Leacock had brought with him to New York City a certain measure of notoriety; continually identified in a series of vicious assaults in Queens—a lot of local cases would be closed once Leacock was in custody—he had become an even higher priority to the deputies working the case. Three days after he had cut to ribbons the flesh of Klein's hands and face, he sliced the throat of a younger man living in the neighborhood, using the same linoleum knife, breaking his victim's fingers in an attempt to remove the man's jewelry. He had hit the Most Wanted list for a reason. Deputies in the district all wanted a piece of his arrest, and were volunteering to work overtime going on night surveillance. Gerri Doody, in addition to carting in the trunk of her car a duffel bag filled with her equipment, was carrying a list of telephone numbers of the friends and relatives of various deputies, numbers at which the deputies could be reached if the arrest went down on a weekend.

"I never took my gun off during the Leacock investigation. And I don't. I used to take it off during the day when we were sitting around the office. But those days are gone. You have to be ready to go out the door. I have my vest, I have my side. You get the call, you just grab everything and run."

But that day as she stood there in the nurse's office, ready or not, Gerri Doody admits, she had just about had enough. Two weeks earlier she had returned from a Caribbean vacation that she had scheduled long before, a vacation she had considered canceling until events had finally caught up with her.

"The hours, the concentration, you know, you become obsessed with that one person. We'd work early morning, we'd go on surveillance at night, places we thought he might return to, just going out there, going out there, and each day we'd come back without him. We knew he was there in the area and we had all these different leads, but every time we got somewhere, he was somewhere else. We'd sit out till eleven at night, surveilling in different vehicles, just sitting in the car, staring, looking and praying and hoping. I'd gotten calls, I'd be home in bed. We'd get false alarms. I don't know if it'll ever happen again, but I just couldn't think of a thing except him."

And so she took the vacation. She returned. And nothing changed.

Paying necessary attention to her other warrants and to those of her fellow deputies (they made their arrests as a group) and thus going out, with regularity, on routine 6 A.M. hits, she was still working days, nights, and weekends. What personal time she was able to steal she was determined to devote to her father; she was unfailing in her visits to the hospital, as she would continue to be until eventually he died there of cancer.

It was hard to see how things could get worse.

When Gerri Doody finally heard that Garnett Leacock had been arrested, she heard it from a police officer in Queens. She had been circulating copies of Leacock's photo when the officer gave her the news.

"Yeah, we locked that guy up," he said.

Garnett Leacock, after losing a very brief car chase to them, had gone on to lose a follow-up fistfight to two New York City cops. No sooner had he staggered the first cop with a sucker punch to the nose, than the second kicked Leacock so hard in the chest that he knocked the fugitive out cold. After taking him to the hospital, the cops took Leacock to jail and booked him under the alias Jerome Jackson: black male, five-seven, with brown eyes, black hair, and a one-inch scar on his right cheek. They charged him with assault, resisting arrest, and possession of stolen property, locked him up, and misclassified his fingerprints.

Her fugitive, the officer told Gerri Doody, had been in police custody for three days.

Three days, three weeks ago.

"He was allowed to post bond. We released him."

Because she was talking to the nurse at the time, Gerri Doody, that March afternoon, did not take the call that came in from the informant she had spent so many months rigorously cultivating. All she remembers is walking back to the squad room and Dave O'Flaherty's bearing down on her:

"Grab your gear," the supervisor shouted.

Oboyski sped past with the shotgun. Everyone was racing for the door.

Some later claimed that O'Flaherty, that day, as he hung up the telephone, actually yelled the words "Saddle up." Whatever he first said was unimportant, they agreed, because the next thing he said was "Leacock." In the projects. Right then. In a sixth-floor apartment. O'Flaherty had the number.

Six deputies, on the move, all visibly armed, clutching bullet-proof vests and raid jackets, one of them carrying a twelve-gauge riot gun out onto the streets of Brooklyn, engineered a familiar broken-field run, under the eyes of several court-security officers, through the pedestrian traffic in the lobby of the Federal Building.

(To suggest that such behavior, which was nothing short of routine, might give a moment of pause to those citizens looking for, say, the office of the Internal Revenue Service, is to indulge, one discovers, in the obvious. As Gerri Doody explains it: "They're horrified.")

A three-mile drive to the Albany projects, it was lights and sirens until the entry teams were two blocks away. In front of the projects, hanging out when the three two-man teams pulled up, were maybe a dozen people. Most of them were teenagers. All, not most, of them scattered instantly when Oboyski hit the grass. On the run, with the shotgun out, the 235-pound Oboyski, entering the building, did not take either ramp, he went straight across the lawn and vaulted a four-foot fence. O'Flaherty's instructions, transmitted over the radio as the deputies approached the projects, were immediately to seal the staircases.

"Keep him from the lobby."

With no fire escapes, and with the apartment six floors up, it was Leacock's only way out.

If, in fact, Leacock were still in there.

Gerri Doody and deputy Marvin Mack, moving fast, took one stairway, deputies Tony Crook and Billy Thrower the other. O'Flaherty and Oboyski (the senior men) took the elevator.

"Me being the supervisor," O'Flaherty explains, "I take the elevator. [And] I want my guy, who goes in the door first with the shotgun, to be fresh. . . . First guy going in the door, I want him to be ready." On the elevator, O'Flaherty acknowledges, "My weapon's out . . . because if the elevator door opens and Leacock's standing there, I want him to meet . . . my friend."

Everyone arrived at the apartment door wired, pumped up, shaking under a rush of adrenaline, sweating under the weight of a second-chance vest and the nylon of a raid jacket.

Everyone had his weapon out. Everyone was breathing hard. And everyone was hugging the wall.

Another day at the office.

Dave O'Flaherty gave everyone plenty of time to calm down.

"Relax," he told them, "we're here. He can't go out the window. If he jumps, he deserves to get away. Anything above the third floor, hell, if he jumps, he deserves it."

In a rapidly conducted tactical meeting, held there at the threshold of the apartment, the deputies decided against immediately breaking down the door. Instead, they would first try to open it, and they would do so with Marvin Mack.

Deputy U.S. Marshal Marvin Mack, fifty-two, was no stranger to the Albany projects. He had grown up in Bedford-Stuyvesant. Today, and too often, unfortunately—because it was so often on business—he found himself back in the neighborhood. If Mack was breathing as heavily as everyone else, it was probably for different reasons—at five-eight, weighing 260 pounds, Mack had just run up six flights of stairs, and to him it had felt like twelve. Not that Mack was unaware of the danger he and the others faced.

Garnett Leacock, who had assaulted one police officer, and in an earlier confrontation had escaped by ramming a stolen vehicle into the patrol car of another, was, according to the informant, in possession of a gun. He was, far more importantly, facing the rest of his life in prison. He was a man with absolutely nothing to lose. It was very possible that there would be some shooting on the other side of the door.

"You don't go out there intending to kill somebody," according to Victor Oboyski, who has been out there more than once. "You don't go out there intending to harm someone. You're happy if *you* don't get hurt. If *you* don't get hurt, you've won."

On the landing that day, outside the apartment, everybody was frightened, and everybody had been there before. But not one of them knew the meaning of sheer, flat-out terror the way Marvin Mack had experienced it.

It was October 1973, he had been two years on the job, dispatched on special assignment to the U.S. District Court in Baltimore. Mack was standing in a hearing room adjacent to the defense table—the defendant standing before a judge—when his supervisor turned to him and said:

"Marvin, if he's remanded, I want you to take him."

It was then, as he confronted the prospect of actually throwing handcuffs on the felon in question, that Marvin Mack experienced The Fear.

"I stood there thinking," Mack recalls. "I wondered if my legs would move. I was proud to be where I was, for my family, for my race, I'd come a long way. But I was worried that, if the time came, my legs wouldn't move. What a country. I was Marvin Mack, a kid from Bed-Stuy, and I was going to put the vice-president of the United States in jail."

Marvin Mack, DUSM—who had been there the day Spiro Agnew resigned the American vice-presidency, pleading *nolo contendere* to a single charge of income-tax evasion—now back in Bed-Stuy, holstered his Smith & Wesson. He turned his navy-blue raid jacket inside out, obscuring the embroidered patch and the large yellow lettering that identified him as a deputy marshal, and zipped it up to conceal his body armor ("100% Kevlar Aramid," better living through chemistry from the wonderful people at Du Pont). He knocked on the apartment door and announced that he was from the Housing Authority, an agency whose personnel were always conducting inspections.

Standing to the right of the door, his back to the wall, was O'Flaherty. Oboyski stood to the left. In the several minutes they had waited there listening, they had heard, inside the apartment, both men and women talking. If no one had answered the door, they would have slammed through with no hesitation. Using any one of three very rudimentary tools with which they traveled, the deputies, with a nod from O'Flaherty, were prepared to take the door out fast—"I guarantee that door would have been down in a matter of a minute . . . the Halligan, the ram, or the sledge"—knocking it broadside into the apartment, carrying the entire door frame in with it.

The woman who answered Marvin Mack's knock did not open the door to him, she asked whom he wanted to talk to. Mack gave the name of a second woman, the apartment's tenant of record.

Oboyski would be the first man through—as soon as the door

was off the latch, Oboyski, with the field pump, was going. Having loaded the five-shot in the car coming over, he had refrained from chambering a cartridge. He would go through, he announced, holding the action back, the ejection port would be open.

"When I get inside, I'm gonna slide one in. I want them to know I'm rackin' a round."

The sound is an irreplicable one, and natively unmistakable— *a round in the chamber*—a noise so ominous it is audible to the deaf.

Especially when it happens in your face.

Billy Thrower, who went in *behind* Oboyski, would later tell Gerri Doody that when he heard it, he "jumped out of his skin."

The second woman opened the door.

Gerri Doody, commenting on the roles played by the various participants in the events that immediately followed, would give a far more accurate indication of her own personality than of that of any of her colleagues, volunteering, as she did, in endearingly honest fashion, what many considered to be an understatement of oceanic proportions.

"Dave and Victor, they're not the kinds of personalities to stand around in the background. They're pretty rambunctious, yeah."

Yeah.

Gerri Doody stands just under five-foot-eight. Her hair is blond, her eyes are hazel. Her skills, in the words of her supervisor, are those of an "expert investigator." You could write a novel on the subject of Gerri Doody, however, and come no closer to nailing her down than with the simple observation that she is one of those people refreshingly capable of coming up with a word like "rambunctious."

To apply the word to the two men in question is another matter altogether. Gerri Doody was exercising poetic license. It is a measure of her charm. To think of these guys as rambunctious is to miss the point so completely as to invite comparison to some offhand observation, say, that boa constrictors eat.

Victor Oboyski is six-foot-three, Dave O'Flaherty six-foot even, and together—unarmed—they weigh 460 pounds. If you have federal paper outstanding against you, and you run into either one of these two people, negotiating a transaction that could be considered in any way favorable to your circumstances, even on a good day, is like playing basketball in street shoes; strategically it crosses the line between optimism and delusion. The only thing worse than coming up against one of them is coming up against the two of them together. It is like looking over a cliff. And these guys went to college.

Add to the hallucination the likelihood that one of them is staring at you over the bead of a cut-down, twelve-gauge smoothbore, charged with double-ought buck, and it gives an entirely new meaning to the concept of misfortune. A Remington 870 pump-action street gun fitted with a fourteen-inch barrel and a pistol-grip stock offers a memorable course of study in thermodynamics, the single most baffling theoretical question being how to hold on to it after you have fired it; how literally to come to grips, in the absence of a shoulder stock, with the thirty-five to forty foot-pounds of recoil absorbed by your arms.

Oboyski, even when he is smiling, which is most of the time, looks like a guy who has figured it out. (O'Flaherty smiling, in certain circumstances, is probably something you are better off not seeing.)

Of the junior members of the entry crew that day, the heir apparent to the legacy handed down by the two senior men was the youngster, Tony Crook. While he will never be as frightening to look at as either of his immediate superiors, Crook poses as clear and present a danger to American felonry; his enthusiasm for police work is on the order of magnitude of Byron's passion for poetry. Crook, twenty-seven, had just returned from working an extradition in Finland, a four-day trip, and was pretty well wrung-out, when the call came in from the informant, but if anybody beat him going out the door that day, nobody beat him by much, and there are only three deputies in the Service— O'Flaherty, Oboyski, and the chief himself, Pizzi, the cop whose legacy it is—who are likely to beat him going in.

Billy Thrower, thirty-six, the only male member of the group to whom the height-weight chart represented anything other than mere hypothesis, had almost four years on the job at the time. A Brooklyn native, as were most of the deputies in the district, Thrower had come over from the Immigration and Naturalization Service, but it is unlikely that anything at INS, let alone college or the United States Navy, had prepared him for the kinds of partygoers that he was crashing through doors with these days. Like every deputy in Eastern New York, Thrower had his own warrants to work, but of those who were present at the projects that day, only he and Marvin Mack had the broader duties typical of district operations. The other four worked warrants exclusively—the occasional exception, of course, being Victor Oboyski, who, in what might be construed as a career move, spent much of his off-duty drinking time, though he was not much of a drinking man, in the spontaneous composition of rap tunes, required listening and performed in that spirit, to hell with last call, the only 235-pound, Polish-Irish American Jam Master with nationwide power of arrest.

This assorted half-dozen—call them the authority behind the warrant—having delivered themselves to the door of an apartment in the Albany Housing projects in Brooklyn, on the afternoon of March 8, stood on a sixth-floor landing, waiting, not altogether impatiently, to serve a piece of paper, representing the American taxpayer with guns in their hands.

The woman did not actually open the door, she was simply responsible for unlatching it. Oboyski opened it with his foot and a unit of energy equivalent to what was later determined to be some function of his 235 pounds multiplied by the speed of light squared. Or something like that. At any rate, his linear momentum carried him over the woman who opened it, propelling him directly into the living room of the apartment, about six feet distant from the door, where he ended up standing before a coffee table racking the Remington into the faces of three men seated on the couch.

". . . and just very simply told them, in the nicest terms possible, that if they moved they might upset me."

Actually Oboyski was screaming, O'Flaherty, who came in behind him and immediately over him, was screaming, and everybody behind O'Flaherty was screaming as he or she came through the doorway: "Police . . . U.S. marshals . . . freeze . . . don't move . . . put your fucking hands up!"

Gerri Doody came through behind O'Flaherty, immediately freezing the woman who had unlatched the door, a woman to whom Oboyski and O'Flaherty now had their backs. Clutching a child and screaming herself, she was one of two women standing there when the feds came crashing through—a total of twelve people, then, all of them terrified, at least six of them armed and on an emotional trigger, wreaking pandemonium in the room.

As Oboyski, jacking a cartridge into the chamber, loomed there, bellowing, his voice amplified by adrenaline as he shouted instructions—many of which were almost irrationally repetitive, all of which began with what sounded like the word "don't" and came down to the proposition that as an acceptable form of behavior not even breathing was encouraged—O'Flaherty jumped over the coffee table with a pistol in his hand and started throwing people onto the floor. Crook and Marvin Mack moved in behind him, and while he and they held their weapons to the heads of the three men there, Oboyski and Billy Thrower moved quickly to the back of the apartment where, with the shotgun, they swept the bedrooms. They found a young woman with an infant in one, two unattended infants in another, gathered them all together, told the woman to stay put, and wasted no time returning to the chaos in front.

The woman who had opened the door was by now struggling to leave the apartment, screaming so hysterically "Don't hurt my child!" that Gerri Doody had holstered her revolver to try to keep her under control and at the same time protect the baby. Other apartments on the floor had started emptying into the hallway, residents, at the sound of the young woman's screams, crowding around the doorway, firing questions and screaming themselves.

"You really can't hang out in the projects too long. Once you get your man, you get out. We were no more than five minutes in the apartment."

Dave O'Flaherty, who earlier had said the investigation had been so intense for so many months that he "could pick this guy out without a picture," was not encouraged by what he had on the floor. As, left to right, he studied the suspects who were pinned face-down in front of him, he thought: The first two, they're definitely not him. The third man did not make O'Flaherty much happier. The only way this character was going to be Leacock was with some hair on his face and a lot more weight on his bones. It was a cinch that there was paper on the man somewhere—for whatever that was worth—because whoever he was, O'Flaherty concluded, the guy clearly had been living like a real street skell.

Cops, especially street cops—*real* cops, as opposed to, say, the FBI—have a lexicon unique to their work. The expression "skell," if not exclusive to New York, enjoys a currency there unequaled in other parts of the country. Probably derived from the word "skeleton" and applied by police to criminals of sickly, somewhat scurvy appearance—the drug-addicted, the diseased, the manifestly vertebrate and nothing more—the expression is employed frequently by Brooklyn deputies (who exhibit many characteristics of the nuclear family, among them a shared vocabulary) in its adjectival form, for example, "the guy really looked skelly." There is a generic term for members of the criminal class that is in far more common use in New York, not only among deputy marshals, but among local police as well. NYPD calls them all "mutts." Tony Perez, who oversees the Marshals Service's 15 Most Wanted program out of headquarters in Washington, D.C., a legendary bodysnatcher who helped pioneer the Service's Fugitive Program and who has worked all over the country, is a cop who knows only one synonym for "criminal." To specify the object of a manhunt, he uses the word exclusively, and he uses it as casually as civilians use specific nouns to denote gender. Among police nationwide, it is like Received Standard English, a word universally embraced, unanimously employed, and as indispensable to their verbal commerce as such words as "man" and "woman." To Tony Perez, and to cops everywhere, the accepted expression for any individual subject to felony arrest, whatever else he or she happens to be, is invariably and quite simply "an asshole."

When Vic Oboyski returned to the living room, O'Flaherty was taking names. And it was Oboyski, the entry teams' public-relations director, on behalf of everyone assembled, who congratulated the asshole under the barrel of O'Flaherty's automatic —third man from the left—when the latter identified himself as Jerome Jackson. Oboyski initiated the cheer. Smiling quite jovially at his most recent acquaintance—"Jerome, we been looking for you"—he conversed with him until Gerri Doody took over.

Lost on Leacock, almost certainly, was the chivalry:

O'Flaherty cuffed his hands, Oboyski his ankles, together they hoisted him off the floor—less like a dragon slain, more like a road kill—and presented him to his case officer, the way one might surrender a trophy.

"Gerri," they said, handing him up in as courtly a fashion as possible.

The chivalry may have eluded Leacock; the poetic justice did not.

It was Gerri Doody who explained very clearly to the rapist that he was being arrested by a woman—not another of whose company he was going to enjoy for a while, she wanted him to understand; Gerri Doody, armed and dangerous, speaking for so many of his victims, when she looked Leacock in the eye and told him:

"Take a good look, it's going to be your last."

They carried him out face-down, parallel to the floor.

Gerri Doody, who had come off the civil desk at thirty-three, had brought in a 15 Most Wanted. Before the year was out, she would find herself in Jamaica—the Caribbean island, not the Queens, New York, neighborhood—and from there she would bring in another.

Where Gerri Doody went wrong was in the assumption that she was the last woman whose face Garnett Leacock would get a good look at.

At a federal hearing scheduled to have him classified a Dangerous Special Offender, Leacock, soon after his capture, enjoyed the company of various women in a Syracuse, New York, courtroom, at least one of whom testified against him; he was to do so again when the state of New York held a similar hearing, the prosecutor there prevailing where the U.S. attorney did not. Judged a Predicate Felon in the latter proceeding, Leacock received a guarantee from the Empire State that, as long as he lived, he would not see a prison from the outside. To say that he will not see the light of day for a while is something of an exaggeration—he currently sees it, according to Assistant U.S. Attorney Craig Benedict, for fifty minutes every twenty-four hours in a four-by-six exercise pen located in the maximum-security facility at Marion, Illinois. When he sees it, he is alone. Under twenty-four-hour lockdown, like everyone at Marion, the federal system's only Level 6 penitentiary—it replaced Alcatraz—Leacock spends the remaining twenty-three hours and ten minutes of the day indoors, in isolation, in a cell three stories below ground. After he serves his twenty-seven-year federal stretch, from wherever it is that he serves it—the average stay at Marion is thirty-three months—the state of New York will take him into custody and lock him away for the rest of his life.

3.

Westward the Star of Empire

"Even police officers . . . in my earlier days on the job, I'd go into the precincts and say I'm with the U.S. marshals; they'd say, 'Where's your horse?' I'd hold up the star and they'd say, 'What, are you with Texaco?'"

Gerri Doody is employed neither by Texaco, the international petroleum giant whose corporate trademark is the same five-pointed star behind the authority of which Pat Garrett, Virgil Earp, Bill Hickok, and others either advanced or managed to delay the closing of the American West, nor by the Texas Rangers, the mounted police force of the union's Lone Star State with whose history her agency's is frequently confused. One of 2,700 sworn deputies who, among other things, execute fugitive arrest warrants in the nation's ninety-five federal judicial districts, she works for the president of the United States. Under the supervision of the U.S. Marshals Service, she and her fellow deputies in 1988, the year they captured Garnett Leacock, hunted down and arrested 14,000 fugitives from justice, more than all other federal law-enforcement agencies combined.

Truly the long arm of the law, and increasingly acknowledged as such today in police precincts throughout the country, they are heirs to a legacy which enjoyed its most dramatic expression on the American frontier, a heritage which came to romantic flower over a century ago, when the deputy U.S. marshal was "the law west of Fort Smith." It is a tradition that in the fall of 1880 was anything but new. When Pat Garrett set out from Lincoln County to bring in Billy the Kid, the inheritance he acceded to was just short of a hundred years old.

The United States Marshals Service, postdating by fewer than six months the inauguration of George Washington, is the oldest federal law-enforcement agency in the country. Embroiled since the birth of the nation in its every labor at self-realization, it is an institution which, often foundering, itself has labored to survive. The fact that the average citizen knows between little and nothing about its mission today comes as no surprise to the people who carry that mission out. Theirs is an agency whose experience with organized law enforcement followed by better than fifty years the organization of crime. The changes the agency has undergone in its turbulent 200-year history, remarkable on their own, seem dwarfed in their significance by the very fact of its continued existence.

Established by the Federal Judiciary Act of September 24, 1789, the offices of United States marshal and deputy marshal were instituted by the First Congress as a part of the same legislation that empowered the third branch of American government: the Supreme Court and the federal judicial system. Marshals and their deputies, mandated to administer to the newborn nation's federal courts, were assigned to serve all legal process—writs, warrants, summonses, subpoenas—make arrests, handle prisoners, disburse fees and expenses, and, in general, ensure the orderly conduct of the administration of federal justice. Commissioned to carry out within their districts the orders not only of the courts, but of Congress and the president as well (in the years leading up to the Civil War they enforced the nation's neutrality laws against several armed expeditions aimed at Canada, Cuba, and other countries; they took the national census every ten years until 1880), they projected federal authority across the far reaches of the young republic, providing local representation of an emerging national will, the only civilian police power available to the constitutional government.

Marshals, as they continue to be, were appointed by the U.S. president—the original thirteen were appointed by George

Washington—subject to confirmation by the Senate, and until 1853 they reported directly to the secretary of state. After 1853 their supervision came to rest with the office of the attorney general, but not until the end of the century, some thirty years after its founding, did the Department of Justice develop a bureaucracy capable of overseeing them. Even then the individual marshals were autonomous in their districts. Paid on a fee basis until 1896, when Congress established a salary for both marshals and their deputies, escaping national organization until 1961, when a chief marshal, James P. McShane, was appointed, they continued to hire their own deputies until 1972, a full three years after the superimposition upon the districts of an agency: the United States Marshals Service.

Under its first three directors, the Service began rapidly to professionalize recruitment and training. Its fourth, Stanley Morris, by 1988, had engineered legislation that ensured that his successors would be appointed not by the attorney general—as Morris and his predecessors had been—but by the president himself.

The deputy marshal, today, is the embodiment of both personal and institutional survival in modern America. His story is the story of the survival of the institution itself, its passage from vitality to eventual morbidity to ultimate, almost miraculous, recovery; its achievement of a renaissance at a time when history was just about to call in the embalmers.

For more than a century after ratification of the Constitution, marshals and their deputies remained the only federal officers with power of arrest; and because they represented that essential barrier between civil and military control of the union, it was their destiny thus to become the general practitioners of American law enforcement. Their broad federal mandate (the varied nature of which would come to ill serve them in an age of specialization, the constitutional weight behind which they have only recently manipulated to their advantage) put them at every critical juncture in the history of the republic.

The story of "men and women [who] fought and died in support of the ideal of self-government," according to Marshals Service historian Frederick S. Calhoun in his official history of the agency, *The Lawmen: United States Marshals and Their Deputies, 1789 to 1989,* "the story of the clumsy, inefficient, and peculiar method by which we Americans choose to govern ourselves. . . . the history of the U.S. marshals and their deputies is a history of Constitutional implementation, of how the Constitution has worked—or failed to work—over the past two centuries."

In the decades between ratification and the War Between the States, that history insistently expressed itself as a struggle to strike some balance between federal and regional interests.

In 1794, five years after its founding and three years after the republic's first secretary of the treasury, Alexander Hamilton, endeared himself to the people of the new nation with an excise tax on domestic spirits (among other things there was a Revolutionary War debt to pay off), the grain farmers of frontier Pennsylvania honored Hamilton's boss with the first armed insurrection against the United States government. U.S. Marshal David Lenox, riding out of U.S. District Court in Philadelphia to serve summonses on seventy-five distillers who refused to pay the tax, did not inspire what was to become known as the Whiskey Rebellion—west of the Allegheny Mountains, where liquor was a staple in a hardscrabble economy, they had been tarring and feathering federal revenue collectors for two and a half years —but Lenox took the initial gunfire. Some five months later, setting out from the nation's capital with a 13,000-man militia, raised by four states on the orders of the president and marching under the command of Virginia governor and former Revolutionary War general Lighthorse Harry Lee (Hamilton, the lunatic Federalist, went along for the ride), Lenox was one of three civilians required by the commander-in-chief to take the field against the rebels. Lenox was there to make the arrests, establishing by his presence, instantaneous to ratification, the law-enforcement authority of the constitutional government.

At those points in American history where parochial and federal interests inevitably came to collide, the office of the marshal, as the personification of federal power, was very often the target of most immediate opposition, exercised not only by the regional population but by regional governments as well. Upon no circumstance prior to the outbreak of civil war—a century later it would be an outbreak of civil rights—was the collision between those interests to be more dramatic than it was on the issue of slavery.

One of the few political victories over the propagation of slavery enjoyed by the North in the years preceding secession was an 1819 measure enacted by Congress equating the importation of slaves from Africa (formally prohibited in 1808) with piracy, a crime that was punishable by hanging. Over the same period, concessions to the South, which had been necessary to the very creation of the Union, were characteristically more numerous and, in at least one instance, more inflammatory. Among the separate measures passed collectively as the Compromise of 1850 was an infamous Fugitive Slave Act more drastic than that originally provided for by the U.S. Constitution (a document which institutionalized slavery and, by necessity, its quaint sequela, the notion of "fugitives from labor"). Numbered among the casualties in the political war engendered by these two statutes were the marshals mandated to enforce them.

Local people (natives, traditionally, of the districts in which they serve) not entirely unaware that a patronage job was a temporary one, that upon expiration of their commissions their occupational well-being grew out of the good opinion of the community, marshals inevitably found themselves caught between their sympathies and their duty. Sworn to uphold the 1819 law, southern marshals, many of whom were slaveowners, boarded vessels intercepted offshore by the navy, confiscating the "cargo" and bringing merchant captains to justice, only to confront recalcitrant jurors, reluctant witnesses, and the derision and scorn of their neighbors. Sworn to enforce the Fugitive Slave Act, northern marshals, who were dragged into court periodically by state and local officials in challenge to federal authority, met with vilification, riots, and bloodshed. The death by gunshot in 1854 of Deputy U.S. Marshal James Batchelder—at the hands of an angry mob of Massachusetts abolitionists attempting to liberate the captured Anthony Burns—best illustrates what federal lawmen in the free states confronted in the ten years of accelerating conflict that foreshadowed the capture of Fort Sumter.

With the inevitable collapse of the Union, marshals throughout the South resigned their commissions to join the Confederacy.

It was during the Civil War that greenbacks were introduced, and by that time as much as a third of the legal tender in circulation in the United States—until the twentieth century American money existed in a variety of forms—was counterfeit. The

United States Mint, which up to the war had printed only fractional currency, was striking gold and silver coins, hundreds of individual banks were issuing notes of their own, and counterfeiters were forging just about anything they could move.

The Treasury Department on occasion hired detectives to investigate the traffic—Allan Pinkerton, the original "private eye," who would also serve as a Civil War spy, had gained fame cracking a counterfeiting ring as an undercover cop in Chicago—but such special agents were rare, and until 1865 the suppression of counterfeiting was assigned to the U.S. marshals. An investigative mandate, the first of its kind, requiring undercover work and the development of informants, the assignment was lost by the marshals to the creation that year of the Secret Service, the government's first true investigative agency.

Organized under the authority of the secretary of the treasury, the Secret Service, at the outset, enjoyed limited power of arrest; in its pursuit of counterfeiters, the new agency would rely on the assistance of deputy marshals until the end of the century.

In the twelve years that passed between Lee's surrender at Appomattox and Rutherford B. Hayes's election to the American presidency, United States marshals, entering the most dangerous period in their history, would take casualties as the vanguard in a losing war to ensure the rights of the nation's newly enfranchised Southern Republicans, citizens who were being systematically victimized by their former owners throughout the South.

(It was a war deputies would come back to win, but not until a hundred years later.)

Reconstruction of the South saw the states of the former Confederacy occupied by the Union Army. Under control of the federal government, they were forced to modify substantially their political and social institutions and, prerequisite to full readmission to the Union, to ratify the Fourteenth Amendment to the U.S. Constitution. Washington's determination to prohibit the South from denying the rights of citizenship to former slaves gave rise as early as 1865 to such night-riding social clubs as the Ku Klux Klan in Pulaski, Tennessee, and to the subsequent legislation designed to suppress such organizations.

By 1877, deputy marshals, backed by the army, had arrested more than 7,000 people for violations of the civil-rights laws, the most radical of which were the Klan Acts of 1870 and 1871. The marshals paid for their success; attempting to serve process, they faced arrest by state authorities, but that, of course, was the least of it. Carpetbaggers and scalawags in the eyes of the South, many of them simply were murdered.

The federal government's power to defend citizens from one another, a power which theretofore had fallen to the respective states, was eventually denied by the Supreme Court, which in 1876 ruled the more forceful provisions of the Klan Acts unconstitutional. In his bartering for the presidential election of 1876, in which he had lost the popular vote (Samuel Tilden had carried the majority), Hayes, in exchange for the electoral votes of Louisiana, Georgia, and Florida, promised to pull federal troops out of the South.

By 1877 Reconstruction was over.

But the killing of deputy marshals in the South had only begun.

The region's determination to resist the authority of the U.S. government continued to be expressed in its citizens' outright refusal to pay the reinstituted federal excise tax on whiskey.

The Moonshine Wars, in which more deputies would lose their lives than in any theater of operations beyond the boundaries of Indian Territory, were a legacy of the larger conflict in which North and South had so recently engaged. The excise tax which had resulted in the Whiskey Rebellion during George Washington's second term, a tax repealed by Congress in 1809, was revisited upon the nation in 1861. It and the nation's first (temporary) personal income tax had been legislated to underwrite the Union Army. At an original seventy cents per gallon, the tax inspired the Whiskey Ring scandal that typified the corruption in which the presidential administration of Ulysses S. Grant was so thoroughly soaked. With its rise to ninety cents per gallon, the customary bribery of revenue agents gave way to the more profitable practice of clandestine manufacture.

The authority of revenue agents extended no further than the seizure of illegal stills and whiskey. Power of arrest lay with the U.S. marshals and their deputies, some of whom reported entire counties in rebellion. The murder of a federal officer was not a federal offense, and local authorities, in their opposition to a government from which they had fought to secede, were more readily inclined to prosecute deputies for destruction of private property—to wit, the stills in question—than to prosecute the moonshiners who routinely gunned the deputies down.

Not until 1889 did the Supreme Court provide the federal government with the means to protect its officers from the authority of the states. That year, Deputy U.S. Marshal David Neagle, assigned to protect the life of Supreme Court Justice Stephen Field, shot and killed, in the discharge of that duty, a man named David Terry. Charged with murder in California, Neagle, appealing to the Ninth Circuit Court (on which Field also sat and after a brief hearing from which he abstained), was ordered released on a writ of *habeas corpus.* The Supreme Court decision upholding the order, *In re Neagle* (from which Field also abstained), did little to discourage state authorities from arresting federal marshals but created a precedent for releasing them.

The federal government would continue to chase moonshiners well into the twentieth century. Distillers of white lightning would enter the nation's popular mythology, roaring in and out of the hollows of the rural American South, pursued by U.S. authorities into that era of specialized law enforcement characterized by a superannuated deputy marshal. Indeed, it was Internal Revenue's Alcohol Tax Unit (precursor of today's Bureau of Alcohol, Tobacco and Firearms), inheriting the marshals' turf, that would oversee the most radical change in the way the country conducted its police work.

In the words of retired Customs investigator William Hughes, a former Special Agent in Charge in San Antonio, Texas:

"ATU invented the conspiracy case. They could put eighteen guys in prison with a Mason jar, two pounds of sugar, and a Ford."

In age-old American moonshine, modern law enforcement would eventually be born.

In the returning Confederate soldier, in the bitterness of his defeat, flashed a spark of lawlessness sufficient to ignite a prairie fire that would burn for a quarter-century across the American West. And across the scorched earth of that untamed frontier, the deputy marshal would ride into folklore.

Nowhere did the bitterness to fuel the combustion exist in greater abundance than in the ravaged landscape of postwar Missouri.

Missouri, whose regulars had fallen fast, had been occupied by Union forces as early as 1862. Resistance was sustained throughout the war by well-trained guerrilla armies, riding under such famous commands as those of William Quantrill and Bloody Bill Anderson. Denied amnesty after the war, unlike their brothers-in-arms across the South, the Kansas and Missouri raiders entered civilian life as outlaws.

Emblematic, in their vilification, of the lost Confederate cause, they nursed their grievances collectively and, in the hearts of the local population, their grievances found support. The brutal experience of the Missouri farmer under Union occupation was amplified in its aftermath by an unsympathetic government's failure to address his desperate struggle for economic recovery. A victim rather than a beneficiary of postwar federal policy, he bore little respect, if any, for the nation's institutions.

Least of all for its banks.

It was on the tinder of this resentment that the fire of lawlessness would feed. And never would there be more successful keepers of the flame than a pair of young Missouri irregulars named Frank and Jesse James.

The James gang virtually *invented* bank robbery.

At that moment on Saint Valentine's Day, 1866, when William Bird, clerk of the Clay County Savings Association in Liberty, Missouri, was told, over the barrel of a gun, "I'd like all the money in the bank," he entered the annals of American criminal history—so rare, so up-to-the-minute as to be unimaginable, was it that an American bank be knocked over during business hours.

The take was estimated at $60,000.

Imitated but never equaled by desperadoes for over a century, their like never to be seen again—they *owned* the railroads, *and* the stage lines—Frank and Jesse James, by measure of sheer innovation alone, would stand forever unchallenged as the first family of American crime, not the least of their accomplishments being that they managed to remain at large for more than fifteen years.

On April 3, 1882, Jesse James was murdered, shot in the back of the head by a guest in his house, fellow outlaw Bob Ford, who had made a deal to save himself with the governor of Missouri. Frank, who thereupon surrendered to Governor Thomas Crittenden—he was tried for murder and, with dispatch, was acquitted by the people of rural Missouri—would live to the age of seventy-two, dying on the eve of the First World War steeped in the rhetoric of communism.

In the shadow of these two men, across the Great Plains, rode outlaws such as the Daltons, whose cousins, the Younger brothers, had gained fame riding against the banks as members of the James gang. The three Youngers were taken alive in the great Northfield, Minnesota, raid in 1876. (A penitent Cole Younger, after serving twenty-five years, would take to the American lecture circuit.) Emmett was the only one of three audacious Dalton brothers to survive the failed 1892 raid on two banks, simultaneously, in Coffeyville, Kansas. He would serve fifteen years in prison. Others came and went, but it was the death of one outlaw, more than that of any other, by which the end of the era was measured.

Uninvited to take part in the catastrophic Coffeyville raid was a Dalton understudy named Bill Doolin. Doolin's death in Oklahoma Territory in August 1896 was a significant moment in the triumph of law and order on the American frontier. And it was just as significant a moment in the history of the U.S. marshals.

Between the end of the Civil War and the turn of the century, more deputy marshals were killed in the line of duty than at any other time in their history. A dozen died fighting the Klan. Two dozen died in the Moonshine Wars. But of all those slain in the 200 years since their office was established, no fewer than a quarter lost their lives on the 74,000 square miles of real property that is occupied almost entirely by present-day Oklahoma: between 1872 and 1896, 103 deputy marshals were killed in what at that time was known as Indian Territory.

"A rendezvous of the vile and wicked from everywhere," in the words of a Fort Smith, Arkansas, newspaper, Indian Territory, unorganized until the Oklahoma land rush of 1889, had been officially established by the Intercourse Act of 1834. Until congressional passage of the act, which was designed to protect Indians from depredation by whites, the territory had existed as a vaguely defined wilderness of undesirable land upon which the Five Civilized Tribes, as they were called, had been resettled by the government after being forced to vacate the East, the region to which they were indigenous.

Indian Territory was the sorrowful product of the nation's Indian removal, journey's end on the Cherokee Trail of Tears.

In 1870 the only authorized permanent residents of Indian Territory were 50,000 native Americans, principally Cherokee, Choctaw, Chickasaw, Creek, and Seminole, whose ancestral lands had been stolen from them by settlers of European descent —tenants bent on ownership of a chiefly coastal region that would one day exhibit the approximate boundaries of the Southeastern Conference of the NCAA—but by that time history had begun to repeat itself. In the wake of the Civil War, Indian Territory had become swollen with squatters, the worst of the nation's whites, drawn there by commerce and the utter absence of local law enforcement.

Tribal law, the local law of the land, did not cover the behavior of the white man.

America's unorganized territories were just that; not until their populations of free white males reached 5,000 were provisions made for local government. (Territories thus organized, once that number reached 60,000, were then nominated for statehood.) Previous to organization, federal law prevailed.

Jurisdiction over Indian Territory emanated from the United States Court for the Western District of Arkansas, which in 1871 had been moved from Van Buren to the town of Fort Smith. Situated on the Arkansas River, no more than a hundred yards from the territory's eastern rim, the court, maintaining its jurisdiction over thirty Arkansas counties as well, had become so corrupt by 1875 that the district judge, his clerk, the U.S. attorney, the U.S. marshal, and most of his deputies had all been forced to resign. Into the vacuum of authority created by their departure would step, that year, a thirty-six-year-old former two-term U.S. congressman from St. Joseph, Missouri, to make more than twenty years of judicial history.

Isaac Charles Parker, appointed U.S. District Judge for the Western District of Arkansas by Ulysses S. Grant, arrived in Fort Smith with his family on May 2, 1875. Within nine weeks of his arrival he had sentenced six men to hang. Simultaneously. The gallows built upon his orders were designed to execute twelve at a time. None of the condemned was a famous outlaw, but each, in his anonymous way, was typical of the vermin whose sheer numbers choked Indian Territory. Parker—among other things, a great ally of the native American—in his twenty-one-year tenure, would sentence hundreds of such criminals to prison, 160 to die. After appeals and commutations, a total of seventy-nine would be executed. In his first fourteen years on the bench, Parker sent forty-six men to the gallows for murder or rape.

The condemned did not make their way to Isaac Parker's court voluntarily. Keeping the "Hanging Judge" busy, a force of 200 deputy marshals, over a period of twenty years, scoured Indian Territory on horseback, riding out of Fort Smith on the most celebrated manhunt in history. The motives of some deputies were questionable. Some had questionable pasts. The dark futures of some—the Dalton brothers—would bring them greater fame. All had only one thing in common. Their skills were those of the gunfighter.

Of the deputies who "rode for Parker" the most famous was a native Georgian whose reputation as a frontier lawman was well established by 1886 when he was recruited out of Texas. Quiet, resolute, almost avuncular in appearance, he would ride into modern history as the prototypical Western marshal. Take away the ivory-handled six-shooters, the lever-action Winchester .44-40, and the fabled number-eight shotgun, talk him out of the badge and the knee-high boots, stand him up for a photograph in a three-piece suit, and Heck Thomas still looked saddle weary.

He once rode into Fort Smith out of Indian Territory with thirty-two prisoners in custody.

Heck Thomas, in August 1896, was riding for E. D. Nix, U.S. marshal for Oklahoma—the territory carved out of Indian land and opened to white settlement in 1889, then expanded by the 1893 rush across the Cherokee strip—when he finally caught up with Bill Doolin. The outlaw had been brought in once already, captured by famed deputy marshal Bill Tilghman after being tracked to Eureka Springs, Arkansas, but had managed to escape the territorial jail in Guthrie six months later. Thomas tracked Doolin to his father-in-law's farmhouse in Lawson, where the outlaw was holed up with his wife and young child. On the night of August 24, as Doolin and his family, under cover of darkness, were setting off from the house, Thomas and his posse got the drop on him. After a brief exchange of gunfire, in which Doolin managed to discharge first his Winchester then his six-shooter, Thomas, as he explains it, "got the shotgun to work and the fight was over."

The death of Bill Doolin, leader of the last of the great outlaw gangs to ride out of the Midwest, did not put an end to crime on the frontier. It did, however, provide evidence that law enforcement in the territories had finally become organized. The manhunt itself signaled a change in the tide of local civilian support —running in favor not of the outlaws, but of the lawmen who pursued them.

But Bill Doolin, alas, did not ride off into the sunset alone.

With the closing of the West and the onset of the new century, the deputy U.S. marshal would enter upon a twenty-five-year decline and a plunge into obscurity that lasted another twenty-five.

With the organization of the western territories came local rule on the frontier, and with the emergence of local, county, and state police forces there, the deputy marshal eventually fell victim to operational atrophy. After that, it seemed he was doomed, when he received attention at all, to receive only negative attention.

In the spring and summer of 1894, led by its founder Eugene V. Debs, the year-old American Railway Union, fresh on the heels of its first victory in a strike against the Northern Pacific, struck the Pullman Palace Car Company just south of Chicago. Protesting massive wage cuts, 18,000 workers walked off the job, bringing rail operations across the Midwest (and across much of the far West) to an abrupt halt. The federal government, as it would continue to do well into the next century, sided immediately with management. Citing, as an excuse, interference with the movement of the U.S. Mail, Grover Cleveland's attorney general, Richard Olney, obtained an injunction against the union, and authorized the deputizing of 5,000 men, most of them thugs in the employ of the railroads, to break the strike. Eventually followed in by over 2,000 soldiers, the deputies served as the shock troops in what proved to be a stunning setback for organized labor. For the better part of the next forty years, the deputy U.S. marshal would provide the federal muscle in the government's war with the American labor movement.

(During the First World War, deputy marshals arrested, delivered, and registered enemy aliens, who were then interned by the army; they provided perimeter security against saboteurs on the nation's docks and around its industrial plants. During Prohibition they provided arrest power for Treasury agents. They also conducted the property seizures. In June 1925 the U.S. marshal's office in Chicago averaged eighteen arrests a day; on July 1, 1926, marshals had forty-nine seized distilleries and breweries in custody. It was deputy marshals, one of them a woman,

Norma Haugan, on warrants issued in the Northern District of Illinois, who in 1931 arrested Al Capone.)

The deterioration of the office was accelerated in the new century by a rapid expansion of the federal bureaucracy. New law-enforcement agencies were chartered, and not only were they specialized, but more important than that they were centralized, headquartered in Washington with ready access to the decision-makers who controlled their destiny. Their growth was assured.

The decline of the deputy marshal would be cast sharply into relief in the 1930s when, capitalizing on manhunts for such celebrated gangsters as John Dillinger and Pretty Boy Floyd, a publicity-savvy bureaucrat named J. Edgar Hoover transformed a minor agency in the Justice Department into what was soon to be the most famous law-enforcement organization in the world.

With the rise of the FBI (established in 1908 as the Bureau of Investigation and granted power of arrest in 1934) the office of the deputy marshal would substantially depreciate.

Once the long arm of the law, the deputy was by now reduced to bailiff and professional process server. A glorified jailer. With no central headquarters to lobby the federal bureaucracy on his behalf, he was civil servant without a career path. Held to no professional standards, he was a lawman at the occupational pinnacle of whose job sat local ward heelers, party hirelings, and well-connected sewing-machine salesmen. For a quarter-century the office of marshal would serve as a refuge for aging political hacks, sustained solely on the fruits of congressional patronage.

Eventual revitalization of the office had its roots in the American civil-rights movement. When communities in the South, in the wake of the 1954 Supreme Court ruling *Brown v. Board of Education of Topeka, Kansas*, defied federal court orders to desegregate their schools and public facilities, the Justice Department turned to the United States marshals to enforce the courts' decisions.

It was deputy marshals who in 1960 escorted black first-graders to school in desegregated New Orleans, who in 1965 walked from Selma to Montgomery with Martin Luther King, Jr. But it was on the night of September 30, 1962, in Oxford, Mississippi, in pressing the most incendiary confrontation of the era, that the deputy marshal walked out of the obscurity cast by the shadow of history to recapture the errant glory that was destined to be his again.

By the end of September, 1962, several attempts to secure the registration of James Meredith as the first black student at the University of Mississippi—his admission having been ordered by the Fifth U.S. Circuit Court of Appeals—had been thwarted by state officials under Governor Ross Barnett. Attorney General Robert Kennedy, to guarantee Meredith's enrollment, detached to the Ole Miss campus, on the afternoon of Sunday the 30th, 123 deputy marshals, their force augmented by specially deputized Border Patrol and Bureau of Prisons officers, a total of 536 men.

By 5 P.M. they had attracted a crowd. By nightfall the crowd had grown violent. In the vanguard of the riot that ensued was a small corps of university students. The mob that eventually formed, however, was dominated by outsiders; over the course of the confrontation their number would reach 3,000. Backed by the white columns of the Lyceum, the antebellum building which housed the office of the university registrar, helmeted deputies, who had been ordered to hold their fire, soon started hitting the ground under an onslaught of rocks, bricks, and vials of acid.

Using tear gas, they held their positions.

Gunshots eventually erupted and the deputies were forced to take cover. They took sniper fire throughout the night. By 2 A.M., when the army arrived and cleared the campus of rioters, there were, among the officers who had taken part, 180 casualties, 27 of them wounded by shotgun or rifle fire. Five were cited for bravery. There were two fatalities that night, one a young Mississippi spectator, the other a working French journalist. Both died of gunshot wounds.

Marshals arrested 200 rioters, fewer than 50 of them university students.

At 8 A.M. Meredith, a transfer student, registered for classes. He would remain on campus for almost a year. Until he graduated—until August 18, 1963, when he received a bachelor of arts degree in political science—he was guarded by deputy marshals twenty-four hours a day.

The fight for civil rights did not end with James Meredith, but after Oxford, the days of state-defended segregation in the

United States were clearly numbered. That night in Mississippi was a turning point, not only in the social history of the nation, but in the history of its oldest law-enforcement agency. Enrolling Meredith and keeping him alive for a year, deputy marshals, demonstrating not only their professionalism but the flexibility of their authority, would go on to desegregate the South. Their new stature in the eyes of the public and in the ranks of the federal bureaucracy gave rise to a period of expansion and rebuilding that would bring them, belatedly but dramatically, into the twentieth century.

In 1969 the United States Marshals Service was established. By 1974 it had achieved bureau status within the Department of Justice. (In 1988 that status was reinforced by congressional statute.) Headquarters enjoyed control over the Service's budget, over the hiring and training of deputy marshals, and over the nature of the Service's various missions. The ninety-five U.S. marshals themselves, the political appointees, were tolerated.

By the time of the marshals' bicentennial, the Marshals Service had secured a broad operational mandate that was reflective of its deputies' unique status in the federal bureaucracy. Because they are both officers of the federal courts (the judicial branch) and law-enforcement agents of the attorney general (the executive branch), theirs is a widely diversified mission.

The Marshals Service, as it has been for 200 years, is responsible for the security of all federal judicial proceedings. That responsibility includes the personal protection of judges, magistrates, jurors, witnesses, prosecutors, and officers of the court, both in and out of the courtroom. The Service responds to all reported threats against members of the judiciary; in 1990 there were 496 verified threats against court officials, 193 as of April 1991. Responsibility for the physical security of the more than 500 judicial facilities in the ninety-five districts was consolidated within the Marshals Service in 1983. To that end the Service implemented the Court Security Officer Program, under which CSOs are hired by contract to provide building perimeter security, to screen those entering the buildings, and, in sensitive trials, to augment the security details to which deputies are assigned. In 1990 CSOs detected some 138,000 weapons at courthouse security checkpoints—10,809 of them illegal.

The Marshals Service receives, processes, and takes custody

of all federal prisoners brought before the court for arraignment. In 1990 it processed approximately 87,000 of them. It contracts with state and local jails for housing unsentenced prisoners when federal facilities are not available. (On average it costs forty dollars a day to rent space in a city or county jail.) On March 30, 1991, in one place or another, the Service was holding a record 15,000 prisoners for trial or sentencing. (On that date there were 61,225 people serving time in federal prison in the United States.)

The Marshals Service is also responsible for transporting all federal prisoners, producing them for legal hearings and meetings with counsel as well as for trial. (In 1990 deputies produced prisoners for 437,538 court appearances.) The Service moves sentenced prisoners to penitentiaries and transfers them between penitentiaries. Short-distance prisoner moves are handled by district personnel in surface vehicles; long-distance moves are accomplished by the Service's National Prisoner Transportation System.

NPTS in 1990 moved over 125,000 prisoners. Budgeted at up to $18 million annually, it operates a scheduled airline by which it moved a third of them. "Con-Air," a sixteen-plane fleet that includes two Boeing 727s, was launched in 1984. With stops at some thirty cities and six military installations around the country, it flies five to six days a week at an industry-enviable capacity of 70 percent. Headquartered at Will Rogers Airport in Oklahoma City, where aircraft, pilots, and engineers are based—prisoners are processed at the El Reno Correctional Institution thirty miles away—it moves state and local as well as federal prisoners and charges state and local authorities for the service. Cheaper and infinitely safer, if not faster, than commercial transportation, Con-Air has enabled local authorities, reluctant to seek extradition of felons because of high transportation and personnel costs, to do so at a fraction of the expense traditionally incurred.

As administrator of the National Asset Seizure and Forfeiture Program, the Marshals Service is custodian of over $1.4 billion in cash and property seized in criminal cases brought by the various agencies of the Justice Department. (The Customs Service manages a similar, though smaller, program in the Department of the Treasury.) It is the responsibility of the Marshals Service under NASAF to secure, inventory, appraise, store, maintain, and ultimately dispose of the assets seized. The Comprehensive Crime Control Act of 1984 authorized the equitable sharing of the proceeds of property forfeited to the federal government with state and local law-enforcement authorities; the Assets Forfeiture Fund, also administered by the Marshals Service, provides for distribution to those authorities in proportion to their participation in the case in which the property was seized.

The Marshals Service is still responsible for the expeditious service of all federal process; it executes some 354,000 court orders, not including warrants, every year. Because its deputies, on the nation's public highways, have arrest powers not granted to the Department of Defense, the Marshals Service provides security assistance to the Strategic Air Command during the intermittent movement of Minuteman and cruise missiles between military installations; as part of the Service's Missile Escort Program, deputies escorted close to 1,400 missile convoys in 1990. The Marshals Service oversees the security of all international spy swaps; it accepts custody of fugitives surrendered to the United States by foreign governments pursuant to extradition or expulsion; it is one of the principal U.S. agency participants in INTERPOL. To respond to emergencies—civil disturbances, terrorist incidents, hostage takings—and to provide security during high-threat trials and prisoner moves, the Marshals Service maintains a paramilitary force, the Special Operations Group. (It was they who put the handcuffs on General Manuel Noriega in Panama in January 1990.)

A modern law-enforcement bureaucracy, sustaining and expanding a jealously guarded federal mandate, the Marshals Service owes much of its new purpose to its Office of Congressional and Public Affairs. As engineer of the Service's publicity, the office has successfully promoted the agency, constructing an image for the deputy marshal modeled on the prototype of his frontier predecessor. Notwithstanding the agency's professional handling of the programs outlined above, however, mass production of that image would have been impossible prior to 1979.

The year of the Fugitive Program.

That year, in a Department of Justice policy move, responsibility for the majority of federal fugitives fell to the Marshals Service. Under a memorandum of understanding between the Service and the FBI, the Marshals Service assumed authority over certain categories of federal fugitives, including those who had violated the conditions of their parole or probation or had jumped bond after being convicted. The backlog of fugitives at the time had grown to unprecedented levels, primarily because the FBI was giving them no priority. (In investigative agencies, no institutional credit is given for fugitive arrests; agents are rewarded for opening new cases and making *initial* arrests.) The Marshals Service inherited 8,500 FBI fugitives. Ordered to devote more of its resources to the infiltration of organized crime and the arrest of white-collar criminals, the FBI had that much more reason to unburden itself of what it considered to be a lowly mission; when several years later the Bureau went to war with the Marshals Service on the matter of federal fugitives, it was not really over the loss of the program as such, but over the consequent and quite cavalier theft of international headlines that had once been the Bureau's exclusive property.

With the Fugitive Program came jurisdiction over those who had escaped from federal prison. And with that authority the Marshals Service made its first, well-calculated move in the campaign that would eventually carry it to the forefront of American law enforcement.

Christopher Boyce, it is arguable, when he broke out of maximum security at Lompoc, did more for the United States Marshals Service than he had ever done for the KGB. The young California native, celebrated in the book, and subsequent film, *The Falcon and the Snowman,* who was convicted in 1977 of selling American satellite secrets to the Soviets, escaped prison in January 1980. He remained at large for over a year and a half. It was deputy marshals, invigorating their reputation as the law west of Fort Smith, who brought him back alive. The Service capitalized on the attendant publicity with such shameless sophistication that its budget and manpower were summarily increased. With the trackdown and capture of Boyce (chronicled in a sequel to the book) the deputy marshal as manhunter was clearly on his way back.

Just as celebrated was the apprehension in 1982 of rogue CIA operative Edwin P. Wilson. Indicted in April 1980, Wilson had been wanted on several charges, including illegal weapons trafficking—he had supplied Libyan colonel Muammar Qadaffi with explosives and had trained an army of international terrorists in their use. Assistant U.S. Attorney for the District of Columbia Larry Barcella, who had made the case against Wilson and was seeking to extricate the former agent from his sanctuary in Libya, turned to the FBI, under whose jurisdiction Wilson fell. The Bureau, finding the political risks of involvement too great, and citing as futile, at best, any effort to bring Wilson to justice, wanted nothing to do with the case and made their disinclination plain to Barcella. The young prosecutor, finding a court of last appeal in the Marshals Service, approached Howard Safir, its Associate Director for Operations. The stratagem that lured the cunning Wilson inevitably into Barcella's trap (the case is documented in detail in the book *Manhunt* by Peter Maas) was both a coup for the United States Marshals Service and a significant embarrassment to the Bureau.

Under Safir's direction, deputy marshals attracted international attention again when in 1985 they tracked down the Nazi "Angel of Death," Dr. Josef Mengele—last seen at Auschwitz forty years earlier—corroborating his death in South America and ultimately exhuming his body in a Brazilian cemetery.

But these and other successful high-profile fugitive efforts were merely the more dramatic plot points in the larger story. Capitalizing on the restoration of its historic authority, the Service inaugurated various Special Enforcement Operations run out of headquarters, the most successful conducted under the acronym FIST, for Fugitive Investigative Strike Team. Designed to grab headlines and boost arrest figures—engineered unashamedly to make numbers—and conducted in cooperation with state and local agencies, the nine major FIST operations engineered between 1980 and 1987 (there were regional equivalents, run out of various districts) resulted in almost 15,000 felony arrests, over 13,000 of them on state, not federal, warrants. While grounded in traditional police investigative techniques, the operations often attracted attention for the innovative nature of those arrests, for the scams occasionally employed by deputies to snare fugitives *en masse,* several dozen at a time, without violence.

The United States Marshals Service, with a work force that hovers in the vicinity of 3,300, is about a tenth the size of the New York City Police Department. (The FBI is staffed at about 24,000.) Of the 3,300 personnel, about 2,700 are sworn, operational people; 150 of those are women; 9 to 10 percent are black, 5 percent Hispanic.

A man or woman of action, typically drawn, when not to a second career, to a career happened upon by chance—rare is that American child who, when he or she grows up, wants "to be a U.S. marshal"—today's deputy survives, and productively so, in an agency at the outer reaches of which bureaucracy has only lately begun to coagulate. Answering to Washington is a recent phenomenon, and the game of political survival played out at headquarters is one in which the deputy need not participate; had he any natural talent for it, he probably never would have found his way to the Service in the first place. The deputy is an individual whose personal ambitions have never been those of an administrator. His survival into the next century may change that, as his enthusiasm for everyday police work is outpaced by the operational ambitions of his agency.

A deputy's livelihood, like that of any cop, incorporates survival in its most elementary manifestation. His is an endeavor where mortality is a preoccupation. The typical deputy marshal devotes a large part of his average workday to averting violent death on the job. Even at its most routine, the job is decidedly dangerous. Prisoner transportation, "almost half of what we do," puts a deputy in continual contact with some of the nation's more desperate people.

"They are ingenious," as one deputy explains it. "They have twenty-four hours a day to think of how to beat you."

Survival is the story of the deputy marshal in another, ironic way.

To the survival of members of the criminal class, a large part of the Service's resources are dedicated. Public-relations successes aside, the future of the Marshals Service, in the absence of anything else, is secured by the one activity it does not go out of its way to advertise, an activity by which the course of law enforcement in this country has been changed forever.

The United States Marshals Service is proprietor of the federal Witness Security Program.

It is with the Service's assignment to witness protection and relocation in 1971 that the modern era of the deputy marshal truly begins.

4.

California
Dreamin'

For Bud McPherson, chivalry had died a long time ago. When the charter touched down in Cedar Rapids, he expected the women on board to remain seated. There was, in McPherson's unique line of work, a protocol for deboarding an aircraft, a code of established conduct, and it was one he had been enforcing for years:

The people wearing guns exit first.

The plane, a small, twin-engine job, was on time out of Kansas City. On board that day, in addition to the pilot, were three deputy U.S. marshals; McPherson's dark-haired, blue-eyed wife, Claudette; and a small, plump, clearly delusional young native-American woman named Myrtle Poor Bear.

The two women and the pilot were unarmed.

Claudette McPherson, viewed in the context of her marriage, had led a relatively sheltered life, but only as sheltered as is possible for a clever Italian-American girl who had grown up on those streets of Brooklyn, New York, controlled by the Gambino crime family; a resourceful young woman who had gone on to marry a former cop, one day to be promoted to Region XII Chief, Witness Security Division, United States Marshals Service.

Claudette McPherson had grown up legit, but she had not,

as her husband might artlessly put it, "been hiding under a rock."

Still, that day in 1976, in Cedar Rapids, Iowa, as she was violating procedure—as she came storming out of that airplane ahead of the security detail assigned by her husband—Claudette McPherson was unprepared for what awaited her on the runway below. For the first time in her husband's *most recent* career, and to what would prove to be his surprise, she was suddenly compelled to ask questions.

And the first question she asked, as McPherson remembers it, was:

"Are you trying to get me killed!!?"

Donald "Bud" McPherson, like many of his contemporaries in the Marshals Service, had come on the job with a background that one could honestly describe as checkered. His was one of those career histories that impress personnel directors the way calls to jury duty impress the gainfully employed—bringing them immediately down with inexplicable illnesses and mysterious prior engagements . . . *No need to call back, Mr. Mc-Pherson, we'll call you.* His résumé was of an admittedly . . . *eclectic* . . . nature, of that somewhat fanciful variety identified more readily with the method actor and late-blooming novelist than with the typical civil servant.

A "pre-Miranda cop" in Brooklyn, New York, McPherson had quit the force at thirty, resigning with an associate's degree in police science and fewer than ten years on the roster. He joined the New York City Fire Department in 1963. In 1966, leaving the city, his first marriage, and that job behind, McPherson followed the Dodgers. He moved to southern California. There he went to work as Burns Detective Agency supervisor and, after that, as a firefighter for Warner Brothers Studios—he helped save the castle on the back-lot *Camelot* set—eventually being laid off. He tended bar for a while. He then bought a truck. In time, he landed a contract to haul furniture for Global Van Lines. He did that "a couple of years." In the fall of 1970 he was sitting in his rig in a rainstorm (he was now hauling for Mayflower) unable to load because of the weather, when he ran across a newspaper item announcing a test for sky marshals.

And far be it from Bud McPherson to ignore any opportunity to broaden his occupational horizons.

Air piracy, as a criminal occupational specialty, came into its own in the early years of the Nixon presidency. Responding to its sudden, worldwide popularity, the White House issued orders that armed undercover agents, as expeditiously as possible, be placed aboard U.S. carriers. Sky marshals, as they came to be called, operated under the authority of U.S. Customs, the search-and-seizure power of whose personnel was long established at the nation's airports. Their authority as Customs Security Officers to enforce the U.S. Code was amplified by their simultaneous commission as special deputy U.S. marshals.

Bud McPherson went to work as a sky marshal, but, characteristically, not for long. In August 1971, hitching his perpetually double-parked career wagon to a familiar five-pointed star, he applied to fill one of two openings for deputies in the office of the United States marshal in Los Angeles.

In 1990 he was still there.

How McPherson, in the winter of 1973, came to be standing in a blinding snowstorm in Rapid City, South Dakota, dressed in yellow golf pants is a story which as accurately as any illustrates the day-to-day vicissitudes of the career into which he had stumbled.

McPherson (who went through basic training with Marvin Mack, attending the school when it was located "above the Safeway in D.C.") had not been on the job a full five months when he applied for duty with the Service's paramilitary wing, the Special Operations Group, a year-old unit of volunteers, organized to respond within hours to civil disturbances and national emergencies and activated only "as needed," its deputies on call from their various district assignments pending permission of their respective marshals. The group, at the time, conducted its tactical training at the U.S. Border Patrol Academy in Los Fresnos, Texas. Soon after he trained there in 1972, McPherson found himself on SOG duty in Washington, D.C., where that November's Trail of Broken Treaties march had, with significant justification, escalated to a five-day occupation of the Bureau of Indian Affairs. McPherson, a combat veteran, who as a teenager had served with the 187th Airborne in Korea, took to the prospect of rappeling out of a helicopter onto the roof of Washington's BIA building with a certain measure of equanimity. (Ultimately the plan was abandoned in favor of negotiations.) He did not, however, see in Special Operations his future as a deputy marshal.

McPherson recalls SOG, in the early days of its existence, as being composed principally of "good ol' boys . . . a bunch of ex–drill instructors"; in its members he saw crystallized all those negative characteristics by which the twentieth-century deputy marshal had come to be identified. Summed up in an expression that today enjoys semi-official status in the lexicon of the Service, the old days were the days of the "size-46 polyester."

(By the time of the marshals' bicentennial, the United States Marshals Service would boast a growing population of sworn personnel who were able to discourse more poetically on the subject of traditional tailoring than on the relative merits, even at the most fundamental level, of various operationally approved firearms.)

Three months after he returned from the nation's capital, on a sunny February morning in Los Angeles, McPherson received orders to report to even sunnier San Diego on a routine court-security assignment. Those who know McPherson well will tell you that what he grabbed first were his golf clubs. No sooner had he packed a suitcase, however, than a second call came in, instructing him to go, not leisurely but at once, to Los Angeles International Airport. And there his itinerary was changed. From Los Angeles he was flown to Denver, where they clearly were not playing golf at the time, and where he was joined by other deputies assigned to Special Operations.

In Denver, McPherson was briefed.

He was dispatched immediately to South Dakota, there to touch down in the aforementioned Rapid City snowstorm. He hit the tarmac running, like a paratrooper for the PGA—dressed rather optimistically, he discovered, for what would prove to be the opening round in the ten-week occupation of Wounded Knee—diligently, and quite cheerfully, prepared to impose his presence on that year's San Diego Open.

Colorful clothing, of course, would be the order of the day.

Within hours he was wearing a royal-blue jumpsuit—SOG patch and silver star—an orange neckerchief, and combat boots. He was about to participate, however reluctantly, in the continuing history of his government's oppression of those people native to North America, a continent which, somewhere in the dark backward and abysm of time, had given majestic rise to the gold-latticed, coal-and-uranium-rich real estate that would come to be known as the Black Hills.

After helping deny access to the BIA building on the Pine Ridge Reservation to members of the Oglala Sioux Civil Rights Organization—a five-day assignment—McPherson returned to Los Angeles. Again, as it happened, rather optimistically. He had been home no more than two weeks when several hundred Indians, under the leadership of OSCRO and the American Indian Movement, occupied the Pine Ridge village of Wounded Knee, site of the December 29, 1890, massacre in which more than 200 defenseless Sioux—men, women, and children—had been slaughtered by President Benjamin Harrison's decorated Seventh Cavalry. Within twenty-four hours of the occupation, the community was surrounded by federal officers—FBI agents, BIA police, and deputy U.S. marshals, McPherson among them —equipped in short order with armored personnel carriers, semiautomatic rifles, and enough ammunition to make the original massacre measure up like a motor-vehicle fatality.

The siege lasted seventy-one days.

"This is not Korea, this is Wounded Knee," McPherson would later explain of a photograph taken of him at the time, a snapshot in which he is pictured, armed with a modern assault rifle, aboard an APC. "We were shooting at each other every day."

Royal blue inevitably gave way to camouflage.

According to John Haynes, a Special Operations deputy who would go on to become the unit's commander, "Practically every day, there was a firefight . . . shots exchanged. Three, four hours sometimes. We had night shoot-outs. . . . Every night, every so often, we'd pop flares to illuminate the area. . . . We had everything imaginable. We had .270 Weatherbys, .300 Magnums, M1 rifles, M16s. We had every kind of weapon you could think of, all semiautomatic fire, no full-auto."

The armored personnel carriers were brought in, Haynes remembers, to enable forces to traverse the snow.

"The first night we went out there and set up at a thousand meters we got hit by a snowstorm, and we stayed in our cars for about forty-eight hours without any food, and the cars ran out of fuel. . . . There was snow up about fender level, and one of us would have a candy bar or one thing and another and we would ration that out. They finally brought a helicopter out and started picking us up and relieving us. . . .

"The snow stayed on like that. . . . We were right out there in the middle of nowhere. . . . Thousands of rounds were exchanged. . . . It was real strange for me, having been just out of the military and back from Vietnam. . . . To be in the United States, to be involved in the same kind of thing right here in your own country. . . . They say it was the longest siege on American soil that's ever taken place."

Exclusive of secession, the siege at Wounded Knee stands as the longest civil uprising in American history.

"We figured," Haynes concedes, "we could have ended it within six hours, anytime we wanted to. But nobody wanted another Wounded Knee massacre, like the original thing that happened. Nobody wanted that . . . nobody."

Storming the hamlet was estimated by the military to be possible at a cost of 50 percent casualties to the assault force. As negotiations were pursued, the siege dragged on into the spring.

"We were settin' in the same positions that the Seventh Cavalry had set in. And you would visualize, here we are, the cavalry, settin' up there, lookin' down, just like they were back then. We set in and deployed in some of the very same positions. And to sit up there at night and listen to them beatin' their tom-toms and dancin'. . . . We all grew up watchin' cowboys-and-Indians movies and stuff . . . it was a hell of an experience."

The siege, when it was over, was marked by the deaths of two Indian fighters and the permanent paralysis of a visiting U.S. marshal whose spine was severed by a rifle round.

"When we went down in there, I tell you, I don't know how there weren't more people killed . . . I mean there was bullet holes through everything. They had killed 'most all the cattle in and around there that they could. They butchered them up, and there'd be a hindquarter layin' over here, or the carcass of a cow over there."

For Haynes, a Vietnam combat veteran, a man born and raised in former Indian Territory, the memory of the uprising would be an indelible one. Reflects the native Oklahoman:

"The damndest thing I've ever been to."

And the experience was no less surreal for the native of Brooklyn, New York.

"At Pine Ridge we didn't have any cars," Bud McPherson remembers. "We were leasing them, using them at roadblocks and taking cover behind them. After a period of time, Hertz put out a teletype, instructing all its offices not to rent any more cars to U.S. marshals. Hertz was getting them back with bullet holes in them and with the windows shot out."

McPherson, engaging the Indians, was simultaneously engaging the FBI, an agency which, according to the locals, provided many of the villains of the uprising. McPherson, who harbored few illusions about things, was nothing if not a self-starter—initiative, for better or worse, being the *sine qua non* of the deputy marshal for close to 200 years. And the last thing he needed in a firefight was the advice of an aspiring bureaucrat, especially one in whose particular agency a show of initiative, as a matter of policy, was greeted like an outbreak of anthrax. As McPherson informed one special agent who was unwilling to return fire without authorization (presumably from the ghost of J. Edgar Hoover himself) and indignant that McPherson would do so:

"I'm thirty-nine years old, I've been shot at a lot of places—Korea . . . Brooklyn. . . . I wouldn't be here if I had to get permission to return fire."

It would be the FBI, three years later, having tested to the limit its peculiar in-house blend of ambition and incompetence, that brought McPherson back to the Badlands, the FBI that in its self-induced aphasia invented the pitiful Myrtle Poor Bear.

By then, however, McPherson would have reached a point in his career where the process of formal assignment had become little more than a matter of etiquette, a conventional social gesture, all but purely ceremonial—by then, to find out where he was expected to report on any given day, all McPherson would have to do is pick up a newspaper.

Bud McPherson's evolution as a witness-security specialist began in 1972. The United States Marshals Service, still in the embryonic stages of its development as an agency, had yet to envision law enforcement as being akin to the study of modern medicine. The deputy marshal at that point was still a general practitioner, but the time was rapidly approaching when he would be welcome to specialize in almost anything.

It was from graduates of its Court Security School, which McPherson had attended within a year of his basic training, that the Service took its witness-security specialists in the early days of the program. Advanced training in WITSEC itself—which some in the Service like to think of as the law-enforcement equivalent of a brain surgery residency, a discipline that Mc-Pherson, one of the program's pioneers, actually helped to create—had yet to be formalized, and until such time as it was, WITSEC remained a subspecialty of court-security work.

McPherson, as a court-security specialist, had handled, among others, the trial of Daniel Ellsberg, the erstwhile defense analyst and failed academic who, taking oddly to heart the expression "publish or perish," had in 1971 leaked the Pentagon Papers to the *New York Times*. It was as a court-security specialist that McPherson had been ordered to San Diego, when like a hallucinating Arnold Palmer he had shown up in the onslaught of that developing snowstorm on the outskirts of Rapid City.

It would be upon his return from Wounded Knee in 1973, with a year of court security behind him, that McPherson was assigned as a district specialist to WITSEC. And if he was looking for a clue to his future, he did not have to look very far.

The call came in from Washington. McPherson's orders were simple. He was to meet an American Airlines flight at Los Angeles International Airport.

The orders ended there.

"Your man will be on it, you'll recognize him."

End of conversation.

Security on the witness was that tight.

"In the early days of the program everything was a secret. Not only did they operate on a need-to-know basis, but they wouldn't even tell you when you needed to know."

McPherson, with two cars stationed outside the American Airlines terminal, put a low-profile, three-man detail on the arrivals gate, and waited, ready for anything, open to whatever wild card headquarters had decided to deal. Studying passengers as they deboarded the transcontinental flight, McPherson made his man immediately. Blond, bespectacled, all-American, a young man of medium stature, the fellow was unimposing in the extreme, yet at the same time unlikely to benefit from any serious attempt at disguise. Not even a marginal attempt had been made. He was dressed the way McPherson had always seen him dressed, a little bit less than elegant, a little bit more than uptight. A lot, indeed, like a lawyer.

"He comes over to me and says, 'You must be Bud.' *He* knew

who he was meeting. I guess he had a need to know and I didn't."

Washington had not been fooling. McPherson's man was recognizable. Unmistakable, in fact. A television celebrity, he had been playing second lead to the star of what had proved to be one of the more compelling daytime dramas of the decade. Given that, it was only fitting that the man should take up residence in southern California. He was using the name John West, and he and his wife would spend a part of their time with McPherson looking to buy a house in Los Angeles. His real name was John Wesley Dean, and he would spend the rest of his time helping to orchestrate the inevitable fall of the political administration of the thirty-seventh president of the United States.

In the summer of 1973, virtually all participants in the Witness Security Program were members of organized crime. John Dean, the White House counsel, far from being typical of the witnesses McPherson was assigned to protect (a majority of the American public probably held racketeers in higher esteem), was not even *in* the program, which presupposed relocation and the formal erasure of one's identity, the offer of which services Dean, for obvious reasons, had declined and for which he really had little need. Dean, officially, was just one more federal witness, a cooperating one, to be sure, but he was so high profile a witness— he had been testifying against the president—that security on him was essential. Not only was Dean vulnerable to death threats, but simple injury to him, however slight or demonstrably accidental, held a promise of political embarrassment the enormity of which the Justice Department could ill afford. What Dean shared with McPherson's other witnesses, really only a couple of things, were things as prevalent in Washington as they were on the New Jersey waterfront—a couple of things like (a) a felony indictment and (b) a desire to trade.

"I'd been around a lot of guys who got religion because it was in their best interests. But I liked Dean, I believed him."

McPherson would grow friendly also with Watergate superstar G. Gordon Liddy, whom he was charged to deliver, not as a witness but as a defendant, in the 1974 conspiracy trial that stemmed from the burglary of the Beverly Hills office of Daniel Ellsberg's psychiatrist.

"Behind his back, we referred to Liddy as Unit Twenty-six. We figured he was playing with half a deck. His best buddy in [the Federal Correctional Institution at] Terminal Island was [New York mobster] Bill Bonanno. They jogged together."

In witness security, a line of work in which forced camaraderie was an essential condition, McPherson would eventually develop a soft spot in his heart for an array of racketeers, crooked politicians, and twisted individuals in general, especially for their innocent families, ambivalence being inevitable in a job that brought one into intimate contact with some of the more treacherous characters on the planet. But the collapse of the Nixon administration, which had overseen so dramatic a shift in the destiny of the deputy marshal, which in fact had engineered the very revival of the office itself, posed a singular irony for the specialist working witness security. It was under Richard Nixon's attorney general, John Mitchell, that the Service as such had been created, under his authority, by way of the Organized Crime Control Act of 1970, that WITSEC had been codified and entrusted to the Service as an essential component of its mission. McPherson's assignment to protect John Dean coincided with Dean's testimony in the Watergate-related trial of John Mitchell and Maurice Stans, and he was up against the politics not only of a critically convulsed Justice Department, but of an institution both older and closer to home.

As McPherson explains it:

"The U.S. marshal here [in Los Angeles] is appointed by Nixon. His rabbi, it is said, is Bob Mardian—the man who got him appointed—who has Watergate trouble of his own. There's a Republican administration going down. No one wants to protect John Dean."

McPherson was selected, he feels, on the basis of his reputation; he was a deputy who could be trusted to handle things, a do-it-but-don't-tell-us-about-it magician, anything but a size-46. Because he was competent, he was a very *credible* choice, but his credibility, he speculates, was only the more obvious half of it. The other was his expendability. The thinking in Washington, McPherson theorizes, went something like this:

"We'll put him on, and if something happens, hey, we did the right thing, we assigned the guy with the credentials, and [more important] he's easy to give up, we don't have to give up the marshal."

Everybody, McPherson insists, was hands-off on John Dean.

"The marshal told me, when I walked into his office, 'Look, I don't want to know anything you're doing with him. Don't keep me informed. I don't want to know, I can't be involved.' And that was the political climate. All the political appointees owed their livelihoods to people who were getting indicted."

McPherson's association with Dean predated the discovery of the White House audiotapes which were to corroborate Dean's testimony and to provide back-beat to the inevitable collapse of the Nixon administration. McPherson had been a cop for too long, he had been around too many witnesses, to take anything Dean said on faith.

"In the beginning I didn't know, and I tried not to make a distinction. . . . You don't know, they've got to prove it to you one way or the other. With John, I got to like him, and I got to appreciate the situation he was in. He was tough. Most people hated him—he's the snitch, he's talking about the president, trying to save himself—he was [perceived as] a lowlife. . . . [But] John was basically a decent human being when you got to know him, and as I got to know him I was pulling for him. Still, I didn't know for sure. I was hoping he was right, you know, and what he said made an awful lot of sense. It led me to believe he was telling the truth."

McPherson was with Dean the day Dean and the rest of the world learned of the existence of the tapes, and McPherson says that Dean's euphoria that day was an expression impossible to fake.

"In the beginning, I was pulling for him . . . but that day, when he found out about the tapes, I would have bet my life on him."

McPherson was not alone in his growing to like the soft-spoken man who routinely, over the telephone, identified himself as John West. Claudette McPherson, following the Watergate hearings on television, like many incredulous Americans, had early on in the proceedings become somewhat enraptured by Dean.

"I watched, I think, every minute of Watergate," Claudette McPherson recalls. "John Dean totally fascinated me. I wanted to know—because I really liked Nixon, I was a believer in Nixon—is this guy Dean for real, what kind of a person is he?"

"She never knew, until later, that she was getting calls from him every day."

Dean came under McPherson's protection upon completion of

his testimony before the Senate committee investigating the Watergate break-in; he had been called as a prosecution witness in the Mitchell-Stans trial in New York. He and his wife, Maureen, before buying a house in one of the canyons, were living temporarily in a condominium in Marina Del Rey. Like many of McPherson's witnesses in the days before electronic satellite paging (during office hours, deputies, very likely to be in court, were more often than not unavailable), Dean, when he needed him, telephoned McPherson at home.

Claudette McPherson, who ran a print shop during the day, took most of Dean's calls in the evening:

"I'm following Watergate, and this guy kept calling at different times. 'God damn it, Buddy, it's that John West again.' I'd be watching the [taped] hearings on television [at night] and this man would be interrupting."

When her husband was not at home, Claudette McPherson would take messages. And he was not at home a lot. Her husband was not at home, for instance, when John Dean was called as a rebuttal witness in the Mitchell-Stans trial in New York.

Claudette's epiphany came one late afternoon as she was catching the news at work.

"The first time I saw Bud on television . . ."

There on the screen, as the two men were leaving court together, Claudette saw McPherson and Dean.

"I was at work and I saw him on TV. I got so mad at him. He called me that night, and I said, 'I saw you on television, and I know what you're doing, and now I want to know everything.' "

McPherson's blown cover was inevitable, he admits.

"When you're running around New York in the same suit every day, and you're on the network news with John Dean, it doesn't take a genius to figure out what you're doing."

Dean's delivery to New York for the trial had followed an eleventh-hour decision by the prosecution to put him on the stand.

"Get him there," McPherson was ordered.

McPherson's instructions were to fly out immediately.

"It's like a twelve-o'clock flight to Newark. I look at my watch, it's ten-thirty. There was no time to pack or pick up any clothes. I had a promise from the chief deputy in Los Angeles: 'Tell your wife to pack a bag and we'll get your clothes on the next thing smokin'.' "

The luggage arrived four days later.

The memory of it strikes McPherson with terrible impact, much the way mushrooming hollow-point tears through the chest.

"Every night we're the lead item on the network news. I was on television every day in the same suit."

In fact, the marriage of WITSEC and modern tailoring was one that was sanctified after that; the John Dean assignment predated the inclusion of Image Awareness as a course of study in the Service's basic-training curriculum. Protecting Dean was a seat-of-the-pants operation conducted by deputies who had yet to start calling their pants "trousers," and it demanded much of the ingenuity upon which McPherson and they would continue to draw in the days before authorship of an enforcement manual.

"There was no equipment, no money to get the job done ... we didn't know who could be trusted. I remember times when we'd get on planes and move every two days for maybe three weeks until we could sneak a guy into court."

There were few safe-houses at the time, and while prisoners could sometimes be held in secure county jails and government offices—the former were difficult to trust, the latter required heavily armed deputies—non-prisoners, like Dean, had to be handled outside the system.

Travel vouchers from headquarters came cheap—official Government Transportation Requests were issued to the typical WITSEC deputy as freely as ammunition:

" 'Here's a book of GTRs ... go somewhere ... keep him alive.' "

And, by the way, keep him happy.

Dean, going over his testimony at the Nashville, Tennessee, home of government prosecutor James Neal, wanted to visit Opryland USA—take in the Grand Ole Opry and the Country Music Hall of Fame, maybe hit a couple of rides at the amusement park.

"I finally said okay," McPherson remembers. "I assigned six or seven guys to the detail. I told Dean to dress *down*."

The snapshots would tell the story. They would show Dean seated with McPherson and Maureen, a hat jerked down over his eyes, superimposed stiffly upon the backdrop of a crowded Opryland USA, smiling as naturally as a man waiting for dysentery to kick in.

"He got nervous," McPherson says, "when he saw a lot of guys staring; he said maybe we better leave."

McPherson, who was more than happy to oblige, did not share his suspicions with Dean:

"They were looking at Mo . . . I don't mean to sound . . . you know . . . but . . . she was really built."

Maybe they were looking. Maybe not. Maybe McPherson should have known better than to take the guy out of a suit. But rarely again would it be as much fun to speculate. Later in his career, entrusted with the care and feeding of Jimmy "the Weasel" Fratianno, McPherson, acceding to a similar request, would face far less entertaining imperatives when he took the cigar-smoking hit man ice-skating.

With Watergate behind him, McPherson was promoted to inspector. (Until 1977 he would be one of only five.) In late 1974, he was transferred to Kansas City. And not long after his arrival there, through the good offices of the FBI, he found himself west of the Missouri once more—once more in the unenviable position of pissing off the Indians.

This time the possibility of incoming gunfire was an experience he was able to share with his wife.

On June 26, 1975, precipitating a confrontation with members of the American Indian Movement, two FBI agents, Jack Coler and Ronald Williams, were shot to death in a gunfight that took place on the property of Harry and Cecelia Jumping Bull, a few miles southeast of Oglala and some twenty miles northwest of Wounded Knee on the Pine Ridge Reservation. An Indian, Joe Stuntz, also lost his life in the shoot-out.

The combination of circumstances in which the tragedy was rooted and all that inevitably followed will forever be subject to debate. What has never been open to question, however, is that the tragedy was compounded in a hurry when the FBI, in its effort to assure the conviction of AIM member Leonard Peltier, who may or may not have been guilty (charged on two counts of first-degree murder, Peltier was eventually sentenced to consecutive life terms in prison), induced the false testimony of a pathetic, easily manipulated, dysfunctional young woman by the name of Myrtle Poor Bear.

For that period in 1976 in which her whereabouts were unknown to her family—in which the FBI was securing from her what proved to be coerced and wholly fabricated evidence—

Myrtle Poor Bear was living under the official protection of witness-security inspector Bud McPherson. Women in the Marshals Service were in short supply at the time, and it was not unusual for deputies, where female witnesses were concerned, to call upon the custodial services of their wives—often, they were ordered to do so—whom the Service was only too willing to pay as matrons on an hourly basis. Thus, Myrtle Poor Bear, when she was outside what in WITSEC is called the "danger area," was housed in various hotels in Missouri, not far from the McPherson residence. Claudette McPherson, always in the company of at least one sworn deputy, pulled regular twelve-hour shifts on the detail, and seven days a week, over a period of almost three months, the McPhersons' two-year-old, Jennifer, was entrusted to the care of a babysitter.

It was on her first and only trip into the danger area—on that flight to Cedar Rapids—that Claudette felt compelled to ask questions.

"Her knowledge [of my work] was pretty limited. I never told her much; (*a*) I didn't want to scare her, and (*b*) it was none of her business. So I assumed, and it was the wrong assumption, that she knew more about the realities [of my work]. . . . She never saw me with guns, I'd always put mine in my briefcase before I came home . . . stuff like that, so . . . She was not prepared for Myrtle Poor Bear."

Indeed.

Had Bud McPherson, a few years earlier, been paying closer attention, he might have picked up a clue.

Myrtle Poor Bear was not Claudette's first assignment. Her first had been a prisoner that McPherson, early in his career, had been charged to transfer from Terminal Island in southern California to the San Francisco County Jail.

As McPherson would recollect:

"I grabbed Claudette, we picked up the prisoner at T.I. We shackled her up, and took her to LAX [Los Angeles International Airport]. I'm arranging for the tickets, and the lady has to go to the restroom. Claudette takes her in. And they're gone an awful long time. And now I'm getting nervous. They finally come out and Claudette has a sheepish look on her face. The girl is giggling like hell. Come to find out, I'd never thought to tell Claudette how to take the handcuffs off. So after a crash course from the criminal . . ."

"She taught me how," Claudette volunteers. "They were

double-locked, and I didn't know how to get the double-lock open . . ."

Which would prove to be the least of Claudette's problems.

"I would really be the wrong person," she explains, "to get involved in law enforcement, because I get emotionally involved with people. I felt so sorry for this woman. I really did. I'm not what you would call an objective person. . . . By the time we finished this plane trip, I was cursing the Marshals Service. I did not even want him to put her in prison."

It was, McPherson reports, Claudette's first look at a jail:

"And the San Francisco County Jail makes the L.A. County Jail look like the Hilton."

Claudette departed crying.

"It was horrible. I did not want him to leave this poor woman there. She had children. At that point I wanted him to quit the Marshals Service."

A routine prisoner trip, before WITSEC, before SOG, it was probably the second trip McPherson had made.

"Everybody did it [put his wife to work], they considered it a plum at the time, because you got away, you got to spend a night in San Francisco in a hotel. Your wife made, I think, a big five or seven dollars an hour. They considered that a plum. You got away from the everyday stuff, your wife made a few bucks, and you got a night in San Francisco."

"We argued all the way back," Claudette recalls. "This woman was raising three children and she got involved with the wrong man. She was really young, she was twenty-five, and he was like forty years old . . ."

Claudette was the same age as the prisoner. McPherson was twelve years older.

". . . and he manipulated her into delivering these drugs. She was a really nice person. She was at the wrong place, at the wrong time, and basically took the wrong road."

The woman, according to McPherson, was sidetracked only briefly:

"Maybe she was doing a dime. She wasn't about to get out, but she wasn't doing real heavy. Three and a half years in the federal system. She had another indictment in San Francisco."

If prisoner operations found Claudette unprepared, WITSEC would hit her on the blind side.

Claudette's first WITSEC assignment, McPherson points out, was "a Mickey-Mouse district case." The deputy he assigned, of the old school, was "very immature," he admits, but he disputes his wife's characterization of the man.

Claudette remembers him as "a wacko."

"These people were not for real, okay? He told me—this deputy, he was really a trip—if you see anyone with firearms coming at you, I want you to jump on the witness. I'll try and shoot them, he said. I looked at this guy and said, 'No way.' He said this is the way you have to do it. I said, 'No disrespect, Jim, but no way. If I see anyone with firearms, I will hightail it out of here as fast as I possibly can.' "

McPherson acknowledges that "it was classic overreaction on the guy's part. This is the same guy that . . . we had Harry 'the Greek' Coloduros, who was a 300-pound enforcer, testified against the Mob here, and I used to sneak him through the corridors, in and out. So one day this deputy tried to get him out that way, he was going to copy what Bud did. And the two of them got locked in the post office. They closed the door behind them and they couldn't get out. Fortunately they found a live phone, and I came and got them. We're taking the same Harry the Greek out of the federal building to the strike force. Harry's in the back seat, I'm on the passenger side, the same deputy's driving the car. We pull around the corner, there's a light and he stops for the light. In California we can go right, we don't have to stop for these lights. A guy pulls up next to us and starts asking directions. [The deputy] rolls down the window, he starts giving the guy directions. Now the guy could throw anything in the car, right? I yelled, 'Get the hell out of here.' I'm screaming. I scare him, and he gets the car moving. He said, 'Bud, you want me to be impolite?' "

McPherson's deputies displayed an aptitude for following orders that Claudette judged to be almost preternatural. In fact, their loyalty to their boss, as she was about to experience it, would find its nearest parallel in the allegiance that was traditionally exhibited only by the Ton Ton Macoute.

The eventual trial of Leonard Peltier was preceded by that of two other suspects, Robert Robideau and Darelle Dean Butler, for which McPherson was providing witnesses, and prosecutors in that trial wanted to talk to Myrtle Poor Bear. McPherson, in Cedar Rapids, overseeing the security detail, called his deputies in Kansas City:

"Look, she doesn't like to fly, but get her on the damn plane.

There's no time to get anybody else, and we have got to get Myrtle here."

The "she" who did not like to fly was Claudette McPherson.

"I had told him that I would never go to Cedar Rapids. I'm deathly afraid of flying and I've never been in a small plane."

In fact, Claudette McPherson had flown only once before in her life, and on a large commercial carrier. Her flight to San Francisco. Before and especially after that, she had managed, one way or another, to avoid flying altogether. Her husband, for security reasons, was flying witnesses into Cedar Rapids by way of a series of small landing strips surrounding the city, and even the veteran flyer would have been unimpressed with the size of the aircraft McPherson was using.

"He puts these three goons on me. . . . we were driving, they told me we were going to *drive* to Cedar Rapids, and I said, 'Fine, then I'll go' . . . and this one guy in charge, he keeps looking back at me, and I know something is wrong. . . . We were driving and all of a sudden, I see these airplanes . . .

" 'Where are we going?'

" 'I have strict instructions from my supervisor for you to fly on this airplane with Myrtle.'

" 'There's no way you're going to get me on that airplane, I'm not going.'

" 'Sorry, you are going.'

"And they picked me up, two marshals, physically picked me up, and put me on the plane, and I started cursing and screaming, and I was now ready to kill him, I definitely was going to kill Bud, my mind was made up that he's dead."

Myrtle Poor Bear, for her part, found it all completely hilarious.

"Don't forget, this was Myrtle's big thing," McPherson submits. "Myrtle was on, she was the star, she was happy as hell to be the focus of all this attention."

(After all the comings and goings, the debriefings and depositions, after all the trials had run their respective courses, the government would maintain that everything Myrtle Poor Bear had to offer was entirely worthless. "The Indian network was not very sophisticated," McPherson contends. "So while she was lying, either they didn't know she was lying, or they thought she would get away with her lies. Her life was still in danger. That was an absolute fact. You couldn't believe anything she

said. And I think Leonard knew [that]. But he had a lot of sup-
porters who wanted to die for the cause, and they might *not* have
known.")

Claudette's fear of flying was exacerbated by acute claustro-
phobia.

"It was horrendously small, tight, it was horrible. I was just
totally freaking out. I stood up all the way. The plane is landing,
and they're all telling me to sit down. 'I don't want to sit down,
you're not making me sit down.' There was no way I was listening to anybody. So they open up this airplane door, and I go
charging out of the plane, and I start screaming at [Bud]. And all
of a sudden I look around . . ."

"She was totally unprepared for the degree of security I had
waiting for this plane."

Deboarding the charter in Cedar Rapids that day, on the
threshold of a domestic argument, Claudette McPherson was
rendered momentarily, yet literally, speechless. On the tarmac,
waiting, just outboard of the aircraft, were three late-model sedans, doors open, motors running—had they been horses, they
would have been breathing heavy. They were surrounded by
deputy marshals.

"We had a minimum of four people to a car. Two automatic
weapons and a shotgun assigned to each."

Beside the middle car stood her husband—which of the others, the lead car or the follow car, was actually called the "crash
car," Claudette did not care to know.

"[The rear car] is really a weapons car. You put some of your
more physical people in it, with some of the heavy weapons. If
an emergency goes down, these are the guys you want to have
covering you. They have no responsibility other than watching
your back."

Claudette, immobilized, physically suspended on an intake of
breath, had not been given time to exhale when, through the
rear door of the middle car she and the witness were whisked,
unceremoniously hustled, and the door slammed shut behind
them. Her husband, taking a seat in front, turned to Claudette
and shouted:

"Claudette, lie down on the seat. Myrtle, get on the floor."

Tires screeched, the cars throttled up. The motorcade pulled
out of the airport.

"We had perimeter security throughout the airport, we had a

couple of posts on the way in, and on the roof of city hall we had a guy with a sniper rifle."

Claudette McPherson, whose final effort this would be on behalf of the United States Marshals Service ("After that, he could not talk me into it, he could not force me into it, he could not order me into it, that was it"), actually had to scream at her husband in order to make herself heard.

"Are you trying to get me killed!!?"

McPherson, expressing his disbelief, shouted back:

"You been hiding under a rock all these years? What did you think I did for a living?"

5.★

The Two Tonys and Other Tales

What Bud McPherson did for a living, he continues to do today. He simply does it at a higher level. He does it out of an office in the Federal Building in Los Angeles as WITSEC chief for Region XII, which encompasses the states of Washington, Oregon, California, Hawaii, Alaska, and parts of Nevada. McPherson's responsibility is twofold. Not only does he direct the security of all federally protected witnesses over the course of their testimony in his region, he oversees an enormous share of the relocation program that WITSEC in practice represents.

One September day, which was a typical day at the office, with a single exception—that he was actually *in* his office—the explanation he gave for his imminent departure therefrom spoke to the ongoing needs of racketeer redocumentation.

"I gotta go get some birth certificates in Nevada," he muttered into the telephone.

Soft-spoken, articulate, management material to the max, McPherson, a twenty-year resident of southern California, has been hanging out with hoods for so long that there is little hope now that the Brooklyn will ever leave his voice. His speech, by no means inelegant, carries with it a vaguely perceptible, upper-register rasp. Issuing occasionally from the side of his mouth, it occupies that phonetic no-man's-land where federal civil servant meets administrative-level Mafioso.

Over the phone he sounds like a very upscale underboss.

Taking pains ever to dress as though he were on emergency call to photographers for *Gentlemen's Quarterly,* as do most of the people who work "metro"—district jargon for WITSEC— McPherson appears to pay more for his clothes than many deputies pay for their cars. He is a cop who invariably in public sports a matching tie and handkerchief and until recently could be seen driving around greater Los Angeles in a late-model BMW confiscated by the Service under its National Asset Seizure and Forfeiture Program. He is six-one and weighs 195, he has a full head of light-brown hair steadily going to gray and blue eyes you will never see: he is a man with a flair for the dramatic. As something of a personal trademark, he always—day and night, outdoors and indoors—wears shades.

"And I'll be wearing sunglasses," he told a stranger over the telephone that day as the two made arrangements to meet. Detailing the afternoon's apparel, as precisely and unashamedly as a fashion coordinator, right down to the accessories, McPherson asked for no such sartorial inventory of the man he expected to encounter, making it clear without having to say so that reading people, getting a rapid take on total strangers, was a part of what he did for a living.

Among the many telephone messages that awaited him when he returned from the meeting that day were two from a celebrated television producer who had been courting him as a source of material for the better part of a year and whose efforts had doubled in the advent of McPherson's retirement, which was now fewer than two years away. McPherson at the time was one of several Marshals Service veterans facing mandatory retirement—at least three of them fending off serious offers— whose life stories were being sought by various people in publishing and the entertainment business.

Had they cornered Bud McPherson that afternoon, they would have found him stretched pretty thin.

One of McPherson's more pressing problems concerned an Asian witness he had relocated years before. The witness's daughter had just been accepted on a full scholarship by a medical school in Chicago. She had lived in the United States almost all of her life but was not a U.S. citizen. As the expatriate of a friendly nation, she was ineligible for asylum, and the Immigration and Naturalization Service would not grant her immigrant status. Without proper documentation she would be denied a physician's license, rendering her acceptance meaningless. McPherson was trying to get her a green card.

McPherson's difficulties were exaggerated by the fact that he was, as was often the case, operating short-handed. One of his top field inspectors, Bill Wagner, for example, was in New York supervising the Marshals Service's annual participation in the State Department security detail assigned to members of the United Nations General Assembly.

In addition to everything else, that day, McPherson, with the help of a SOG detail, was overseeing the security of a high-threat trial being conducted across the street. In the lockdown of the U.S. courthouse, a focal point of media attention, he had René Verdugo and two other high-profile prisoners—one had been convicted, the jury was still out on the others—implicated in the 1985 kidnapping, torture, and murder outside Guadalajara, Mexico, of U.S. Drug Enforcement Administration agent Enrique Camarena. These three, collectively, were going to be put away for several hundred years (Verdugo, alone, would eventually draw 240), they had access to an effectively unlimited source of cash, and it did not take much of an education to judge the risk of their escape—or their murder by confederates in the drug business, should they choose to cooperate with the government —to be a serious one. Witnesses by no stretch of the imagination (McPherson did provide protected witnesses during the trial), they were nevertheless, as defendants, the responsibility of WITSEC, which handled all of the Service's sensitive, high-threat, high-profile moves and most of its international action, spy swaps being an example.

On top of all that, McPherson had his *routine* duties.

It was Bud McPherson's habit, earlier in his career, to arrive at his Los Angeles office at around four o'clock in the morning. One hot day in July, he arrived to receive the following message on his telephone answering machine:

"Bud, you know Tony died . . ."

McPherson knew Tony had died.

". . . He's got to be buried in the Bronx. I put him on the red-eye."

The red-eye from Hawaii. It was scheduled to land in Los Angeles at 6 A.M., local time.

Tony had been an associate of the Genovese family, the old Lucky Luciano crime family, back in the Bronx. Heavy into narcotics and facing the rest of his life in prison on a couple of murder charges, Tony, about ten years before, had cut a deal to save himself. Testifying against his former benefactors, he served a stretch of four or five years before finally being relocated. He was in his sixties when he died.

McPherson knew him as a "stone killer."

And, having said that, only Bud McPherson would find it necessary to add:

"And not a nice guy, either."

One look at old Tony, McPherson maintains, and you knew "he'd kill you in a heartbeat if he could make five dollars off you." He had done a lot of his time in safe-houses back east, especially the old safe-house in Providence, Rhode Island, and even the witnesses there who had known him on the street, McPherson contends, were afraid of him.

To McPherson's way of thinking, Tony "was not a nice person."

And?

"I didn't like him," McPherson admits.

Tony, at his own request, was to be buried in the family plot. The plot, located in the Bronx, was handled by a wiseguy funeral parlor owned by a capo in the Genovese family, against whose members Tony had given testimony. It was McPherson's responsibility to prevent the Mob, for a variety of reasons, from learning that Tony—late though he may have been—had been relocated to Hawaii.

McPherson's task was manifold. He had to oversee the transfer of Tony's body from United, the airline on which it was to arrive, to American, the carrier that would take it to New York. He then had to remove the burial-transit permit that accompanied Tony's remains, a permit issued in Hawaii, exchanging it to assure that the body arrived in New York on a permit that could be traced no farther than Los Angeles. And he had one other thing to do, but he did not want to think about that yet.

What he needed was a funeral director, and he needed one pretty fast. The air temperature in southern California that day was forecast to reach 110 degrees Fahrenheit. McPherson's fellow deputy in Hawaii had done nothing more than throw Tony in a box and put him on the red-eye; the air quality in Los Angeles, lousy to begin with, was going to get lousier in a hurry if McPherson did not get a move on.

Funeral directors, on their own, in McPherson's experience, did not start showing up for work until about three in the afternoon. McPherson, a member of the American Airlines Admirals Club, figured that, with the telephones available to him there, his best bet was to get to the airport and start making deals on the scene.

Working the phone for close to an hour, McPherson had come up with nothing when Tony's body touched down. McPherson was going to have to take care of the paperwork himself. No problem there—he was, after all, custodian of the body, it *had* been shipped to him, and he had seen funeral directors handle bodies often enough—but he himself was going to have to move Tony from United air-freight to American. And he had that other thing to do. And he was running into a time problem.

This body is going to start to rot on me, he was thinking, stepping out of the Admirals Club, wondering how to go about putting together some transportation.

It was then, as he was lost in thought, that McPherson crossed the path of the second Tony to step out of his past in the course of the previous two hours.

"Hey, Bud."

"Hey, Tony, how are you?"

The second Tony, an airport maintenance man, had known McPherson from the days of the Air Piracy Program. He knew, or at least he thought he knew, a little bit about McPherson's job. A soft-spoken, Italian fellow, whom McPherson knew to be a family man, he was an elderly gent "who would plant roses in his garden and he wouldn't step on a bug." The two, when they met, had taken a liking to each other and over the years had maintained a passing acquaintance.

As a literary device, in the drama of McPherson's morning, Tony would serve as *deus ex machina.*

"Say, Tony, you still got your pickup truck?"

"Yeah."

"Can I borrow it for a minute?"

"What's the matter?"

"I got to pick up a package at United air-freight."

"Bud, I'm just getting off. Not only will I loan you the truck, I'll take you."

Better than nothing, McPherson figured, in classic confusion of movement with action—pick up the body and see what happens. From there he would play it by ear.

At United, with Tony waiting outside, McPherson signed for the corpse. He got on the phone, made arrangements for American to receive the remains, and requisitioned a burial-transit permit from funeral director McPherson, Los Angeles International, to funeral director McNeil (Alf McNeil, WITSEC's Region V chief) at JFK in New York. That took care of the paperwork. Now he had to move the body from United to American. And before he attempted that, he had to say something to Tony.

Tony, the living.

"Look, Tony, I'll be honest with you," McPherson said, as the two of them stood by the truck. "The package I got to pick up, it's a body."

Old Tony did not take it well. Call it a look of confusion. McPherson thought a joke might help. He saw a fork-lift coming. It carried a package about a foot around and maybe thirty feet long. It looked to be some kind of antenna.

"Here comes Tony now," he said. "He was a tall, skinny guy."

Tony, believing it was all a joke, gave himself up to laughter. And he was thus that much more crestfallen when, behind the first, a second fork-lift arrived carrying the crate bearing Tony-the-other.

Very gingerly did he assist McPherson in loading it onto the bed of the pickup.

Leaving United behind, the truck pulled onto Century Boulevard, Tonys front and back, McPherson in the passenger seat. Neither man had said much since the arrival of the second fork-lift. Tony, it seemed, was for all practical purposes constitutionally *unable* to speak. McPherson had other things on his mind. There was that one thing he had yet to take care of. Spotting an alley coming up on the right, McPherson asked Tony to pull in.

Tony was on auto-pilot, he did as he was asked.

"Wait here a minute," McPherson said, stepping out of the truck.

As though there were any way Tony was going to follow McPherson when he saw where McPherson was going.

McPherson opened the crate. And he started checking the dead man's clothing for labels. Identifying tags, anything that smacked of Hawaii, had to be removed from the killer's body.

All a part of the job. Of the glamorous life of the deputy marshal. For California's Bud McPherson, just one more day in paradise.

Tony-the-living, motionless—his eyes visible in the rearview mirror as he stole the occasional glimpse of the horror that transpired behind him—sat there literally dumbstruck while McPherson rifled the murderer's remains.

And now McPherson was laughing.

If LAPD ever finds me, they will throw a net over me, was all he could think, standing there, prosecuting the desecration in broad daylight.

Outside American Airlines, over coffee, when the two men finally pulled up, sat a citizen of no certifiable occupation.

"He's got a better job than I got," McPherson would say later, "because he's been sitting there about an hour."

If the cortege made any impression on the fellow, the man was keeping it to himself.

"Tony, wait here," McPherson said, stepping out of the pickup. "I got to go in and take care of the paperwork."

"Bud, you know . . . ," Tony began, and McPherson could see it coming. Tony had had enough. The old fellow had grown really pale. All McPherson needed at that point was to have two bodies on his hands. "I just remembered," Tony continued, "I got to take my wife to the doctor."

"Sure, Tony," McPherson said, expressing his appreciation as, together, he and the older man removed the crate from the truck.

Tony climbed aboard, and immediately put the truck in gear. He leaned his head out the window.

"Bud, can I talk to you for a minute?" Holding the clutch down with his workboot, Tony raced the motor while he spoke. "Bud, you know, you're a nice guy, and I'll help you with anything," he said, "but, please, no more of this James Bond shit."

He left McPherson standing there with only the one Tony for company—Tony and the guy drinking coffee, who had yet to utter a word.

"Excuse me," McPherson said, speaking to the more animated of the two, though the difference was somewhat marginal, "will you watch my body while I go inside?" The look on the man's face prompted McPherson to add, "I just don't want anybody to steal it."

The man sipped his coffee and answered:

"Who the hell would want it?"

McPherson, having completed the paperwork—he paid with a GTR—was standing in the sun with Tony when a fork-lift arrived on the scene, followed in short order by an American Airlines employee who was appropriately dressed in black. The guy who was paid to drink coffee sat there bearing silent witness. McPherson's biggest fear at this point was that if he ever started to laugh he might never be able to stop.

"Sir," the man in black asked, addressing McPherson solemnly, "would you like to accompany the remains to the plane?"

McPherson gave it a second. He glanced at Tony, then turned to announce:

"He was a pain in the ass when he was alive, and he's still a pain in the ass. No, I don't want to bother with it."

Tony was carried off, à la carte, to keep his rendezvous in the Bronx.

As McPherson turned to commence what promised to be a long walk back to his car, the man drinking coffee spoke:

"Sir, can I ask you a question?"

McPherson could not wait to hear it. He said, "What do you want to know?"

"Does your company always operate this way?"

McPherson said they did:

"We kind of specialize in no-frills funerals."

He laughed all the way back to the car. And he continued to laugh. On the San Diego Freeway he was laughing so hard, he had to pull over to the side of the road.

Forever McPherson would wonder what might have happened had his telephone answering machine in some way malfunctioned, had he simply not gotten the message, had he been out of town that day. The deputy who had called from Hawaii, so eager to get rid of the body, had placed more faith in modern technology than McPherson could ever have mustered, more faith in McPherson's comings and goings than was justified by experience. Tony, God bless the old son of a bitch, might easily have enjoyed his everlasting reward, waiting to depart this vale of tears, sitting in air-freight at United. McPherson likes to think it is possible that Tony might be there today.

. . .

Bud McPherson's routine duties as a witness-security inspector can best be appreciated in light of a legal opinion once eloquently rendered by Louisiana mob boss Carlos Marcello. When the late "Mafia Kingfish" was finally indicted for labor racketeering, a piece of artwork he treasured was confiscated—it had hung from the wall of his New Orleans office, mounted there much like a sampler, catching the eye of many a dignified visitor like the proud needlework of a properly educated young lady. Imprinted thereon was an adage, an observation that might easily serve as the unofficial motto for WITSEC. It was a quaint statement of forensic principle, and it was the adage by which the old racketeer lived. It read:

"THREE DO NOT MAKE A CONSPIRACY IF TWO OF THEM ARE DEAD."

Call him the Oliver Wendell Holmes of wiseguys.

Honor among thieves as a keystone in the edifice of Crime has always been of questionable strength. When you see it at work, if you see it at all, you can safely bet that what you are gazing upon is the archway over the door to the Enforcement Division. The willingness to betray one's brothers-in-arms did not begin with the Witness Security Program. What WITSEC did was simply to elevate the song of the stool pigeon to a legitimate American art form. Squealing in this country is a vocation as widely admired today as was the Sicilian policy of *omerta* in its day. (A mere convenience in the exercise of criminal behavior, it is a flat-out *requirement* of media celebrity.)

There *was* a time when *doing* time was an acceptable part of the cost of doing business. And as often as not it was an essential part. Rare was the made guy in the Italian rackets who had not proved he could take a fall. An indoctrinated member of La Cosa Nostra, a right guy, a wiseguy, was by definition a stand-up guy. He could be trusted to do what was correct.

"Dad's *at college* for a couple of years, he's *away* at college. He was never *in jail*, he was always *away*."

The moral compunction attributed to the old Mafia bosses, the Mustache Petes, on the matter of narcotics is nothing more than a literary convention—what the old men-of-respect knew was that the heavy penalties for drug trafficking increased the possibility of the rank-and-file's cooperation with prosecutors. Heroin, as it happened, was to be the least of the bosses' problems.

The sentences that came down under the nation's modern racketeering statutes, those, for example, associated with the conduct of a Continuing Criminal Enterprise (CCE), were enough in the absence of narcotics to push family enforcement operations to the limit.

With the coming of the Witness Security Program, the code of silence was all but dead.

Until Congress passed Title V of the Organized Crime Control Act of 1970, protection of an individual government witness was the responsibility of the investigative agency making the case in which that witness was testifying. With establishment of the Witness Security Program the following year, that responsibility, on the attorney general's authority—the authority of John Mitchell—was entrusted to the Marshals Service.

The truth is, nobody else wanted it.

Underfunded and understaffed to begin with, the program instantly became the Department of Justice equivalent of bureaucratic Siberia. If you were in trouble at Justice, according to McPherson, you could count on becoming WITSEC chief, or director, or whatever DOJ was calling it just then—the title changed, it seemed, with every new man who was condemned to the job, and it seemed to change every six months.

In the beginning, it was thought that between thirty and fifty people a year would require the services of the program, which was funded at under $1 million. It was not long, however, before the program was taking on 400 and 500 principals annually. (By the end of September 1990, 5,600 witnesses, 97 percent of whom had extensive criminal records, and 7,000 dependents had been protected, relocated, and provided new identities. By fiscal year 1991 the federal budget line for the program had reached $43 million.) While the program enjoyed immediate, quantifiable success from a prosecutorial standpoint (the government claims a conviction rate of better than 86 percent in cases where protected witnesses are used, and a recidivism rate among program participants that fluctuates between 17 and 23 percent, which is less than half the national average), the program, at the outset, was in every other way a disaster.

Because the program, by design, was so heavily layered in security, it generated publicity only in its negative manifestations. Disgruntled witnesses went running to reporters with disturbing regularity, while the details of the program's triumphs, out of necessity, remained a secret. Not the least of the program's unqualified successes was that of those witnesses who followed its guidelines, none had ever been killed. (To date, according to the Marshals Service, no witness following security guidelines has been harmed. Thirty of those who have left protection have been murdered.) The program's perfect record at providing protective services had much to do with the ingenuity of its early deputies, but not in the way one might assume.

McPherson is very candid about it:

"We never got caught in those days—*we* didn't know what we were doing, how could the wiseguys know?"

In the days before the 1978 Memorandum of Understanding, a document requiring the signature of every witness entering the program, deputy marshals took the heat for a lot of case agents and U.S. attorneys. It was they, not the deputies, who made the deals that resulted in the trigger-man's turning state's evidence, and in doing so they were inclined to make outrageous promises upon which the Marshals Service, by law and often by any measure of common sense, could never deliver. When the witness did not get the new Cadillac he was promised—that mansion in the Cayman Islands, the Park Avenue plastic surgery, and the 3,000 Balinese dancing girls he dreamed of—battle lines were rapidly drawn. It was the witness, the case agent (usually FBI), and the U.S. attorney on one side and the WIT-SEC deputy on the other.

"The case agent's the guy's rabbi," McPherson is quick to point out. "He's the one the witness goes running to. The case agent and the U.S. attorney. He's testifying for *them*. And *they're* getting something in return. We're not. We're providing a service to these other agencies. They're not restricted like we are."

Not, at any rate, until the Memorandum of Understanding, which stipulated that the only promises that were in any way binding on the government were those that were made by the Marshals Service itself.

In 1977, McPherson acknowledges, he relocated a horse. He will not identify the U.S. attorney who originally made the promise, nor will he identify the U.S. marshal who so readily agreed, in writing, to honor it, except to point out that both were politically appointed and that the two "were close." And of course he will not identify the witness, a female witness, he says. Her thoroughbred required a legal name change. A tattoo change as well.

"The woman," he explains, "we sent first." He is parsimonious with the details, adding only: "The woman was easy."

McPherson no longer redocuments animals. WITSEC will pay for their transportation—the Service does relocate housepets—but the reproductive future of any animal is the responsibility of the witness. To breed or show a relocated animal under its pedigree is a violation of security.

"It's like the Vehicle Identification Number on a car. And we won't let you take the car. Though we relocated an airplane once."

At least one witness has declined to enter the program because McPherson was unable to provide new papers for the pooch:

"Give him a haircut," the witness was told, "and change his name yourself."

McPherson says, "I'd never ask a person to come into the witness program if he had any other option. I tell people before they come in, 'It's the toughest thing you'll ever do.'"

The Witness Security Program is a relocation program. The lifetime protection of the Marshals Service presumes redocumentation and relocation, a permanent identity change for every member of the family and permanent extirpation of that family from the community in which it is rooted. Communication with relatives and friends, when it is permitted, is handled through secure mail-forwarding channels administered through the Marshals Service. There is no going home ever again . . . no weddings, no baptisms, no high-school graduations . . . one minute you are in New York, taking commissions on your six-figure extortion contracts, dividing up the draw on your investments in bookmaking, loan-sharking, prostitution, and narcotics . . . you are carting warm minks and hot jewelry home to the wife—maybe you have one or two girlfriends—you are pinning new hundreds to the vestments of a statue of San Gennaro . . . and the next minute you are sporting a new haircut and selling second-hand Oldsmobiles for short money to a community of Mormons somewhere in Utah.

Nobody said it was going to be easy.

Take all the problems any family ever had, add to them an emasculated father, a man from whom the making of all major decisions has been taken away, who is everything he hated most in the world from the moment he learned to shake hands, namely a stool pigeon, which is the wiseguy equivalent of being a child molester—a fact that his wife is only too ready to throw in his face along with the sauce pans when they happen to go flying— a wife with no girlfriends to talk to, who misses talking to her family, not to mention the Coupe De Ville in the driveway and the occasional Saturday night at the Copa, and children who, when they finally make friends, have to lie to them on a regular basis, and you have a day in the life of the typical WITSEC family.

One mistake by anyone and it is a new name all over again and maybe this time you are promoting Chryslers to Lutherans outside Des Moines.

"These people leave everybody," McPherson explains. "They come out here, the only one they have is you. They can't be going to AA to tell their stories, because they'll be blowing their cover. In the old days we didn't offer psychiatric help. Today we do. We get a psychiatrist cleared, that's different. But in the old days you didn't have any help. They had a problem, you were the rabbi, you were the minister, you were the priest, you were their adviser, and by virtue of that, especially when they had young kids, you became close to the people. And it's human nature that you're going to get closer to some than the regulations permit."

Tell them, Claudette.

"You get involved because you can't help but get involved, because these people are stranded, they're away from their families, away from their friends, away from everybody. They feel so totally alienated. Bud was out of town and this woman called up, she was stuck in a hotel with three or four kids . . ."

"I had a detail on her."

"She calls me up and she's totally panic-stricken because they won't let her use her car. The Marshals Service wouldn't let her use her car. So I said to her, maybe she could have it towed to Sears, and *see* if there's a bomb in it . . ."

"Could you see this . . ."

"I felt so sorry for her because she was trapped in this room with these kids and she was going crazy, and none of the marshals . . ."

"It was a blown cover. Her husband got in trouble and the cover was blown. We had to get him out of town. The car was in another part of Los Angeles, and I said don't use your car. When I get back from out of town we'll get it looked at . . . and all we're going to do is take it somewhere when it's safe and get it sold for you. You can't use the car [anymore, because it can be traced to you] . . . not to mention . . . there could be a bomb in the car. She wanted the car because the kids were driving her nuts in the hotel room, and she's a bit of a wacko, and she calls this wacko, and they hit on this brilliant plan. Fortunately, Claudette had enough sense to tell her . . ."

". . . Before we do it, let's check with Buddy . . ."

"You can imagine my reaction . . ."

"I could tell by the tone of his voice that it was not a good idea."

"Could you see that poor mechanic at Sears: 'Oh yes, lady, I'll find the bomb for you.' "

The relocated family's lifeline is the WITSEC inspector, a combination of social worker, religious worker, doctor, banker, and body guard. A deputy must have a year in grade as a journeyman before applying for advanced training in witness security, a curriculum which includes courses in counseling and psychology and methods of documentation as well as a refinement of such basic-deputy skills as defensive driving and protection of high-profile dignitaries.

(With the reorganization of WITSEC in the late 1970s emphasis was placed on identifying the better, more upwardly mobile deputies in the agency and channeling them into the program. Selection carried a higher rank and grade. It was as a means of encouraging application to WITSEC that the rank of inspector was created.)

Transfers within WITSEC are not encouraged. Essential to the success of the program is that the deputy be an insider, that he make a long-term commitment to the relocated family. Continuity is the glue that holds the arrangement together. And a knowledge of the witness's case is very often as crucial to the arrangement as the establishment of a personal rapport. Inexperience, of course, creates the ultimate nightmare—the witness walking all over the deputy.

"These guys," McPherson advises, "are protecting the best con men in the world."

McPherson hypothesizes a WITSEC inspector working in the American heartland. His boss is in Washington, D.C. The deputy sees him only at conferences. He gets "chummy with a witness out in the boondocks."

McPherson paints the following picture:

"Then comes a time you tell the witness he's got to go to work, he's terminated from funding. Now, all these witnesses, no matter what you tell them in the beginning, they want a pension for the rest of their lives. Smart witnesses, when it comes time to work, say, 'You got to relocate me.' Why? 'Well, this inspector, I think he's dirty. He went out to dinner with us ... I bought dinner for him ... I met his wife ... I been in his house ... his wife's been in my house ...' The deputy gets in trouble. He either gets fired or shifted out of WITSEC. And this witness, he's got a certain amount of credibility, he's got to be relocated. Now he starts all over again."

And does not have to go to work right away.

For the naive deputy, it is very easy to get sucked in, very often trying to do the right thing.

McPherson has lost a lot of good people.

"A conservative guess? Twenty to twenty-five inspectors over the history of the program. ... Compromised by the witness. That's only since '78. Before that, there were no rules."

One of McPherson's deputies went into business with a witness. Many deputies get fired, some go to jail.

"WITSEC is very dangerous that way."

Or as WITSEC inspector Bill Wagner puts it:

"I'm paying for my own damn coffee."

Off the record, there are few WITSEC inspectors who will go out of their way to deny that the federal witness program, in principle, is morally corrupt. Their defense of it is as a necessary prosecutorial tool. But as such it is quite cynically applied—not to serve the cause of justice, but to generate positive statistics. And to do so at any ethical cost. No punishment is so out-of-proportion that a prosecutor will not invoke it to force a witness to testify. No crime, no criminal history, is so heinous that a U.S. attorney will not overlook it in the effort to boost the government's conviction rate, and by extension to advance his career. Very rare is it that innocent people enter the program. Its rewards are directed primarily at career criminals, and in the end what it rewards is treachery.

An individual's acceptance into the Witness Security Program is the decision of the Office of Enforcement Operations in the Criminal Division of the Department of Justice. Application for protection is made by the various U.S. attorneys' offices and Organized Crime Strike Forces throughout the country. A witness's case agent makes simultaneous application, presenting a threat assessment through his national headquarters.

The suitability of an applicant, according to the Marshals Service, is determined on the basis of the following information: the possibility of securing similar testimony from other sources; the relative importance of the testimony; the risk the witness might pose to a relocation community, as determined through psychological evaluation; and assessment as to whether acceptance will substantially infringe on the relationship between a child who would be relocated and a parent who would not.

(In cases where only one parent enters the program with a child, the Service arranges and monitors secure visitation between the child and the non-program parent. It also oversees visits between relocated witnesses and non-program children pursuant to court orders allowing them. Inspectors, nationally, arrange between fifteen and eighteen child visits a month. The visits take place in a neutral location—away from both the danger and the relocation areas.)

In 1987 the Marshals Service opened the Witness Security Safesite and Orientation Center in metropolitan Washington, D.C., through which all witnesses now enter the program. The Center, which can accommodate six families and four prisoner-witnesses, includes temporary living quarters, interview and polygraph rooms, and medical and dental examination facilities. Here, witnesses, before being relocated, complete a comprehensive admission and evaluation program and receive psychological counseling to prepare them for the move. It is here, also, that they sign the Memorandum of Understanding that enumerates their responsibilities and outlines what they can expect from the Marshals Service.

Participation in the program is voluntary, and a witness, by formally releasing the Service of its protective responsibility, may terminate his participation at any time.

Upon acceptance of a witness into the program, redocumentation begins. And it begins with a court-approved name change, the new name being chosen by the witness himself. With the change in effect, most agencies will supply back-stopped identity papers, the basic portfolio including birth certificate, social-security card, driver's license or state I.D. card, and school and medical records. The Service, which has provided everything from passports to nurses' and mariners' licenses, will issue only those documents to which a witness is actually entitled. A diploma will not be issued, for example, to a witness who has not graduated from high school. Every witness must pass a driver's test before he or she is licensed. Foreign nationals are not given proof of citizenship; they receive immigration papers instead. Those who have entered the United States legally can petition to become citizens once they have met the residency requirements; those who have entered illegally are allowed to remain and work in the United States until they break the law, at which time they are subject to deportation.

"You get a new family, you're going to deal with them on a daily basis, a Monday-through-Friday basis, for maybe a month," says WITSEC inspector Bill Wagner. "You're going to spend a lot of time with them when the process first begins. Schools, furniture, medical records . . . to obtain the records is a piece of cake, but to do with them what we do with them and then finally get them into the family's hands is a lengthy process. There are a lot of things in the program that take a lot of time, and that's probably the major complaint. You need the cooperation of literally eighteen agencies. And not everyone cooperates with the federal government, believe it or not."

Many federal agencies cooperate only reluctantly, and marginally at that—the Immigration and Naturalization Service being a good example—while a lot of state and municipal agencies will not cooperate at all.

Modern WITSEC guidelines require that all new paper be legal. The guidelines are about ten years old. Bud McPherson was redocumenting people when there was no redocumentation program in the Service, making it up as he went along, manufacturing birth certificates in an instant print shop to get relocated children into the Little League.

"I relocated a witness once and I get a call from him four years later. He wants to talk to me about Angela. His daughter. She can't get married behind the altar rails, according to the priest, because she has no proof of baptism. Who ever thought of baptismal certificates? So, I go see my friend, Father Reilly. Well, for a long time everybody that got baptized in the witness program got baptized at the Holy Name in [a community in the archdiocese of Los Angeles]."

McPherson, who has witnesses with numbers like 0009, still

gets calls from some of those he handled as far back as 1971. Many will deal only with him.

"I can't tell you how many graduations I get invited to. How many weddings. To the kids, I'm Uncle Bud."

Few things are more difficult than finding employment for the program's participants, the vast majority of whom are career criminals. To say that they have limited job skills is something of an understatement. The Marshals Service, which employs various psychologists, administers a battery of vocational inventories to incoming witnesses, who receive a stipend from the Service until such time as they are self-sufficient; the amount of the allowance, based on the size and geographic location of the family, is determined by the Bureau of Labor Statistics. During that time the Service also covers the cost of any necessary medical treatment.

Essential to a witness's successfully going legit is what the Service picturesquely refers to as "a readjustment of expectations"—its way of saying that selling cocaine pays better than pulling the night shift at the International House of Pancakes. The Service will not support a witness indefinitely, and the disgruntled witnesses whom the public generally hears from, those who complain that the Service has cut them loose, are typically those who have simply been cut loose from funding.

Regulations require that the Service notify prospective employers of a witness's participation in the program and of a criminal record, if any. Where documentation is required, and either is unavailable or represents a security risk, the Service, rather than provide records, will "make representations." The days of phony identification—of instant "pocket litter"—are over, and today there are regulations governing every move the deputy makes. The mechanisms for redocumenting foreign nationals are especially cumbersome and employment opportunities are slim. Birth certificates and passports from their countries of origin are impossible to come by; INS refuses to provide them with similar documents and in many cases will not even give them green cards.

In WITSEC, frequent reference is made to "mechanisms for keeping them in country."

A foreign national who violates security is subject to termination (as is any witness who does so), and consequently to deportation by the Immigration and Naturalization Service, an extremely rigid bureaucracy which is not in the habit of making exceptions.

"That's a death sentence," McPherson argues. "You don't want to sentence him to death. There should be more you could do. I don't know of anybody that got sent back, but the loophole's there, and some day somebody is going to get killed."

Many problems for deputies arise from the fact that witnesses, especially those from certain Third World nations where everything is relatively crooked to begin with, share with the general public the impression, not entirely unwarranted, that the United States government can do anything it wants, that its employees are above the law. One thing the federal government can do— and continues to do on a regular basis—accounts for the more legitimate complaints about the program, complaints which come not from the witnesses themselves, but from the long-suffering American taxpayer.

Into the communities of law-abiding citizens, career criminals are routinely injected with completely sanitized backgrounds. Gone only are the days of the more severe violations of the public trust, when case agents intervened with local law enforcement on behalf of the protected witness.

When a protected witness is arrested today, WITSEC instructs local authorities to treat him as they would any other suspect, with one exception: WITSEC asks that he not be put where his enemies can get to him. Which rules out putting him in with the general population of a lot of American prisons.

"If that means putting him in the hole [solitary confinement], so be it. But we'll give him up in a heartbeat. And we tell him that [before he comes in]."

Often, local authorities are asked to allow the witness to serve any time he draws in the lockdown of a secure federal facility.

It is not unusual, McPherson admits, for a witness to come into the program, get probation because he has testified, be relocated, and eventually be arrested for defrauding a local businessman.

"The victim could rightfully say, 'If I'd known he was in the program for embezzlement . . .' [but] it's unavoidable. We don't advertise his criminal record, but any police agency that asks, we give them the facts—maybe a sanitized rap sheet . . . six bank robberies, two murders . . . we just won't say where or under what name he committed them. The information is necessary to the court in deciding what kind of sentence to give him."

What comes as a surprise to those who are unfamiliar with it is how many participants in the Witness Security Program are actually relocated to prison.

"There are guys doing life who are in WITSEC."

While many witnesses may benefit from shorter sentences in return for their cooperation, few are the serious offenders who do not draw federal time. Only when they complete their stretches do they qualify for full services under WITSEC. Until then their protection is the responsibility of the Bureau of Prisons. The Marshals Service is involved only in their secure transportation and their delivery to court to testify.

Located around the country, in the seven busiest metropolitan areas, are the respective WITSEC safesites, used to house protected witnesses when they are returned to the danger area for court appearances. Layered in physical and electronic security, the safesites, according to McPherson, are relatively new. Ingenuity, he confides, is as essential as ever.

"I used to rent trucks, mail trucks, bread trucks, a lot of trucks . . . once I rolled a guy out of court in a wheelchair. You take a couple of guys, not drawing attention, no red lights, brakes aren't squealing, you just sneak in, sneak out . . . you can have a guy on the roof with a shotgun, just don't have him carrying an American flag and a searchlight . . . you do it low key, they don't know where you are. . . . But there are times when they know you're coming and times when there are only one or two ways to get in . . ."

And that, in witness security, is when the fun begins. They call it going high-profile. Drawing unashamedly on the power of advertising, it is the quintessential show of force.

"If I'm going to take a guy on a dangerous move, I've got guys on the roof, I've got a couple of inspectors and four SOG deputies with automatic weapons. SOG can wear their black Ninja outfits—if we have a shoot-out in the street, I'd like the locals to see some uniforms. . . . We move a lot of hot people, we use private planes, air force planes, a lot of automatic weapons. It's fun and it's twelve-hour shifts. Everybody in WITSEC wants to be at 37,000 feet with an Uzi. You don't have to worry about the kid with an earache, all the kids the mother can't handle because she's having trouble with the father, the witness, who's having psychological problems. You give a deputy a break, you let him go to 37,000 and get away for a few weeks."

And that is what Bill Wagner had been doing.

6.★

Fast Company

"I was down there fourteen times last year . . ."

WITSEC inspector Bill Wagner was talking about the Carlos Lehder trial.

Lehder, the Colombian cocaine billionaire, who had been in Marshals Service custody for well over a year, had recently been sentenced to life without parole plus 135 years. Security arrangements for his trial, in which six protected witnesses had testified, had cost the Service $2 million, and Wagner had been one of hundreds of deputies who had provided security for the high-threat prosecution in Jacksonville, Florida.

"My joke was, I was going to buy a time-share."

It was a warm September day on the East Side of Manhattan, noon on the 29th. The broad, semicircular driveway sloping away from the United Nations General Assembly Building was choked with foreign bureaucrats. A disembodied voice over the public-address system announced them as they came and went.

The General Assembly was in session. And of those attending the annual, autumnal orgy of international brotherhood, not all were VIPs, not all enjoyed diplomatic immunity. Of those in the crowd that afternoon not attached to a foreign mission, virtually all were armed, each carrying hidden under his or her jacket a service pistol or revolver, spare magazines, and speed loaders, and all appeared to be hooked up in one way or another to a radio.

The place was crawling with heat.

Parading off to lunch, middle-aged foreign ministers stepped smartly out into the daylight followed by eager young men and women carrying an assortment of executive luggage—briefcases, attaché cases, and a variety of odd-looking portfolios, soft-sided valises of hopsack and canvas that resembled nothing so much as they did cue cases and that gave the bright-eyed Americans porting them the look of very dignified pool shooters: travel accessories designed to meet the needs of today's active professional, the man or woman of affairs, vital to whose contemporary success is instant access to the special-purpose, multi-mission submachine gun . . . Uzi, mini-Uzi, the Heckler & Koch MP5 . . . high-tech office gear.

Stretching from gate to gate was the latest in engineering from Detroit. The limousines, all rolling under diplomatic registry, flags flying from the quarterpanels, were armored from the firewall to the rear deck, glass and steel impervious to high-powered ammunition. Federal agents "walked the fenders" as they drifted in and out. All the government sedans, most of them Crown Victorias, high on polish, low on chrome, idled under the weight of the standard Ford police package—motor, transmission, cooling system, suspension, tires, shocks, everything heavy-duty, the batteries and the wiring jacked up to handle the lights, the sirens, and the radios—all of them modified at the factory, built for speed and reinforced to stand up to the J-turns, the bootleg turns, and the high-speed power slides, equipped to jump curbs without falling apart and to maintain their structural integrity as they crashed through vehicular roadblocks. The hot WITSEC cars carried "dispersion systems," smoke and concussion grenades, wired to remote triggers, deployed in the vicinity of the wheel wells.

In the seeming chaos that was noon-hour outside the General Assembly Building, WITSEC inspector Bill Wagner saw the order, the pleasing symmetry. He was able visually to distinguish one security detail from another, to isolate the various elements of a given dignitary's detail at a glance, to differentiate, for example, between a shift leader and an agent-in-charge, and to do so with relative ease. The squawking radio transmissions did not bewilder him. Insistent and absolutely incessant, the electronic voice traffic made walking onto the property like walking into a bird sanctuary, and Wagner, thirty-five, coordinator of the annual Marshals Service participation at the event, had just stepped into the cacophony like a visiting ornithologist.

The lapel pin Wagner wore—gold eagle on black enamel, a serial number engraved on the back—today worn "eagle up," identified him as detailed to the U.S. Department of State. (The United States Secret Service and NYPD Intel each had a pin of its own.) It was Wagner's suspiciously familiar wardrobe that identified him as Los Angeles WITSEC. Under the jacket of a well-cut, dark-blue suit, he wore fashionable red suspenders and a conservative black leather belt, both serving to support his trousers, which was the primary function of neither—the suspenders supported his image as a shameless protégé of Bud McPherson, the belt supported the Model 66 Smith & Wesson holstered to his hip. An inch taller than his boss, ten pounds heavier, almost twenty years younger, Wagner had not yet earned that touch of gray that had insinuated itself so meticulously in the brown of McPherson's hair. But their mustaches were a pretty good match, and if the blue of their irises was not of an identical hue, the same could not be said of their answer to one very obvious question, the answer being:

"My eyes are light-sensitive."

Put these two guys at the bottom of the deepest manhole you can find, close them in, cut the lights, give them a week to tunnel out, and when they finally crawl into starlight both of them will be wearing sunglasses. Following these characters around at night is like hanging out with jazz musicians, a couple of saxophone players, front men for what looks to be an entire horn section that shops at Brooks Brothers.

The Witness Security Program is hopelessly riddled with clones of Bud McPherson.

Ask his wife:

"He'd recruit new people," Claudette says, "he'd bring them to the house and he'd introduce me to them—none of them had dark glasses. Then you'd meet them a year later, we'd have them to the house for a party, and they'd always have dark glasses on. Every single one of them. When Wags came here, he did not have dark glasses. And now Wags has dark glasses. Every one of them wound up buying dark glasses at one time or another. . . . We'll have a party, there are some of my people from the office,

who are all normal-looking people, and there's Bud's crew, all
with the dark sunglasses. They wear them all the time. *In* the
house. Always. They're sort of conspicuous, as far as I'm concerned."

Though times are rapidly changing, America still gets most of
its cops from the same place it gets its commercial airline pilots
—the United States armed forces. Notwithstanding the steady
influx of women into law enforcement's ranks, rare, until recently, was that member of the American constabulary who did
not have military experience, and Deputy Marshal Bill Wagner
was no exception to the rule. An M.P. in the U.S. Army, he had
come into the Marshals Service at the age of twenty-six, but not
before grabbing what was to become the more common and convenient ticket to a career in federal law enforcement, if not for
him then for a generation of American males who came of age
after 1973, the year that saw the end of the nation's Vietnam
draft. He grabbed a college education, a degree in criminal justice.

Married to his high-school sweetheart, and very happily so—
"we had an argument maybe five years ago"—he carried her off
to Los Angeles in January 1980 from Arlington, Massachusetts.
Going on the job in the Central District of California, Wagner
served process for a while, worked warrants under Tony Perez,
then was recruited by Bud McPherson. In April 1984 he returned to Glynco for six weeks of WITSEC training.

PSS, Protective Services, is a part of every deputy's basic curriculum. Advanced PSS training is offered as a specialty to jour-
neymen. Overseeing the General Assembly detail (as is anything
in any way sensitive, high-profile, or even remotely cool, anything, other than warrants, that the Service considers in any way
sexy) is a WITSEC assignment—*all* WITSEC inspectors are certified PSS specialists. The assignment is traditionally twofold.
Members of the General Assembly are to be protected not only
from harm, but from embarrassment. (It is not unknown for them
to embarrass themselves.) It is a job that requires a lot of advance
work, and it is not one that was new to Bill Wagner.

Wagner had worked the General Assembly detail before and
had spent much of his time seeing to it that the ministers from
Iran and Iraq, whose nations at the time were at war, were never
within knifing distance of each other. PSS assignments, Wagner
had learned, differed from WITSEC assignments in significant

ways, not including the most obvious way—the percentage of scumbags in the General Assembly was generally presumed to be lower than in the Witness Security Program—one way being that on a WITSEC detail, the deputy called the shots. Not so on a dignitary assignment. You did not go telling the Soviet foreign minister where he was having his lunch. Nor did you tell him when. And you did not tell him with whom. You were lucky if *he* told *you* with the kind of advance notice you needed to requisition the appropriate number of submachine guns.

The U.S. Secret Service, a branch of the Treasury Department, its principal mission the suppression of counterfeiting, is responsible for the personal protection of the U.S. president, his immediate family, presidential candidates, and visiting heads of state. The protection of foreign ministers—any visiting dignitary requiring protection who is *not* a head of state, including a wife or husband of the latter—is the responsibility of the State Department, which has criminal investigators assigned to seventeen field offices across the country. In addition to serving the functions of physical security and dignitary protection, agents of the State Department's Office of Diplomatic Security gather intelligence, work anti-terrorism, investigate passport and visa fraud, and oversee munitions exports.

(At the Federal Law Enforcement Training Center at Glynco, Georgia, no fewer than sixty-three agencies train cops, all kinds of cops, from Treasury agents to federal tick inspectors—from the Border Patrol to the Bureau of Indian Affairs, the National Park Service to the Library of Congress—and there are two agencies that do not conduct training there, the FBI and the DEA, which share a facility at Quantico, Virginia. Go ahead, you name it—We the People have a cop for it.)

With the General Assembly in session, agents of the State Department inevitably work shorthanded in the fall. Bill Wagner and his fellow deputies were not the only ones helping them out. Also assigned to the detail were agents of the Bureau of Alcohol, Tobacco and Firearms. State this year was stretched particularly thin—in addition to its permanent details on the U.N. representative and on the Secretary himself, the department had a lot of manpower detailed to the Summer Olympics.

The interagency cooperation represented by the General Assembly detail—State appreciated the help—rare enough as it was to see, was nevertheless circumscribed. Characteristically standing apart were what one State Department agent insisted upon alluding to as the Secret Squirrels.

"I like callin' them the SS," his partner volunteered.

The U.S. Secret Service, with the help of the New York City Police Department, which had provided the tactical presence, a few days before had effectively shut down the island of Manhattan.

President Ronald Reagan had come to town to address the General Assembly.

"They closed off the FDR Drive from the U.N. to South Ferry, where his chopper came in . . . they closed down everything in midtown from First Avenue to the Waldorf. Explosive Ordnance Disposal had bomb crews out, sweeping vehicles, sweeping the residences—EOD had the dogs, they were to locate the stuff, the disposal units were all guys from the NYPD bomb squad. There were boats in the river, helicopters up, there were armed men on all the rooftops . . . they closed down the city. . . . the motorcade, it was like nothing you've ever seen . . ."

"Totally armored . . ."

". . . all the Harleys . . ."

Several agents had been caught in the gridlock.

"I had to walk," one of them was saying, "from Ninetieth Street down to here, to the command post at Fifty-first. Take the subway? I couldn't *find* the friggin' subway."

Stephen Baylog, out of Pecos, Texas, had left the command post that morning for the federal courthouse at Foley Square, he and another deputy, and had arrived some six hours later. Baylog's mention of the incident had Wagner trying to remember the names of the two out-of-town deputies who a few years before had vanished underground for the better part of a day, lost in transit, missing-in-action on the MTA, hitting more than one borough en route to the U.N.

All the chitchat that afternoon on the General Assembly grounds (out-of-town investigators and deputy marshals, having decried the elitism of the Secret Service, had turned to querying local cops on the prices of residential real estate in the city of New York) was evidence of the amount of down-time that came with working such details. For deputy marshals, down-time came with working all kinds of details, according to Randy Riggenbach, a deputy from the Northern District of Ohio, whose habit was to take advantage of it.

Riggenbach had worked the 1985 Order trial, the seventeen-week, high-threat prosecution of neo-Nazis in Seattle, Washington:

"He says, anybody want to go help me do an admiralty? I had never seized a ship, what the hell? I said, sure. We went up and seized a 600-foot Greek oil tanker in Puget Sound . . . involved in a hit-skip in Boston, hit-skipped a bridge, caused a million dollars damage. . . . I had never done an admiralty."

Not only was there down-time on the General Assembly detail, but, because State was so short on manpower, there was overtime as well. And as Wagner pointed out, overtime, in law enforcement, was how everyone made money. Another perquisite of duty on State Department details was cause for more pain than celebration. It was not unusual for visiting dignitaries, before departing the country, to offer deputies gifts. And up to $180, deputies were allowed to accept them. Anything of greater value, however, was to be turned over to the State Department, and it had become something of an annual ritual, according to Wagner, for PSS personnel, at the end of the fall session, to line up, "in tears," to hand over the gold Rolexes that had been given them by the Saudis.

The General Assembly detail offered a good look at Protective Services, but it was only one break in the Service's operational slider. Throwing security at a situation was a Marshals Service money pitch, and headquarters knew how to put smoke on it. Bill Wagner, in the summer of 1985, had served to prove how fast the pitch could be delivered.

The call came at 4 A.M.

"Pack your bags, bring your passport . . . can't tell you."

Wagner was told to pack for four or five days. Like every deputy, Wagner carried a war bag in the trunk of his car. Like every deputy, he was ready. He was told to pick up a prisoner serving federal time in Memphis and fly the prisoner from there to New York. The deputy with whom Wagner was paired—who would brief him, he had been told—knew nothing more than he did.

"It was the highest security I've ever been involved in."

Wagner was one of twenty people the Marshals Service had put on the largest spy exchange in history, four convicted East Bloc spies held by the United States for twenty-three spies employed by the West and incarcerated in East Germany.

"We militarily flew these people over to Frankfurt, changed planes, took a C130, and flew up to Berlin. We sat in Berlin for *quite* some time, hopped on a bus with these people, and, once again under *extreme* security, motorcaded across the Glienicke Bridge, which separated East and West Germany. From there it was just a straight swap."

WITSEC would conduct a similar move in February 1986, trading for Soviet dissident Anatoly Scharansky.

In Bill Wagner and deputies like him, Bud McPherson sees the future of the Marshals Service. Which says as much about Bud McPherson as it does about Billy Wags. And it says even more about the Marshals Service itself. For never before in its history has the organization exhibited a sense of its future.

Bill Wagner is good at a lot of things, but there is one thing at which he is better than most who work for the government. As anyone who knows him will tell you, Billy Wagner knows how to smile.

You see it a lot in the Marshals Service.

If there is a virus replicating itself in the bureaucracy today, that virus is *esprit de corps,* and it is only about ten years old.

"In the beginning, it was embarrassing," Bud McPherson admits. "I didn't want to be associated with it. Just a bunch of good ol' boys . . . fighting to get the next prisoner trip, so they could get the ten cents a mile and take their wives. It was very unprofessional . . . just to get a job, you had to know someone who knew the marshal . . ."

(Government cars were introduced to the districts over a period of years, and according to Service historian Frederick S. Calhoun, "Many of the deputies resented the new acquisitions. Government cars robbed them of the ten to twelve cents a mile they earned driving their own cars on duty." Before G-cars, says Brooklyn chief Mike Pizzi, "the senior guy used *his* car for prisoner transportation. To make the mileage money. I was on the job a year before I could use my own car.")

McPherson's agency career vivifies the bridge between the "old" and the "new" Marshals Service. His success as a deputy and as an individual parallels the success of the agency itself. But for several years after he had pinned on the badge, McPherson's commitment to the job had been marginal at best— viewing the Service in terms of a career, McPherson had always been one move away from making another move.

And then McPherson got word that things were about to change.

The word came down from headquarters in 1978. On a trip to the training academy at Glynco that summer, Bud McPherson saw the word made flesh.

. . . and we beheld his glory, the glory as of the only begotten of the Father . . .

His name was Howard Safir.

"We were out on the range, he was firing a Sig Sauer—nine-millimeter semiautomatic pistol—and the rear-sight aperture fell off. Twenty-five meters. And not one of his rounds went out of the black . . ."

Alf McNeil, witness security supervisor, Region V—Bud McPherson's opposite number in New York—describes himself, humorously, as one of "the twelve Apostles in WITSEC." Mc-Neil, like McPherson, is one of the dozen regional chiefs. The parable of the Sig Sauer cited above is McNeil's, but it represents merely one rendering of the episode in question.

The WITSEC Gospels are Synoptic.

And the miracles are always performed by the Service's Associate Director for Operations.

"He can do as many push-ups as anybody in the Service. He can take that wall and motivate it . . ."

Howard Safir was a thirty-six-year-old Drug Enforcement Administration supervisor when in 1978 his boss, DEA administrator Peter Bensinger, put him on loan to the Marshals Service to rescue the Witness Security Program. Tall, lean, square-jawed, the son of immigrant Russian Jews, nephew of a New York City police detective who in 1952 had arrested bank robber Willie Sutton, Safir had grown up in the Bronx. He had entered federal law enforcement in 1965 as a special agent for Customs, and went immediately from there to the Federal Bureau of Narcotics, the Treasury Department precursor of the DEA (which was established in 1973, six years after the FBN was assumed by the Justice Department in the form of the Bureau of Narcotics and Dangerous Drugs). Having worked undercover in New York, Miami, and San Francisco, making drug buys in the days when domestic dope traffic was vertically integrated within the counterculture, Safir, operating out of Washington, worked several temporary overseas details, assigned to heroin interdiction in Southeast Asia, France, and Turkey. Street-cop tough, no stranger to a gunfight (his first shoot-out came six months into the job, and came to an end when he put a bullet into his suspect's chest), Safir nevertheless swelled to full law-enforcement blossom as a bureaucrat.

"If anybody is responsible for the changes in the modern Service," according to Bud McPherson, "it's Howard. Little by little, things got better, more professional . . . money here, a piece of equipment there . . . we started holding our heads up . . . started thinking about the future, instead of just apologizing for the past . . ."

Because WITSEC offered no institutional credit for those rotating out of Justice to oversee the program—with the negative media attention it drew, it promised only to accelerate the damage to a career whose future had already been cast into doubt— prevailing instructions to field inspectors, up to that time, had been *do it but don't tell me about it*. The phone calls out of Washington were always fraught with intrigue: "We're sending this witness to Colorado, but the marshal there doesn't want him, so we'll sneak him into Colorado and fund him out of Kansas."

Marshals in the districts had no affection for the program at all. Run directly out of headquarters, it bypassed them completely. All it did was cost them deputies, whom they assigned as contact men, McPherson suggests, only because they were forced to and only "on a slow afternoon." The deputy assigned, McPherson continues, was more often than not the "least competent" deputy in the district—the marshal, understandably, detailed his better men to the service of judges, the pressing needs of the federal bench being his primary responsibility.

"There was no funding, no staff, no equipment . . . no *regulations*. . . . It was the cause of the bad press, much of which was justified. . . . We were just stickin' our fingers in dikes and there were more holes than fingers . . . and then Howard came along . . . we had regulations, we had a Memorandum of Understanding."

Meeting Myrtle Poor Bear's flight in Cedar Rapids that day, the day that Claudette was aboard, was a motorcade, McPherson remembers, that did not consist of government cars.

"They were personally owned vehicles. They weren't the government cars as you see them today. Forget about armor plating. We had one government car, and the radio [in it] didn't work. We had my car and two others, and we happened to have CBs in them, so we're communicating, 'Easy Money to Charlie the Coffee,' like that, you know. We're communicating on an infrequently used channel on CBs, because in those days government equipment was nonexistent."

McPherson, seeing in Safir the breath of air that would carry WITSEC out of the doldrums to which it had been condemned, was not above running an occasional con on the new chief in the interest of accelerating the pace of change.

"I set Howard up a couple of times. We're at Fort Hamilton in Brooklyn with Fratianno, he's going to testify [in New York]. I can throw a snowball from Fort Hamilton to [boss] Joe Colombo's house, to [Genovese boss] Funzi Tieri's house. We're in an abandoned WAC barracks. It's a nice brick building, we're upstairs. There are all kinds of army beds, you know, with box springs and mattresses. And at the downstairs door, absolutely no security. We didn't have any. In those days, the wiseguys went on the mattresses, *we* went on the mattresses. They had better equipment, but at least we knew what to do. So I got some wire coat hangers, and I hung some beer cans above the door. For blackout curtains, I used box springs and G.I. blankets tacked over the windows. And that kind of nonsense . . . little trip things in the hallway . . .

"We were in the confines of a military base, so we had a *modicum* of security. I know the wiseguys. They are *not* going to come onto a military installation. Maybe terrorists will, maybe some crazy Colombians will, but wiseguys have a book of rules. They know their book and I know their book of rules. So there's no problem. I knew Howard was coming, so I overplayed it to show him what we needed. We were there cooking spaghetti, big pot of spaghetti, Fratianno was our chef, and we're on the mattresses just like the wiseguys go. And Howard comes in and sees my elaborate beer cans strung up, sees the army blankets tacked over the windows—he didn't know me well, he knew me a little bit and he knew my reputation—so we start talking and he says don't you have any [anti-intrusion] equipment? I said we don't *have* electronic devices. We've been promised them for years, but no one ever gets them . . .

"Howard says, you'll have them. A couple of months later we had them all. [Infrared seekers, motion detectors, video surveillance.] Now we can wire windows, we have control units, perimeter security . . . the stuff we should have had all along. We got it. We got it fast . . .

"I overplayed it with Howard a little bit. Once we leased cars.

We leased Malibus and they were pigs. Two-year leases on the Malibus, station wagons, supposed to be ideal for picking up families at airports. I wouldn't want to run away from anybody in one of them, because they could catch you on a skateboard. Howard comes into Los Angeles and he has to go to San Bernardino for a meeting, and he needs a car. I had some good cars, we had some Chevy Caprices, and I know he has to pull this Kellogg Hill. I give him a Malibu. We got rid of the Malibus after that.

"He would react to this stuff. And I would *over*react to make sure I got my point across."

Howard Safir, to his everlasting credit with McPherson, did not do what everyone supposed he would do up front. He did not shit-can the cowboys who had held the program together, however questionably, through its disastrous beginnings.

"To this day, no one at headquarters [acknowledges that contribution]. Instead they say, 'Can you imagine doing that stuff? You'd go to jail for that today.'"

The first major turn in WITSEC's path to elitism was Safir's institution of the "metro corridor," an organizational move the result of which was the creation of the twelve WITSEC regions and the chain of command that circumvented completely the politically appointed marshals. Today WITSEC is so layered in security, its individual operations are virtually impenetrable to anyone without "a need to know," including WITSEC deputies not assigned to the operation in question.

"I was in WITSEC for almost ten years," says Flavio "Flip" Lorenzoni, chief deputy for the Southern District of New York. "I went to a conference, as a chief. Witness Security had one room, I walked in, and they're not talking. I said, 'What's going on?' They said, 'We've got to wait for you to leave.' I said, 'Man, out of sight, out of mind.' I'm only gone like a year. I said, 'I don't believe you guys.' Need to know. I shouldn't have been there. There's no need to be there. They're right."

Detailed to the Marshals Service for a year, Howard Safir, at the end of it, was asked to stay. Promoted from WITSEC chief, eventually to become Associate Director for Operations, he would go on to help revolutionize the organization.

The transition between the old and the new Marshals Service is measured by many events—the desegregation of the University of Mississippi; the arrivals, respectively, of William Hall and Stanley Morris as directors; the appearance of Howard Safir; the capture, under Safir's leadership, of Christopher Boyce—but however one measures it, the transition coincides with an observable shift, at the federal level, in the typical cop's notion of organized crime.

It is said that during the presidential administration of Ronald Reagan, the only thing in America that went down in price was cocaine. With the rise in the Reagan years of the Colombian cartels, organized crime in the United States came inevitably to mean dope. When federal lawmen today talk about organized crime, they are talking about the traffic in contraband drugs, and when they do so they manifest what translates as an outright nostalgia for the Mob.

Nowhere is this phenomenon more evident than in the Witness Security Program.

In the words of Bud McPherson:

"Give me wiseguys any day. . . . Who made us experts on Colombians . . . on terrorists? Give me a good old wiseguy any day, I got their book of rules."

With Caribbean nations providing the manpower, Colombia leading the field, the new Prohibition in America offers the opportunities of the original to a very different generation of immigrants. The face of organized crime has changed. New World American gangsters, for example, do not limit their revenge to stool pigeons, they slaughter entire families, the wives and children not only of their enemies but of their competitors as well. Nor do they subscribe to a code of conduct that prohibits their killing the police. The streets of Miami, New York, and Los Angeles sound like nothing so much today as they do the streets of Capone's Chicago. And every day is Valentine's Day.

But with a lock on the nation's headlines, the trade in Southeast Asian heroin and Latin American coke has drawn attention away from the old Sicilian families who, according to Bud McPherson, are as active as they ever were. They may not be playing leading roles in the nation's nightly news, but they still provide the overwhelming majority, not only of the WITSEC honor roll, but of the program's incoming freshmen.

It was the Mob that gave WITSEC life, the Mob that brought it to the attention of the American public at large, and it is the Mob that still gives the program its unquestionable star quality.

The veritable Gloria Swanson of the Witness Security Program is a guy named Jimmy Fratianno.

. . .

Aladena Fratianno, a made guy in the Italian rackets, was born in 1913 in a small town near Naples, Italy. Arriving in Cleveland, Ohio, at the age of four, the son of a landscape contractor, he embarked upon one of the few careers that offer no dignified retirement at about the same time he started calling himself Jimmy because Aladena sounded too much like a "broad's name."

A precocious gambler, Jimmy "the Weasel," as he would come to be known, was making book at local tracks and hanging around the clubhouse of the Italian-American Brotherhood on Cleveland's Mayfield Road before he was out of his teens. He progressed rapidly from gambling to sticking up gambling joints, and by 1935 he was cracking heads for the Teamsters, who were out to organize the Cleveland parking lots. He was twenty-three years old when he went to prison for the first time—for roughing up a bookie too slow to pay off.

In 1946, one year into his parole, Fratianno moved to Los Angeles, where, at the age of thirty-three, under the sponsorship of celebrated syndicate tough guy Johnny Roselli, in a winery on South Figueroa Street, he "got made"—initiated into La Cosa Nostra in a ceremony reminiscent of his First Communion.

"For a while, there," he told Roselli, "I felt like I was in church."

The rest is underworld history. Fratianno, who has confessed to committing several murders as a soldier in Jack Dragna's Los Angeles crime family, entered the Witness Security Program in 1977, and his testimony has been nothing if not comprehensive, a treachery-ridden Who's Who of postwar racketeering.

Fratianno collaborated on the first book about his life in 1981. Six years later, he collaborated on another. A darling of the media for over a decade, he single-handedly made WITSEC famous, and in the course of doing so raised the visibility of Bud McPherson, whose destiny it had been to escort Fratianno into the program.

And, as Bill Wagner will tell you, "Jimmy will deal only with Bud."

A questionable distinction at best.

One of Fratianno's more recent attempts to make Bud Mc-Pherson's life miserable was his well-publicized claim that the Marshals Service had terminated him, leaving the public to assume that after years of dedicated service to the government he had been cut loose to fend off the enemies who had contracts out on his life. What the Marshals Service actually had done, much later than Fratianno had any right to expect, was cut him loose from funding. Jimmy Fratianno, the program poster boy, had managed to avoid getting a job for better than ten years. He invented the most popular ploy to that end—once settled in a particular community, and on the verge of ultimate employment, Fratianno would spot a suspicious vehicle, or a suspiciously familiar face, and so convincingly identify a threat that WITSEC would have to relocate him.

Again.

Fratianno has been redocumented so many times, in so many parts of the country, that rare is the field inspector who has not, however fleetingly, met him at least once.

"Not the most pleasant guy in the world to be with," asserts the Service's director of training, Duke Smith, who worked WITSEC early in his career.

Smith's is an opinion held by many who have rotated through the program.

Active WITSEC deputies, on the other hand, appear reluctant as a matter of policy to speak ill of any individual witness.

"Fratianno is used to having things his own way," according to Mike O'Neil, a WITSEC coordinator in New York. Which is probably true of most mobsters, especially those who have been around for a while, many of whom, admittedly, can be very entertaining. "After they get immunity, they tell you Sinatra stories, they tell you Kennedy stories, they tell you everything."

Even deputies who dislike him intensely admit that Fratianno is a great cook. Which, as a personal recommendation, is about as profound as the further acknowledgment that "he never missed 'The Price Is Right.' " It is the kind of endorsement that finds an analogue in the observation by Sherlock Holmes that Moriarty was good at math.

Bud McPherson, for his part, has never had serious problems measuring up to various requirements of keeping the temperamental hitman happy. During one stay in Los Angeles, McPherson, for Fratianno's recreation, supervised several afternoon visits to an underutilized ice rink; deputies, strapping on skates, flanked the murderer as, circling the arena, he relived the more innocent moments of an ill-remembered childhood.

Security to the veteran McPherson was not a significant worry.

"Wiseguys don't carry guns. They got to go home, get a gun, they got to get backup. . . . The same with funerals . . . there's plenty of time to get out before anybody can dime you."

(WITSEC coordinator Mike O'Neil, while no less confident in his ability to respond to danger, took a bring-the-mountain-to-Mohammed approach to the entertaining of a witness he was holding in Orient Point, Long Island. It was the Fourth of July and the witness wanted to watch the local fireworks display. O'Neil, rather than move the witness, talked the organizers of the event into moving the fireworks barge two beaches down shore.)

Fratianno, in his constant relocating, likes to serve as his own travel agent, and one of his more recent requests for transfer was to Saint Croix in the Virgin Islands.

"I took him there," McPherson admits. "We stayed twelve or fourteen days. There were chickens crossing the highway. It cost fourteen dollars for breakfast. And there was only one TV network. He couldn't watch the Cleveland game. It pissed him off. We left."

It is his Fratianno stories among others that McPherson is saving for the publishers and producers who have promised to make him rich upon his retirement from the Marshals Service.

"John Dean was very businesslike," Claudette McPherson explains. "Is Bud home, no, would you tell him John called. . . . Now, Fratianno, I would carry on a three-hour conversation with him . . ."

"And if she wasn't home," McPherson interjects, "he'd do twenty minutes with Jennifer."

"He's a talker," Claudette agrees.

As any deputy marshal will tell you, the ruthless-murderer-as-lovable-curmudgeon is nothing more than a myth, and in Fratianno's case it is a fable nourished by the mobster himself. Fratianno's romance with the press is resuscitated every time he opens his mouth. And in the endurance of Fratianno's notoriety, there is a questionable reciprocity observed: thanks to Fratianno, there are few racketeers in the country who do not recognize Bud McPherson on sight.

When McPherson moved from Kansas City, returning to Los Angeles, he built a house east of the city, in part because he wanted to partake of the privileges of the Via Verde Country Club. Studying the membership list when he joined, however, he saw the name of Louis Dragna, Jack Dragna's nephew, who with Fratianno had been acting co-boss of the Los Angeles family just before Fratianno turned government witness.

As McPherson explains it, "I told my boss, I'm never gonna play golf with the guy. He said it was okay to join. I went to the pro and said, never put me in his foursome."

One Saturday, to play as his guests, McPherson invited two strike-force attorneys and "another law-enforcement guy."

"We're in a foursome right behind Lou."

McPherson and his guests played golf all day, and retired to the clubhouse for a drink. McPherson excused himself to use the men's room. Inside he happened to run into one of Dragna's golfing companions.

"He says [and here McPherson starts talking like he has cancer of the throat], 'Hey, Bud, who are those guys you're playing with?' I told him who they were. He says, 'Bud, play behind us every week, like this. Louis thought there was a wire in the golf cart. He was a nervous wreck, he couldn't make a putt. Heh, heh, we took all his money.' "

To hear Bud McPherson tell Mob stories is to harken back to one's school days, specifically those days on which one walks into one's American history class having wretchedly failed to complete the previous night's reading assignment. McPherson drops contract murderers' names as though they were part of the country's cultural vocabulary, recounting events of routine bloodletting on the cheerfully innocent assumption that they carry the mythic freight of Civil War engagements.

When McPherson and Alf McNeil tell stories about protected witness Joe Bish, "the greatest cook in the world," then start talking about Luparelli, "the button man [who drove the car] on the Gallo hit," you are expected to know that Joe Bish and Luparelli are the same guy, that a button man is a mob soldier, a hood who occupies the lowest level in the Cosa Nostra authority structure, that a hit is a syndicate contract murder, and that Luparelli, after spotting "Crazy Joe" Gallo, "dropped a dime," that is, made the phone call that resulted in Gallo's being gunned down in lower Manhattan's Little Italy in 1972, in Umberto's Clam House on Mulberry Street. When they talk about Fratianno and his disquisition on the matter of putting "the boop-boop to the Bomp-Bomp," you have to know that Frank Bompensiero, Fratianno's good friend turned government informant, took four rounds to the head in 1977 in Pacific Beach,

California. Knowing these things when you talk to these guys is like knowing that Stonewall Jackson in 1863 lost his life at the battle of Chancellorsville.

"You can dislike a witness and not have him know; you can dislike him and not be able to hide it, it's so obvious it shows. Then there are what my wife calls your 'friendly murderers'; you may not like them, but coming from Brooklyn, as I do, you have an ability to understand them."

Coming from Brooklyn, as Bud McPherson does, means coming from Borough Park, a neighborhood of Italians and culturally identified Jews, dominated heavily by the former when McPherson was a kid.

"I grew up with all the wiseguys. Joey Gallo and I went to school together."

In the fall of 1978, preparing to testify in the racketeering trial that followed investigation into construction of the Westchester Premier Theatre, Jimmy Fratianno, under McPherson's protection, was being held at Fort Hamilton, New York (the army base on the Brooklyn waterfront at which McPherson had conned Howard Safir with the makeshift security arrangements). Home to the nation's five wealthiest and most powerful Cosa Nostra families—there were 2,500 made guys in New York—the city was a criminal Disneyland, and one afternoon, with nothing better to do, McPherson, with several deputies, took Fratianno on a driving tour of Brooklyn, pointing out to him all the bosses' houses.

"For Jimmy it was like going to Washington . . . the seat of government . . . *Guy votes on the Commission!* . . . He was like a kid, he couldn't control his excitement . . ."

Bud McPherson brings far more to bear upon his knowledge of the Mob than his merely having grown up in its shadow. McPherson is not shy about asking questions, and for twenty years he has been asking questions of the racketeers under his protection. After all, he assumes, if you want to know how to protect a witness from a professional hit man, who better to ask than the hit man himself.

Working the General Assembly detail in the aftermath of the Carlos Lehder trial, Bill Wagner had not seen his chief for a while.

"I haven't seen Bud since August 2nd, two months ago. And

he's my immediate boss. I just happened to be at the credit union that day—I was on leave at the time—I was going to buy a new car. I bumped into him at the credit union, we looked at each other and laughed, he said, 'I know you . . . you work for me.' "

Wagner could not remember how long it had been since he had seen McPherson before that. Nor could he give you an accurate guess as to when he might lay eyes on him again.

When Wagner finally returned to Los Angeles following duty in New York, McPherson was on his way out of town. He was on his way to the Service's training academy in Glynn County, Georgia, there to deliver the series of lectures he had created as a part of the required curriculum of the Service's Witness Security School. The title of the course, a variation on which had become a part of every deputy's basic training, while exemplary of the spirit that pervaded the Service, was eloquent testimony to the academic credentials McPherson brought to the federal government's endless war on organized crime. Informally known as "Bud's course," it bore the official scholastic title:

Wiseguys 101.

★ ★ ★ ★

Eagle Up

7.

Fire in the Heart

Open to rapid evacuation by both Interstate and Intracoastal, the city of Brunswick, Georgia, gateway to stately St. Simons Island, is situated seventy-five miles south of Savannah in the state's maritime Glynn County. Hence the name Glynco, applied to the former naval air station there, where in 1975, in fulfillment of a congressional mandate, the Federal Law Enforcement Training Center was established as a bureau of the Treasury Department. FLETC, as the training center is bureaucratically known, serving some 16,000 students annually on the outskirts of a city that is home to fewer than 18,000 civilians, is a consolidated facility, providing basic and advanced training for the personnel of sixty-three participating federal organizations; it offers advanced programs in selected subjects for the employees of various state and local law-enforcement agencies as well. The sprawling installation incorporates over a hundred buildings on 1,500 acres of land and approximates nothing so convincingly as a theme park for cops.

Not only does it house the largest indoor firing range in the country, it features four outdoor ranges as well, not including that range which is devoted exclusively to shotgun training. On the average workday, there is more brass flying at Glynco than comes out of the typical foundry in a month. (The federal government airs it out to the tune of nine million rounds annually at Glynco.) The northern third of the facility is given over almost entirely to a Driver Specialties Complex—three defensive-driving courses, two vast highway-response courses, and a pair of water-fed skid pans. Isolated, off in the northeast corner, is an expanse of conspicuously unimproved real estate dedicated to what is identified on the visitor's map as Explosives Demonstration (an activity which, both by definition and by application on a school day, clearly speaks for itself). Adjacent to the outdoor firing ranges on the southwest edge of the complex is the International Border Practical Exercise Area. A scale model is what it is not. Nor are the airplanes, the boats, and the assorted motor vehicles which lie abandoned in various locations about the property for hands-on training in search-and-seizure.

Indoors at Glynco the troubleshooter of the new century may attend classes conducted by the Computer and Economic Crime Division, enroll in Advanced Law Enforcement Photography School, or receive advanced training in Technical Investigative Equipment—acoustics and microphones; the installation, operation, and maintenance of electronic surveillance; audio enhancement; radio frequency tracking; "and others." Glynco offers advanced programs in Marine Law Enforcement, in Archaeological Resources Protection, and in a language called Law Enforcement Spanish, the entire curriculum of the academy the outgrowth of the eight-week Criminal Investigator Training Program (job series 1811) around which the Center was created.

Much of the training here is audible for miles.

Defensive driving at Glynco does not mean what it meant when you first heard the expression in your senior-high driver education class. The water-fed asphalt pads are for practicing controlled skids and performing 180-degree J-turns and bootleg turns; defensive driving is evasive driving, jumping curbs, executing controlled crashes through roadblocks, an automotive skill whose essence is nowhere more clearly articulated than in the program syllabus itself: "Proficiency in the use of various types of firearms is mandatory." Highway Response, as often as not, means highway pursuit at Glynco, it means exercising that which is as fundamental to every cop's training as is the alphabet to the elementary-school student, that which is known as the *felony vehicle stop.*

The sedans parked on the firing range serve the requirements of barricade shooting—roll out, take cover, and fire over the fenders . . . *do not shoot the photographer* . . . there are more pop-up and swinging targets indoors and outdoors at Glynco than in a thousand penny arcades, the characters disporting themselves thereupon occupying some twisted comic-strip no-man's-land, some dark Dick Tracy of the soul . . . Uncle Scrooge on speed . . . the tough guys with five-o'clock shadows flashing press cards or pump-action shotguns, the blond cradling the baby, the brunette clutching the large-caliber pistol, cartoons flying at you from everywhere . . . *fire but don't fuck up* . . . a freeze-frame four-color nightmare, and before you graduate, the Marshals Service sends you through an indoor version of it in the dark . . . loud music, flashing strobes, and amplified human screams . . . you and a partner and—only in the United States Marshals Service—live ammunition. . . . "The Maze is where we really stress 'em out; if they're going to lose it, they lose it there. We've seen them come out weeping."

And then, too, there are those combat silhouettes of the three-dimensional variety, the ones that walk and talk and improvisationally scream obscenities in your face, the skilled labor working on scale—the training center's role players, the actors and actresses, civilians, who portray the criminals and the innocent bystanders whom the students confront on the streets and behind the closed doors of the Practical Exercise Area. A three-block complex of former enlisted quarters, the area, though somewhat seedier, exhibits the look of the typical postwar, suburban subdivision. Here, in some thirty-five abandoned bungalows—the interiors of a couple rearranged to resemble those of marginal commercial establishments, barrooms, for example, in places like hell—potential deputies, upon approach and entry, are tested on what they have learned about working fugitive warrants, most importantly what they have learned about walking away from such confrontations alive.

On a typical day at Glynco, traveling the streets, you will see aspiring Broadway performers—ingenues, song-and-dance men, the theater's best and brightest—growling and spitting and verbally abusing future officers of the law (when they are not trying merely to elude them or possibly to gun them down) as the former are questioned, arrested, jailed, or ignored by the young students in question; you will find them riding in the backs of limousines, impersonating visiting dignitaries or playing cooperating Mafia big shots, as those same fledgling civil servants usher them cautiously around town, sometimes as far as the local airport, lead cars and follow cars executing such evasive maneuvers as the block-and-turn at every intersection, potential deputies walking the fenders as the vehicles cruise to a stop on Second Street, just outside Building 20—the training offices of the Marshals Service.

Duke Smith, director of training, United States Marshals Service, is not of the British peerage. He is not the Duke *of* Smith, not as far as anyone at Glynco is aware. But, then, neither can anyone there, if pressed, tell you what his given name actually is. Officially G. Wayne Smith, born in July 1948, he was going by the name Duke, evidence shows, before Elvis was out of the army. Duke is what his wife Suzy has always called him, and the two have been going steady since Smith was thirteen years old.

An erstwhile amateur opera singer, a former college athlete— he majored in music at Western Carolina University, which he entered on a football scholarship—the bespectacled Smith, if not of the royal family, is the man, it is generally agreed, whom the Marshals Service would send first if any of them needed arresting.

He is the agency's knight errant in residence, its on-call intellectual.

A talented short-story writer in whose prose you can hear the drawl (he thinks Robert Ruark puts Hemingway in the shade and he will not shrink from telling you why), an enthusiastic outdoorsman (he is an avid hunter of North American game and he will tie up the telephone for hours, subjecting L. L. Bean's customer-service reps to an inquisition on the merits of various rods and reels offered in the company's annual Fly Fishing Specialties catalogue), Duke Smith is a contemplative fellow, a gentleman of that variety that only the South produces. He knows which fork to pick up first and can be trusted to know how to go about throwing handcuffs on the queen.

Yet while undeniably open to formal overtures from the House of Windsor, Duke Smith would have more to contribute, clearly, to an audience with the Earps of Tombstone. Six-foot-three and weighing in at 230 pounds, he could easily kick Wyatt's ass—and nothing, one discovers, is likely to make him happier. Whether he could outshoot Earp is another thing. This is a guy who has not made a felony arrest since high-test was a dollar a gallon.

Duke Smith came into the Marshals Service in 1974 in Greensboro, North Carolina. The principal prerequisite of employment at the time was that a deputy own a full-size car. It had to weigh over 3,000 pounds.

"When you signed on in the old days," says International Branch chief Larry Homenick, "before they gave you a gun, they gave you a set of handcuffs and leg irons, that was your equipment."

The mission of the Service, as the local marshal saw it—as U.S. marshals everywhere saw it—was the delivery of prisoners for trial. In default of that, a deputy's duties were limited to the service of process.

In Greensboro, however, neither activity filled up a deputy's day.

"Deputies," according to Duke Smith, "were goin' fishin' most of the time."

For Smith, who had gone to work as a cop before completing college (he returned, eventually to graduate with a degree in criminal justice), it was an inauspicious beginning, the more so given the reality that he had gone to work first in Miami, Hialeah to be exact. (After college he joined the Charlotte, North Carolina, PD.)

"When you're a cop in Miami, that's war every night. There's something happening all the time. You'd just walk into stuff. Once a week I'd come in, my uniform'd be ripped off—I mean, you're out there fightin' all the time. When you're twenty-one years old, and the sap is still rising, when you're full of piss and vinegar, it's a great place to be."

The same could not be said of the U.S. marshal's office in Greensboro. And a casual interchange with the chief deputy there convinced Smith that things were unlikely to change. Smith walked into his chief's office one day and saw warrants all over the desk.

"What are you doing with these warrants?" he asked.

"We have 'em in NCIC—when they catch 'em, they'll call us," the chief replied.

NCIC, the National Crime Information Center, is run by the FBI. Its computer contains the name and fingerprint classification of every wanted person in the country. The information is contributed by, and accessible to, every cop in the United States.

"Who are 'they'?" Smith wanted to know.

"Anyone who picks 'em up."

"Do *we* work warrants?"

"Well, every once in a while the judge'll ask us to go out and pick up a guy who failed to show up for court."

Every once in a while.

"On down-time," it was later explained to Smith by one of his fellow deputies.

Down-time in Greensboro, to Smith's way of thinking, was a metaphysical concept:

"You get a summons, a complaint, to serve, you'd drive thirty miles down the road, serve it, then take the rest of the afternoon and fish."

Smith wondered why he should not ask permission to work some of the warrants stacked on the chief's desk.

"You're gonna be mighty unpopular if you do," he was told.

Smith was ready to call it quits.

"I'd been a pretty successful, an aggressive, policeman." [As a Charlotte cop Smith and his training officer, in one six-month period, made more arrests than all other members of the department combined.] "I went home and told my wife, 'I don't know if this job is for me.' "

Called away to a WITSEC detail in Baltimore, where the Service had a safe-house at the time, Smith returned to Greensboro with a renewed sense of opportunity. But the opportunity lay outside the district. He had not been on the job a year, and thus did not officially qualify, but he knew headquarters needed personnel to fill a SOG class in Jackson, Mississippi. His request of the marshal and chief deputy that he be allowed to join the Special Operations Group was the second-to-last thing Smith would do in the way of alienating them permanently.

"That's run by Washington," they told him. "You don't want to have anything to do with that."

Not only did Smith join SOG, but he spent a month and a half on the western Pacific island of Guam with the unit—several thousand air-miles from his district—repatriating Vietnamese refugees. When he returned to Greensboro, he summoned the courage to press the warrants issue with the marshal. Two days later, the chief, who saw warrants as the equivalent of make-work and who made no secret of his opinion on the matter, approached Smith's desk with three fugitive warrants in his hand.

"You want to work warrants? Have at it."

"And he gave me three cases so cold . . . I mean, people hadn't *looked* at them for years. . . . These people had been gone, like, since Methuselah was around."

One of the three had failed to appear for trial nine years before.

"The advantage," Smith knew, and the only advantage, "was that these three guys had forgotten that anybody was lookin' for 'em."

Smith's alienation of his chief deputy was complete when he cleared the warrants in three days.

"That really pissed him off."

Smith, as soon as the opportunity presented itself, escaped Greensboro by way of WITSEC. It is still the agency fast track. He attended Witness Security School in 1978, a member of the first class of specialists, all of whom were graduated with the newly created rank of inspector. He worked WITSEC for only two years—in a service that was growing rapidly, Smith, with an eye for the main chance, immediately drew the attention of headquarters. In nine years, he would jump ten grades, his ascendance through the bureaucracy unprecedented.

In 1979 the Marshals Service inherited its Fugitive Program, and Smith was selected by Howard Safir to initiate the study that would gain the Service status as a participating member of EPIC.

The El Paso Intelligence Center was founded in 1974, a joint venture of the United States Border Patrol and the Drug Enforcement Administration. Howard Safir as a member of the DEA contributed to the study that created it. Established as a central repository of criminal intelligence on the international traffic in narcotics, it was focused initially on the transportation of marijuana and brown heroin across the nation's border with Mexico.

By the time Duke Smith arrived in 1979, EPIC had grown to include four other participating agencies—Customs, the Bureau of Alcohol, Tobacco and Firearms (ATF), the Coast Guard, and the Federal Aviation Administration, in that order—and its geographical mandate had outgrown its original limits. Since that time, four more agencies have entered into Memoranda of Understanding: the FBI, the Internal Revenue Service, the State Department, and the Secret Service, a total of eleven federal agencies then, whose representatives in 1989 moved into a new $8-million, 52,000-square-foot facility on the grounds of the U.S. Army's Fort Bliss outside El Paso, Texas.

Since 1979 the Center's charter has expanded to encompass tactical intelligence on aliens and firearms as well as dope, the information in and out officially circumscribed thereby, but in reality no restrictions exist.

There is an Air, a Maritime, and a General watch at EPIC, six or seven agents assigned to each, three watch commanders present during duty hours. On the wall of the Operations Room there is a twenty-four-hour clock. And a light that flashes insistently when a visitor is on the premises.

On that same wall, there are large-scale maps—they are mounted overhead like frescoes—and on them one can see the actual movement of drugs and currency, witness the ongoing international satellite tracking of various aircraft and vessels. Lights of several colors give the maps a festive appearance . . . kickouts, land drops, sea drops, white, blue, and green on the aircraft map . . . thefts, crashes, seizures . . . traffic stops . . . vessels seized . . . activity on the Southwest border.

Here, in the engine room that drives EPIC, tactical intelligence is actually tangible. The strategic intelligence is not. Here and elsewhere at EPIC, criminal intelligence of a strategic nature, the sophisticated stuff, is audible.

Data processing is incessant.

The EPIC data base in 1979 was no data base at all. A collection of several automated and manual systems, it was a uniquely American tribute to the absence of one. Even now, much of its software is discrete. DEA uses NADDIS, Customs uses TECS, the OASIS system belongs to the Immigration and Naturalization Service (parent agency of the Border Patrol), the SENTRY system to the Bureau of Prisons. EPIC, a manifestation, for better or worse, of interagency cooperation, owes its very existence to the fact that, by law, the various agencies' computers do not interface.

"We've had evolve in this country," as Smith explains it, "a very fragmented, decentralized, bifurcated, in many ways unproductive, redundant policing apparatus. We have 11,000 different police departments in this country. We don't want a national police force—we don't want a KGB, we don't want the SS under Hitler—we don't want to live in a police state. Our freedom is far more important than our having a really efficient organization for policing ourselves."

Well, to some of us it is.

Not only does EPIC now have its own data base, IT, the Intelligence Terminal, a source and a repository of information shared by the participating agencies (a data base open, also, to queries and to contributions of intelligence by local, county, and state police through a designated narcotics officer on each of the nation's fifty state police forces), the Center has also developed a program called APOLLO, through which all EPIC participants now may gain access to four of the discrete agency data bases currently in operation there.

Reciprocity is mandatory. Information out? Information in.

It was a bright cold day in April and the clocks were striking thirteen. . . .

In fiscal year 1990, EPIC handled 653,922 transactions.

Smith's reception at EPIC was memorable for its lack of enthusiasm. Interagency cooperation in government is a consensual hallucination. Rarely achieving bureaucratic reality, it succeeds only as a state of mind. And a temporary one at best. In 1979, the situation, as Smith confronted it, was made worse by the perception of the Marshals Service, by then no longer justified, as a kind of terminally stumbling stepsister in the federal law-enforcement family. Its participating status at EPIC, which Smith, with a smile and a shoeshine, helped to engineer, contributed significantly to the agency parity that the Service enjoys today.

Smith's sales pitch was very simple:

"We don't want your dope, we don't want your investigations, we want the bodies . . . we want the guys. What have you got?"

In the United States, *initial* arrests account for all the institutional credit in law enforcement. Agents of the DEA, the FBI, and the other investigative agencies—Customs, ATF, the Secret Service, etc.—receive no credit for *fugitive* arrests. The job of an investigator is to *open* cases. And federal investigators are rewarded for the number of cases they *make*. A case is closed with the initial indictment. Smith walked into EPIC on the heels of an idiotically simple proposition, the out-and-out elemental power of which he had first learned to appreciate at Greensboro:

"The only reason we have fugitives," he had come to understand rather dolefully, "is because nobody looks for 'em."

The Marshals Service specialization in fugitives—not simply a priority, but the mission to which its investigative mandate was restricted—would come to be seen not as a threat but as an asset, eventually, by every federal officer with warrants to work (all but agents of the FBI, whose self-image was ultimately at stake).

In October 1979, with the federal Fugitive Program, the Marshals Service inherited some 8,500 FBI fugitives. When Smith arrived at EPIC, he discovered 77 percent of them documented there.

"In over three-quarters of our cases, we had automatic leads. It had been an untapped resource for years."

Acceptance at EPIC gave the Marshals Service access to the Border Lookout System operated by INS. (Access to the State Department's Passport-Visa Lookout System, the only one that catches you *before* you leave the country, had already been engineered out of Washington.) Smith, querying EPIC's computers, also queried INTERPOL. In 1980, when the Marshals Service started dragging in fugitives ("and we do it three times cheaper than anyone's ever done it"), it was not uncommon for the federally departed to greet deputies with statements like the following:

"I've been here for ten years, what took you so long?"

It was by way of his positioning at EPIC that Smith became involved in the Service's hunt for Christopher Boyce, among other things its first international case. Smith would travel both to Costa Rica and to South Africa in search of the escaped Soviet spy. Smith remained EPIC program coordinator until 1983, when he was assigned to Glynco as the Service's director of training.

"Their training's more for real," a federal agent, who has taught at Glynco, will tell you about the Marshals Service.

He is talking about their survival training.

In the words of Duke Smith:

"Our human resource is the most valuable resource we have, something we take very seriously. We stress officer survival. We make it clear, early on, 'you don't do us any good if you're dead.' We put a lot of emphasis on survival skills."

Survival skills in the United States Marshals Service include mental and physical conditioning and rigorous tactical training, but because, more often than not, life-and-death transactions are conducted in an exchange of the all too familiar currency of gunfire, on nothing is greater emphasis placed than on a proficiency with firearms.

Deputy United States marshals do not respond to traffic accidents. They do not rescue cats from trees. They do not search for missing children, take reports of burglaries and auto thefts, or escort elderly citizens across their districts' busy streets. Murder, rape, armed robbery, and other violent felonies, it is not their duty to investigate—they are not in the business of gathering evidence—their interface with crime is with the criminal himself, the indicted, the convicted, the incarcerated, the escaped. They come in after the fact. And virtually everything they do on an operational level requires possession of a gun.

Deputy John Butler, EPIC program coordinator, in acknowledging a rather unique contribution to the Service's recruitment effort, effectively articulates both the realities and the official limits of the typical deputy marshal's job. The occasional recruit, Butler says, when asked why he is drawn to the Marshals Service, will inevitably cite as one of his professional ambitions— often because he thinks it is expected of him—the rehabilitation of chronic felons, the unselfish attainment of those personal rewards that flow from one's helping crooked people go straight.

"I tell him," Butler says, " 'You're in the wrong business. Our job is to put scumbags in jail. Ninety percent of these people need to be rehabilitated by Doctor Smith and Doctor Wesson. And Doctor Glock,' " he adds, in reference to the Austrian semiautomatic pistol currently popular with the nation's cops.

The average American citizen's customary run-in with the law, the young deputy inevitably learns, can be terribly misleading. Not because it enforces a false impression of the typical police officer, but because it fortifies a misconception about the typical criminal in the United States. While the number of those incarcerated for victimless crimes is admittedly growing—the population's determination to dope itself will one day, out of necessity, be handled outside the criminal justice system—and while miscarriage of American justice is not so rare as one would like to believe, the truth is that a plurality of those doing time in the nation's prisons today clearly belong there. And for the rest of their natural lives.

Many are the career felons who, in a strictly clinical sense—stripping the adjective of all but its pure lexical meaning—are uncivilized. They have demonstrated over the course of their lives a chronic inability to coexist peacefully in a society elevated above the primitive. Theirs is a degree of personal development that, in at least one significant way, bears resemblance to the infantile: they are characteristically unable to recognize a connection between action and consequence. For them, the only thing that distinguishes right from wrong is who happens to be doing it. Nor are many able to discriminate between the mortal and the venial—there is a fundamentalism inherent in their pathology—they perceive no difference, for example, between petty theft and murder.

It is for people such as these that prisons were created. They are people whose behavior would be unacceptable in any microcosm on any planet in the universe. And these are not the criminally insane. These are the normal ones. The etiology of their criminality (some are born to it, many more are bred to it by the environment in which they are reared) is worthy of study. But it does not alter the reality of their existence. In abundance. These are people who have absolutely nothing in common with you. Or anyone you regularly see on television. And they inform the core of the nation's prison population. Charlie Manson is in there with people who understand him. To assume anything else about what dwells today in the American penal colony, as fashionable as it may be to do so, is delusional.

And cops deal with these people all day. Every day. It is these people whom cops are dealing with when they are not dealing with you.

"It is interesting to look at them," says Deputy John Haynes, Special Operations Group commander, whose experience with them dates to the early 1970s. "For the most part you see them coming from broken homes, you see them coming from homes where drugs and alcohol were very important. And you see no love for the most part from the parents. There are exceptions, but everything I've seen, that's the basic pattern. So, that person really didn't have a chance to start with. . . . [and] it keeps breeding itself over and over and over."

Haynes admits that routinely coming into contact with such people is not something one takes in stride. It affects the average cop, and it affects him every time it happens.

"Yeah, I think it does. I've never gotten used to it, and there are thousands of penitentiaries I've been in and out of. It bothers me every time I go in a penitentiary."

And his discomfort has nothing to do with fear, Haynes says, though when he talks about it his voice carries the weight of an elemental, almost spiritual, dread.

"To me, when I walk in there . . . to me it's like walking into hell, what hell must be like. I'm not talking about the living conditions, I'm talking about the . . . sin . . . the hatred . . . the perversion. You know, I believe in God. And to believe in God you got to believe in hell. And that to me, when I walk in one of them places, I think that's as close as getting to hell as you can come, because you can just feel the . . . the energies . . . in that place, and I just cannot wait to get out of there, you know, when I put a prisoner in there. And like I said, I'm not scared of them choppin' on me or hurtin' me or anything else, it's just that I get a sick kind of feeling every time I go in one of them places . . . the scourge and the scum . . . not the institution itself, it's the makeup of those people, that can rape people and kill babies and mistreat children . . . ."

Haynes, in his passionate recital, does not restrict his characterization to the nation's maximum-security penitentiaries.

"Any of them. I've been in all of them. The county jail. You can walk in the middle of a county jail, and go down in the tank area, and listen to the guttural talk and the . . . some guy punkin' somebody in the ass over there in the corner and . . . It makes me sick, it just makes me sick. And I'm not no prude or nothing else, you know, I been around the block. I done my shit, too. But you wad it all up together, and to me, that's hell. That's got to be about what it's going to be like, somebody winds up in hell."

It is a vision, Haynes asserts, that the public ignores at its peril.

"I just raised two sons, and as a parent, I tell you, I had a living nightmare. As a parent, to have good children, and to think one of them is going to do something tonight and they're going to haul him down to the county jail and throw him . . . suppose he's drunk, they're going to throw him in the drunk tank. . . . Now, what's going to happen to that kid? It scared me to death to think of one of my kids going into a lockup with those animals. And it happens. Kids get killed in those jails and stuff, they get raped . . . it's sad, it really is sad, and I don't know a damn thing anybody can do about it. . . . They say we're not going to put him in the county jail, we're going to put him in the juvie home. Juvenile home's no different. You got the same scum down there, just at a younger age. You got that shit going on everywhere."

Think of prison, at its most congenial, as serving to further the purposes of an ancient guild. The expression "career criminal" is not a misnomer. To many people crime is a vocation, a calling, as it were, and periodic association with one's fellow practitioners enforces a necessary maintenance of professional standards.

"I've locked guys up," Vic Oboyski maintains, "I say, 'You're selling drugs.' They say, 'Hey, man, I'm a bank robber, I never sell drugs. Don't be accusing me of selling drugs.' Bank robber. That's their occupation."

And going to prison, as the journeyman sees it, is merely an occupational hazard, figured into his losses the way a retailer factors in pilferage. The recidivism of the professional criminal breeds a phenomenon observable in some of them with which every cop is familiar.

"They become institutionalized," Frank Devlin, warrants supervisor for the Southern District of New York, explained one early morning in Manhattan. "The only thing they know is prison life. They don't have to work, they get three squares a day, they get clean sheets. They can't find that on the outside."

Devlin's squad that day had arrested a thirty-eight-year-old fugitive who had served over twenty years—"over half his life" —in prison. A parole violator, the man had walked away from the halfway house to which he had just been released and was captured without resistance at an address at which deputies could be expected quite easily to find him.

"They don't volunteer for the halfway house. They're put out by the BOP [the federal Bureau of Prisons]. He needs to go back to jail. You can only be in jail so long and then you become institutionalized. That's the only life you know and that's the only way you can live—having other people taking care of you. These guys don't have it bad in jail."

There are, of course, inmates who do not see it that way. And for them the luxury of prison is the seemingly endless time it affords one for the planning of escape therefrom.

"They'll just sit there and talk it over and tell you," John Haynes says. " 'It's tight right now, but eventually, four or five years from now, you're going to put us in a minimum-security prison, we're going to escape, and we're going to rob banks again until we get caught. . . . We're caught now, and as long as you keep good security on us, we're going to be here, but first time . . .' And they're right. Sooner or later they'll transfer them, after they play the good boy for a while. Then something will happen. The crime will be so long removed . . . two deputies will drive up to pick them up one day, they'll be about half-ass asleep or have a hangover from a night on the town, and [the inmates] will get the drop on them and escape. [Either that] or [the inmates will engineer a phony trip] to the hospital or whatever . . ."

And never does the thought cross the minds of such criminals, once they have escaped, to lie low, to parlay their liberty into a lifetime of freedom.

"As soon as they get away, they're going to rob banks. 'I'm going to high-roll and live on the edge as long as I can . . . that's a year, five years, whatever . . . then I'm going to jail for ten years and I'm going to do it again.' "

"They *live* to do banks," says Tony Perez, whose capture of two such escapees closed a celebrated 15 Most Wanted case in 1987.

"There's nothing like it," says Haynes. "You're robbing them banks and driving them big cars and flashing that money and gambling and screwing everything that you can . . . that's what blows their dress up. Doing time is just an inconvenience. They'll just sit there, talking it over, and they'll tell you. 'We're good, we're damn good.' And they are. They're damn good bank robbers."

Some inmates are as cavalier about murder. And especially dangerous in the eyes of cops are those who have nothing to lose. Frank Devlin offers the example of two incidents at Marion, the nation's strictest maximum-security facility, separate incidents in each of which inmates killed a prison guard.

"Just to show them they could do it. What else can you do to [punish the killers]. They're locked down twenty-three hours already."

What the typical deputy marshal faces on the street, in the form of parole violators, probation violators, and escapees, is one part desperation immersed in a solution of depreciated expectations.

"The value of human life . . . they know they're going to die anytime themselves," Haynes says, "from overdoses, from the police, from other criminals. They don't expect to live a long productive life. So if you get in their way, that's your problem. 'It's me or you, and it might just as well be you. Why let you live?' "

Survival in the United States Marshals Service is contemplated in the black light of the foregoing realities. And these days, survival, when they talk about it "for real," is inevitably discussed in the dark context of what has come to be known as the "Roanoke Event" or, sometimes, and more simply, the "Takeaway."

8.

Days of Danger

The city of Roanoke, situated in the Blue Ridge Mountains, is home to the office of the U.S. marshal for the Western District of Virginia. By the late winter of 1988, the United States Marshals Service was conducting some 140,000 prisoner movements annually, and Roanoke, covering two-thirds of the geographical area of Virginia, was conducting its healthy share of them.

One of the prisoners in federal custody in Roanoke that year was a career bank robber named John Anthony Taylor. On March 9—the day after Garnett Leacock was captured in New York—Taylor, forty-two, who was being held, pending trial, at a nearby county jail, was scheduled to keep a physician's appointment at the Roanoke Valley Medical Clinic, located on Franklin Road.

A follow-up visit, Taylor's appointment had been made two weeks before. Its date and time, as a matter of policy, had been kept secret from the prisoner. Taylor, an escape risk, remained officially uninformed of its specifics until deputy marshals arrived at the jailhouse to escort him to the clinic.

Taylor, a suspect in several East Coast bank robberies, had been complaining for weeks about chest pains. Though his heart problems were probably genuine, he did, according to authorities, have a history of faking ailments. A convict with a record of armed bank robbery and escape that dated back twenty-five years, he was known, on one occasion, to have eaten a light bulb, on another to have swallowed a razor blade, in efforts to get out of prison.

Taylor was reported to be unusually chipper that afternoon when deputies Mike Thompson and Sherry Harrison picked him up at the county jail. During the checkup, the doctor remarked that Taylor appeared to be in good spirits; Taylor's blood pressure measured much higher, however, than it had on his previous visit.

Mike Thompson, forty-one, married and the father of five, was a fourteen-year Marshals Service veteran. A native of Alexandria, Virginia, he had entered the Service in San Diego, California, and had been assigned to Roanoke in 1979. Sherry Harrison, twenty-four, raised in Stanley, North Carolina, had joined the Marshals Service with a degree in criminal justice after working three years for the Gastonia County (North Carolina) sheriff. She had been assigned to Roanoke in 1986, the year she came out of Glynco, the year Mike Thompson had last received advanced training there.

At 2:05 P.M., Taylor's examination complete, the two deputies walked the prisoner, in leg irons and handcuffs, out the door of the Roanoke Valley Medical Clinic. As they prepared to put Taylor into their government sedan, Sherry Harrison was approached by a heavyset man, who had stepped, quite suddenly, from behind a utility van parked nearby. He had long hair and a beard. He wore a Harley-Davidson T-shirt. His name was Barry W. Dotson, he was thirty-three years old, a self-employed carpenter from Fredericksburg, Virginia. Walking up to Harrison, he raised a revolver and held it to her face.

"Don't do anything," he said, "we're just as nervous as you are."

The word "we" took on meaning as an armed twenty-two-year-old woman came up behind Mike Thompson. Her name was Tina Marie Julian. She was also a resident of historic Fredericksburg, site of the 1862 Civil War battle in which Lee's Confederate forces had repulsed Burnside's drive on Richmond. Identified by a witness as "the woman in pink," she snatched the car keys from Thompson's hand.

Barry W. Dotson had a minor criminal record. He had served

two years at a state prison farm for a couple of small-time burglaries he had committed in his late teens and early twenties. "A follower, not a leader," in the words of a friend since childhood, "he never," according to another, "hurt anyone in his life."

He was a stranger to John Anthony Taylor.

Tina Marie Julian, characterized by friends as "a bubbly person," by federal investigators as "a bubblehead," had no criminal record. She had met Taylor the year before, when he was flashing money around the Fredericksburg bar in which she worked as a cocktail waitress. Taylor had moved in with her shortly thereafter. At the time, she said, she had had no idea that Taylor was a bank robber, adding, for whatever it was worth, that no man had ever treated her better.

It was she who had recruited Dotson, with a promise of money, according to federal investigators.

Having arrived in the city in a pickup truck earlier that day, these two children of God, two hours before their ambush of Mike Thompson and Sherry Harrison, had checked into the Econo-Lodge motel on Roanoke's Franklin Road. From there, carrying bolt cutters, duct tape, and their weapons, they drove to their rendezvous with Taylor, parking the truck within walking distance of the medical center. In constant touch with him, by telephone and mail, during the period of his incarceration, Julian, authorities say, had somehow obtained from the clinic the date and time of Taylor's appointment, and had done so at Taylor's urging.

Taylor, when the ambush went down, gave no indication that he was surprised.

"Give me your gun, give me your gun!" he shouted at Thompson, as he and Julian together proceeded to shake the deputy down for his revolver.

It is the practice of the well-trained deputy marshal never to let a prisoner see his weapon. Never to let him see the holster, even when it is empty. Neither Taylor nor Julian knew what kind of sidearm Thompson carried, nor did they know on which side he happened to carry it.

Marshals Service regulations governing sidearms are not so rigid as they are specific. The weapon issued by the Service is a six-shot revolver, caliber .357 Magnum, usually a Ruger or a Smith & Wesson, and because it is meant to be carried concealed, it is issued with a three-inch barrel. It is the handgun on which every deputy trains at Glynco and on which he must qualify to graduate. Duty ammunition is 110-grain hollow-point. There are those deputies who, for various reasons, often the increased ammunition capacity, prefer an auto-loading pistol over what is quaintly referred to as a wheel gun, and once he is sworn and qualifies on it, a deputy may carry the semi-automatic pistol of his choice; it must be double-action and the diameter of its ammunition no smaller than nine millimeter. And the deputy must pay for it himself. WITSEC occasionally issues to its inspectors the Sig Sauer P225.

The Marshals Service does not encourage the use of shoulder holsters. Neither does it go out of its way to discourage them, however. Cross-draw holsters of any kind are a hazard on a firing line, so deputies are not given an opportunity to train with them. Glynco holds to the proposition that "you play like you train," but, bowing to 200 years of rugged individualism, enforces no standards where holsters are concerned. If headquarters ever institutes a policy on what the industry refers to as leathers, it will not be until Mike Pizzi retires. Not until then is anyone down there going to try to run with *that* ball. The Brooklyn chief carries his revolver on what appears to be the weak-hand side—grip facing forward on his left hip, in a right-hander's cross-draw holster. The fact is Pizzi shoots left-handed. He just carries the weapon backward. Nobody has ever seen anything like it. And nobody asks. A guy like Mike Pizzi could wear his gun on his head and that would be just fine with Washington.

The Service trains its deputies to draw from the hip, from a high-ride holster, on the strong-hand side—the right hip if you fire right-handed, left hip if you fire left—straight up and out. It is all about ergonomics, the efficiency of clearing leather, throwing down on a shooter in a gunfight. Deriving benefit from twentieth-century science and contemporary time-and-motion studies, deputy marshals do it today the way they did it on the streets of Dodge. Because most people are right-handed, deputy marshals being no exception, odds favor your finding a deputy's gun holstered to his belt, inside or outside the waistband, just above his right hip.

It is where John Anthony Taylor expected to find Mike Thompson's gun.

Orthodox in one way—he carried a revolver—Thompson was unorthodox in another. He carried it in a shoulder holster.

Screaming at Mike Thompson, while Dotson's trigger-finger quivered within inches of Sherry Harrison's face, the handcuffed Taylor, standing on Thompson's right, pulled Thompson's shirt out of his waistband looking for Thompson's gun.

"Where is it?" he shouted.

It was Tina Julian, standing behind Thompson, who discovered the weapon in the shoulder holster under Thompson's left arm and reached for it.

Marshals Service historian Frederick S. Calhoun, who contends that "the gunfighting myth says more about how we view ourselves as Americans than it does about the U.S. marshals," characterizes what Mike Thompson did then as a simple "act of bravery."

"It was better shooting," he casually observes, "than Earp or Hickok ever did."

"He didn't think, he didn't reason," Duke Smith maintains, "his motor skills took over. He reacted to a situation. It's a motor response. You're conditioned [by training] to do that."

What Mike Thompson did was what he had done so many times facing combat silhouettes at Glynco.

Reflexively, he drew his gun.

He shook Julian off and favored Dotson with what the Service teaches as the law-enforcement-standard "double-tap." He put one round in Dotson's chest and one in his head, killing him— for all practical purposes twice—before Dotson could pull the trigger on Harrison. Either shot would have been fatal—Dotson was as good as dead before he hit the ground. Mike Thompson did not see him go down; spinning, he fired twice at Tina Julian, whom he had fully expected to have killed him by then (shooting him in the back, giving Harrison time to draw). Thompson hit Julian once in the chest. She collapsed to the pavement, and there she immediately died, Thompson's car keys clutched in one hand, a can of Chemical Mace in the other, a .25-caliber semiautomatic pistol tucked in the waistband of her blue jeans. Only after he had killed her did Thompson realize that his assailant had been a woman. Seeing Julian go down, Thompson threw Taylor to the ground, holding him there with his foot, while Sherry Harrison, with her sidearm drawn, kicked the revolver from Dotson's hand, and the two deputies scoured the parking lot for additional people with guns.

Taylor was sobbing when the police arrived.

The choreography of the encounter, studied carefully and recapitulated, serves as a training model in the Officer Survival course at the academy.

"It went down absolutely by the numbers," according to Frank Skroski, Smith's deputy director for training, "absolutely textbook," he said, adding that Thompson, from start to finish, was in complete control of the situation.

It was Thompson's Officer Survival training in 1984 coupled with his Advanced Deputy training in 1986 that prepared him for the event, according to Skroski. When he arrived at Glynco in 1986, Thompson was a no-better-than-average shooter. Out of a possible 300, he was scoring 240s and 250s. When he left, a month later, he was well on his way to being an expert, consistently scoring 290s. Not only had he sharpened his skills, but he had sharpened his confidence as well.

"So much of defensive shooting is in the mind," says deputy Joe Trindal, firearms instructor at Glynco. Shooting is sight alignment and trigger control, but more than that, he says, "it is mind control."

From his street-survival seminars, Thompson knew that there would be an instant at which Dotson became distracted. It was at that instant, the instant that Dotson's glance shifted, that Thompson drew and fired. The time it took him to clear his holster and release two rounds was probably no more than three seconds. Standing four to five feet from Dotson when he drew, he fired the gun from no more than three feet away. Skroski's description of the wounds as "non-survivable," while classic law-enforcement newspeak, is something of an understatement and applies to Julian's wound as well. Julian, taking the hollow-point in the aorta, was dead when she hit the pavement or within seconds of her having done so.

(Because Dotson had been fingerprinted before they were conducted, paraffin tests run on his firing hand were inconclusive. There was speculation that he might have fired a round before he died, though investigators were unable to establish proof of the fact. There was a spent cartridge in his revolver, and a nurse, who at the time of the incident had been working inside the clinic, testified to having heard a total of five shots fired.)

The "double-tap" formally applies to shots aimed at the center mass of a target, that area between the neck and the groin on a combat silhouette where the most points are awarded to hits in the thoracic region—the five, four, three, two ring on the color-graded Trans-Star target, the ten, nine, eight, seven ring on the old B-27 target. The Marshals Service teaches two rounds to the chest, and one to the head, to account for the possibility that one's assailant is wearing a bulletproof vest. Thompson's performance, remarkable in the light of what he managed to do, was as remarkable, according to Skroski, for what he did *not* do. He did not waste a third shot (nor the time required by one) on Dotson (he did not even watch him fall) nor, having missed Julian with his first shot, did he fire at her again once he saw her go down. Spinning away from Julian, he had two rounds left in the cylinder of his revolver to protect himself from any additional shooters he might encounter.

"You never assume the ones in front of you are the only ones involved," Frank Skroski says. "We teach that if there are two, you think three, if there are three, you think four. You never underestimate your adversaries. You always look for the next perpetrator."

The encounter, start to finish, went down in a matter of seconds. The typical gunfight, which typically takes place in the United States, and which typically turns out to be lethal, transpires, it has been calculated, in about seven seconds and within a range of fewer than ten feet. An average of four rounds is exchanged. A well-trained police officer is expected to be lethal with a handgun at up to twenty-five yards. It is what the points on the target measure. And he or she is expected to be lethal fast —to clear the holster and release three rounds in little more than five seconds.

Rarely, however, do such confrontations go down by the numbers. Unignorable in such matters is the influence of adrenaline. Former homicide detective Charles Healey, U.S. marshal for Eastern New York, tells the story of a young New York City policeman, a department pistol-shooting champion, who was knocked to the ground by two suspects in the Bedford-Stuyvesant section of Brooklyn, both armed and both running away:

"He's on the ground—what better situation is there than that? He's in the *prone* position. I can't tell you where the bullets went. He almost hit a bus driver over on Franklin Avenue."

(Under NYPD guidelines governing the use of deadly force, firing at fleeing suspects is prohibited. As is the firing of warning shots. It is a policy that is followed by most, but not all, police departments in the country. It is the policy followed by federal agents, who are allowed to shoot only in self-defense or in defense of the lives of others. In June of 1990, the FBI took steps toward easing such restrictions on its agents; the new guidelines, however, are controversial and have yet to be implemented in the field.)

Working in Mike Thompson's favor, augmenting his advanced training, was the fact that Thompson, himself, in 1986 had identified his own shortcomings and gone out of his way to improve his skills as a shooter. Thompson took pride in his status as a P.O.D.

"What makes it all work," according to Duke Smith, explaining EPIC, the Fugitive Program, enforcement in particular, and all the high-profile stuff in general, "is that deputy marshal out in the district . . ."

That deputy marshal out in the district, the backbone of the United States Marshals Service, labors under an appellation that came into being in the wake of the 1973 siege of Wounded Knee; taken up initially by the Service's younger deputies in response to the elitism displayed by certain veterans of the uprising, it came later to signify any deputy who chose to embrace it whose ambitions did not extend to working the fast track leading to Washington—the self-styled P.O.D., the "plain old deputy."

As Skroski said of Thompson, he "always did his job and always did it well. He was a rock-solid deputy who never sought to be a supervisor."

Both Thompson and Harrison appeared shaken after the shooting and neither, until later, was able to talk about it to members of the press.

Thompson did, however, call Duke Smith at Glynco.

He said: "Training saved my life."

When Duke Smith arrived at Glynco in 1983, out of a basic-training class of twenty-four students, the academy was losing an average of 10 percent; within five years, with class size increased to forty-eight students, those washing out and dropping out were doing so at a rate reduced to 1 or 2 percent.

"Training hasn't changed that dramatically," Smith asserts, "the screening process has. We're getting a different caliber of cat."

If training has not changed dramatically, it is only insofar as the Marshals Service has avoided sacrificing focus in the interest of scope. In the face of rapid metamorphosis, of changes undergone by the organization in the decade leading up to its bicentennial, demands on the incoming deputy marshal have broadened to incorporate a versatility that would have bewildered all but the truly sophisticated of his predecessors.

"In our profession there is a unique phenomenon," Smith is at pains to explain. "Agents or policemen or marshals, for the most part, are from the middle class. Probably their parents were blue collar. A sense of team and of country is sort of innate. You bring them into a training environment here, and you teach them how to protect themselves—how to drive fast, and how to shoot straight, and how not to get shot—you get 'em all wired up and you send them out of here . . . and they go out and they kick ass and they take names and they kick down doors. . . . and then somewhere in their careers—and it's different for all of us. . . . You get promoted as a supervisor or chief or a manager, and it's like someone has reached over with an anonymous hand and flipped a switch, and now the government says to you, we want you to be sensitive, and we want you to have great interpersonal and communications skills, and we want you to be a people-oriented guy . . ."

The price the Service pays, says Smith, for its higher-caliber recruit is a relatively small one.

"They have no military or police experience, and bring with them no innate sense of chain of command."

Brooklyn's Victor Oboyski, who earned both his bachelor's and master's degrees at night school while working as a deputy in New York, observes that many of the new, better-educated recruits have never been away from home.

"Their maturity level is pushed back; many, as a result of college, are still dependent upon their parents. A lot of guys, their mothers are still making their beds. When I came in, there were nothing but [armed forces] veterans, a lot of guys out of the service. You come in with a military background, you don't question as much as these kids do, you understand chain of command. For many, now, it's their first job. Most of the time you're working long hours, you work twelve to fourteen hours a day, a kid says, 'What? I got concert tickets!' . . . After three or four years they get with it."

It was the Service's deputy director John Twomey who in 1979 replaced the undistinguished, rather pedestrian shield of the twentieth-century deputy marshal with the current five-pointed star emblematic of the lawman's illustrious patrimony. Not long thereafter, Duke Smith instructed his staff at Glynco to develop a course in Image Awareness.

"When I came into the Service," Smith says, "deputies were wearing string ties, high-water pants, polyester leisure suits, and those fruit boots with zippers."

While stressing the importance of making a positive impression and the impact of doing so on one's job performance, the new course grew out of a desire to enhance the shopworn image of the deputy marshal not only in the eyes of the general public, but among other law-enforcement agencies as well. It confronted four-square the reality that deputies spend the majority of their working day in U.S. Court, in the company of judges, federal prosecutors, defense lawyers, and the special agents of other federal law-enforcement bureaucracies. While explaining how the proper image "heightens [one's] promotion potential," the course enforces an understanding among incoming deputies that in the absence of the proper image, high-profile assignments and all that goes with them are simply out of the question.

A single, one-hour lecture, the course touches briefly on grooming, personal hygiene, and the importance of physical fitness, but is devoted in large measure to clothing, the art of buying it and matching it up, as well as manipulating one's wardrobe to the requirements of the job. Not only must appropriate clothing be ready at a moment's notice for the purposes of travel, it must be appropriate for a variety of missions. It must be well made and relatively expensive to stand up to the abuse it is expected to take and must conform, one learns, to some pretty weird standards. Vented suit jackets, for example, must be center-vented; a side vent exposes one's weapon. Loafers look nice, deputies are told, but walking the fenders on a PSS detail, one is likely to walk right out of them.

Brief attention is paid to interpersonal skills and such things as telephone manners, but many of the newer recruits bring some of that training with them, and as Duke Smith points out, "there's no time in basic training to put 'em through knife-and-fork school."

(While the Marshals Service dress code is unofficial, there is an exception to it that apparently is not. If, working warrants, you are not wearing blue jeans today, you run the risk, it seems, of being mistaken for a civilian—blue denim and tactical body armor, over a pair of high-ticket running shoes, are to the modern felony arrest in America what parachute silk was to the invasion of Normandy.)

. . .

As a witness-security specialist, Bud McPherson, very early in his career, had grown accustomed to spending the better part of his working day in the self-conscious company of FBI agents and U.S. attorneys, accountants and law-school grads who looked as if they had been born in suits. And it was part of a personal policy of McPherson's always to outdress them. It was not something the Marshals Service had taught him. If anything it was to be the other way around. McPherson does not remember when he started dressing like a Wall Street millionaire, but neither does he remember a time when he dressed as though he were anything else; it is not unreasonable to assume that, coming from New York, where one of the few crimes of consequence is being out of style, McPherson, like many of his contemporaries, took to it the minute he started paying for his own clothes. Certainly of no little significance, however, is the neighborhood from which he hailed. McPherson had been surrounded by wiseguys from the moment he was able to walk. The neighborhood was acrawl with made members of the Mob, characters who never passed the barber shop without stopping in for a trim, a generation of tough guys who paid more for their shoes than their wives did.

"I didn't know I wasn't Italian until I went to school . . ."

Bud McPherson, his hands in his pockets, was pacing back and forth, laying claim to the academic territory that stretched between an immaculate blackboard and a dozen WITSEC students in a small classroom at Glynco. He had flown in from Los Angeles the day before, arriving by way of Savannah, but apart from the off-season suntan he sported there was nothing West Coast about him. The conservative charcoal threads set off a red-and-blue paisley necktie. The collar bar was gold, presumably eighteen karat. The eyewear was military standard, full-tint, G-15. He looked like a radar officer in the air wing of the Gambino family.

The one-day course McPherson had come to teach represented the academy's entire curriculum in the field of social studies.

"Wiseguys 101, a basic history of La Cosa Nostra in the United States . . ."

McPherson's tale would open in turn-of-the-century Sicily, progressing through the 1920s by way of New York and Chicago, and would move on to postwar Las Vegas before entering the modern era, returning to the present and the realm of Mc-Pherson's personal experience with the Mob.

"I went to PS 179 in Brooklyn, two of my classmates," he would declaim, "were 'Crazy Joe' Gallo and Pete 'the Greek.' ... In the New York City Police Department, I worked in the 62nd Precinct, Bath Beach, that's close to Coney Island. It was Funzi Tieri's neighborhood, boss of the Genovese family.... Joe Colombo lived there. ... It was the home of the Profacis ..."

His voice rising and falling, conjuring star-studded "sit-downs" and perpetual "beefs" among executives of "the liquor business," McPherson now and then would step to the black-board to inscribe there the names of his story's principal charac-ters. And returning periodically, with a sweep of his hand, he would run chalk through the name of each player as he went into corporate transition ... Colosimo: rubbed out (Johnny Torrio and Al Capone move up in Chicago) ... Frankie Yale, in Brook-lyn: whacked ...

Big Jim Colosimo's was the prototype of the gangland funeral ... the long cavalcade of limousines, the huge horseshoe-shaped floral pieces spelling out "So Long, Pal." ... Underworld digni-taries from everywhere paid their flamboyant respects, the cem-etery a sea of double-breasted suits ... spats, carnations, Borsalinos ... pallbearers packing heat, everybody crying dra-matically, even Johnny Torrio was crying, the man who had had Big Jim bumped off ... an ostentatious show of regret, obse-quies which set the standard against which all future burials were to be measured.

"They gave him a terrific send-off."

The Roaring Twenties were rich with stereotypes that make themselves felt today.

When Legs Diamond, working for the illustrious Arnold Roth-stein, pulled his enormously ill-advised free-lance job, hijacking a liquor shipment in 1924 that belonged to Irish bootlegger Big Bill Dwyer, it was Dwyer's partner, a young Italian tough guy by the name of Francesco Castiglia, who went to Rothstein to say:

"Hey, Legs didn't do the right thing, we're going to have to go and collect."

In capitalizing on Prohibition, Rothstein, the underworld gam-bler who had fixed the 1919 World Series, had always been more banker than bootlegger; he was eager to distance himself from the escalating violence, to resume what had earlier been mere fiduciary participation in the liquor business.

He said, "Do what you have to do."

Following Legs Diamond's removal (Legs survived the attempt on his life but he got the message), Rothstein assumed the sponsorship of three young New York hoods. One of them was Meyer Lansky, a Russian-Jewish immigrant to New York's Lower East Side, born Maier Suchowljansky. It was he who would eventually teach members of organized crime to dress like bankers and businessmen, the model being his patron Rothstein. Another of Rothstein's protégés was the young Salvatore Lucania, Charlie "Lucky" Luciano, who, when he was eleven years old on the Lower East Side, in victimizing his Jewish classmates, launched the protection racket in the United States. He would graduate to narcotics after the Harrison Act. The third was Francesco Castiglia.

Born in Sicily in 1891, Castiglia, the oldest of three children, arrived in New York at the age of four. His family settled in East Harlem. After elementary school, he became the leader of the 104th Street Gang. At twenty-one he was arrested twice, but served no prison time. At the age of twenty-four he went away for a year on a gun charge. Like Luciano and Lansky, Castiglia owed much of his eventual success to a thoroughgoing lack of prejudice; he would form business alliances with anyone, regardless of national origin. At a time when it was unthinkable for Sicilians to marry outside their ethnic circle, Castiglia went so far as to marry outside the faith. He wed a Jewish girl named Loretta and remained married to her for fifty years. His street name made him a natural to serve as liaison to the Irish politicians who controlled Tammany Hall (to whom $100 million in graft would be paid out by the end of the decade).

McPherson moved to the blackboard. He said:

"His street name was Frank Costello."

And when McPherson said it, his voice fell apart.

Yes.

That crepitant wiseguy whisper, that classic, stereotypical rasp associated in Mob mythology with the early, elderly dons, is the legacy of Frank Costello, legendary boss and immediate progenitor of what was to become the Genovese crime family in New York. Costello was to the mobsters who followed him what Chuck Yeager was to postwar fighter pilots, what that lisping Iberian prince was to the future of Castilian Spanish:

He was . . . *the Voice* . . . of La Cosa Nostra.

If a speaking voice like a bad set of air brakes was ever an authentic Italian characteristic, it was not a cultural but an economic characteristic. As Bud McPherson explained it that day, immigrants in the early years of the century took their medical problems not to the doctor but customarily to the neighborhood midwife. (Sometimes to the local barber.) Tonsillectomies and the removal of inflamed adenoids, routinely performed on children, were primitive surgical procedures conducted with even more primitive instruments, often no more sophisticated than the cleanest of the kitchen scissors. And botched operations were as common in the neighborhood then as they are in the metropolitan hospital today.

"They wanted their tonsils out, they went down the block . . . and a lot of them went around for the rest of their lives . . . *talkin' like this.*"

Frank Costello was the archetype.

Wiseguys today who affect the growl, in the absence of any pharyngeal damage, do so in tribute to him.

As Bud McPherson's recitation was coming to a close, Mike Pizzi's nonstop flight from New York was touching down in Savannah. Pizzi's arrival at Glynco was anticipated there with an enthusiasm no less palpable than it was infectious. His lecture on District Operations, delivered just prior to commencement to every basic-training class, was legendary in the Marshals Service. It was as popular with the Glynco faculty as it had proved to be with the students. On this occasion, as they came and went, stealing time to put in appearances, as many as seven faculty members at any one time would be observed in attendance at the event.

Respected throughout the Service, even by those who did not know him personally—by reputation alone he was a standout—the Brooklyn chief, a character in every sense of the word, occupied a very small circle in the nationwide chain of command: he was one of the few men under oath for whom affection appeared to be universal.

The mere mention of his name was good for a smile.

"A wild man, a professional Brooklynite," was not an unofficial assessment of him, it was the evaluation of him tendered on the record by the Service's Office of Congressional and Public Affairs.

A tough guy in the eyes of his fellow deputies, Pizzi was that rare member of the Service who had lost none of his street-cop edge in mastering the skills of the effective manager. At the root of his success was an enthusiasm for his work and for everyday life that was almost childlike. Feeding the undercurrent of his personality was a wellspring of potential mischief, and he seemed unwilling, if not actually unable, to suppress it. His first words to McPherson, delivered offhand, betrayed an impulse that could only be called elfin.

"Bud, it's rainin' out, what's with the shades?"

The two, while at Glynco, were staying at the same hotel, and together that night they closed the bar.

A year before, Pizzi had brought down upon the Marshals Service a shower of political sunshine by having orchestrated, where the FBI had failed, the trackdown and ultimate arrest of Alphonse "Allie Boy" Persico, former underboss of the Colombo organized-crime family in New York. A fugitive on the Bureau's most-wanted list since June 1980, a Marshals Service 15 Most Wanted since 1983, Persico had been at large for over seven years. A task force was formed under Pizzi in May 1987. By November Persico was in jail.

"Allie Boy was a very likable guy. We didn't go knockin' on his family's door on holidays."

Pizzi's understanding of the protocol, like McPherson's, had been acquired at an early age. His grandmother's house in Bensonhurst, the house in which he had grown up, looked out on the local wiseguy clubhouse (the "social club" was home-away-from-home to made guys in the Colombo family), and Pizzi's nocturnal comings and goings as a teenager were met by the woman, who harbored no romantic notions about the Mob, with the following:

"La notte e per il lupo."

The night, she told him, is for the wolf.

It was from his grandmother that Mike Pizzi discovered how the typical racketeer reacts when the federal prosecutor plugs in the tape deck for the jury and starts playing the Title III wiretaps.

"Me and my friends would be sittin' around. A bunch of guys, you know how it is. We're sayin' *fuck* every other word. My grandmother didn't speak any English and we figured it would be like any other English word she didn't know. Well my mother comes home, and while I'm standing there my grandmother [in heavy Sicilian dialect] says to her, '*Maria, qui menna ditta questa parola* fuck?' What does it mean, this word *fuck?* My mother asks why, and my grandmother tells her, 'Because every other word he says is *fuck.*' Now every time she says the word, my mother, she's not even lookin' at me, bops me over the head with a broomstick. She's got this broom in her hand . . . 'fuck, fuck, fuck,' my grandmother's saying, and it's bop, bop, bop with the broomstick."

One of Pizzi's childhood friends, one of many who eventually would fall in with the Mob, had as great an influence on Pizzi as did his grandmother's advice about predatory creatures of the night and his mother's ubiquitous broomstick. Pizzi was at Marine Corps boot camp at Parris Island when he received, "from two sources," photographs of his good pal Freddy, the late Freddy, as it happened; the nineteen-year-old, "very handsome, very tough," had been strangled, shot, and his body eventually crushed under the wheels of a car.

"It really wakes you up."

Another friend, "another legendary tough guy," named Tony, was knocked off soon thereafter.

"My career as a wiseguy," Pizzi would say, "was never to materialize."

Pizzi entered the Marshals Service in 1965 and, like McPherson, brought a young Brooklyn woman along for the ride. That night in the hotel bar, the two men traded stories, recalling the indignities to which they had subjected their young wives early in their federal careers. McPherson reiterated the details of Claudette's WITSEC epiphany upon landing in Cedar Rapids in the company of Myrtle Poor Bear; Pizzi recalled an adventure in prisoner transportation from the more scatological moments of which he had tried to shield his wife, Mary.

The events of the latter tale transpired in 1967.

Pizzi, accompanied by Mary, was transporting three female prisoners from New York to federal prison in Alderson, West Virginia. The five were traveling by car.

"It was the only federal women's prison on the East Coast at the time. I think they were going away for drugs."

Pizzi, at the wheel, had covered what he remembered to be about one-half the distance to Alderson when the prisoners, seated behind him, began cracking wise about variations on the sexual congress in which they would have delighted, had they been given the opportunity, with one of Pizzi's fellow deputies. Pizzi, not so sensitive to the slander—"Fucking a prisoner is a felony"—as to the verbal onslaught on the innocence of his wife, pulled off the road into the parking lot of a fast-food joint and suggested that Mary take the opportunity to use the ladies' room.

"I turn around and I slap the three of them, all at once, you know, one hand, just like the Three Stooges . . . like this, ba-ba-bop. I don't want to hear any more talk like that."

It was later that evening, in Harrisonburg, Virginia, that Pizzi stopped to check the prisoners into the county jail overnight. He and Mary checked into a motel. Pizzi was asleep when the telephone rang. The local sheriff was on the line.

"He wants to know what to do. Two of the women, he tells me, are in the cell eatin' each other." If this was a felony, it was clearly a new one to the sheriff. " 'So pull up a chair and put on the lights,' I tell him. What am I gonna do?"

When Pizzi and Mary, after breakfast the following morning, arrived to pick up the prisoners, one of the young women complained.

"He didn't feed us," she told Pizzi.

Pizzi looked at the sheriff, who said:

"They ate enough last night."

The next line, of course, belonged to Mary:

"Mike, what does he mean, they—?"

"Never mind, get in the car."

As the bar emptied around them, the two men talked through the night, a couple of hometown boys going on about the girls they had married, swapping memories of their early days on the streets of the old neighborhood, catching up on the news, updating each other on the latest being carried on the gangland grapevine . . . "You know who else is dead?" . . . and to the residents of Brunswick, Georgia, who staffed the city's largest hotel, these two colorful characters, so clearly from out of town, sounded for all the world like the very troublemakers about whom they were talking. But if Pizzi and McPherson sounded like a couple of wiseguys, it was only to the unpracticed ear. What was audible in their conversation was a singular music: it was not the Frank Costello crisscrossing their speech, it was the tree-lined avenues of Brooklyn.

9.

Only the Dead Know Brooklyn

Ralph Burnside, thirty-six, was a week and a half into a three-week assignment, 1,200 miles from home. He was one of several out-of-town deputies, not including members of the Special Operations Group, detailed to the 1988 sedition and conspiracy trial of fourteen members of The Order, the enforcement arm of the Aryan Brotherhood, being conducted in Fort Smith, Arkansas.

It was just after 5 P.M. and the defendants were about to be moved, escorted down the rear steps of the Federal Building and loaded into a secure van. The prisoners were to be transported back to the county jail now that court had adjourned for the day. There were points of cover in the compound, but Burnside did not enjoy one of them; holding a position, securing the street, he was standing out in the open.

There were six deputies posted on the ground, three vehicles in addition to the van—a lead car and two backup sedans. There were four SOG deputies on the stairway, another six or eight, dressed in tactical gear, holding covert positions on the roof. Burnside, glancing skyward, could catch an occasional glimpse of sunglasses, the intermittent glint of late afternoon light reflected by tinted lenses, by the barrels of submachine guns and semiautomatic rifles, MP5s, AR-15s.

Armed with a WITSEC shotgun, a cut-down Remington 870, Burnside, wearing a knee-length leather trenchcoat over a three-piece summerweight suit, had been standing for fifteen minutes, holding his post, when the sky opened.

It came from Oklahoma.

Burnside could see the squall line as it came rolling in from the direction of the old gallows two blocks north—Isaac Parker's gallows, on the timbers of which seventy-nine men had met their destiny in the twenty-one years that the Hanging Judge had held jurisdiction over Indian Territory—a landmark in old Fort Smith.

Burnside had never seen anything like it, anywhere in the country, thunderclouds off the Great Plains, rain hitting the hardpan . . . *like a cow pissin' on a flat rock,* they said . . . prairie rain, and it was on top of him before the prisoners came out of the building. He had known there would be moments like this. And Burnside knew what was required of him.

In the words of his chief: "Shit-and-jump-in-it."

Burnside did not leave his post. Resolute, redoubtable, rain cascading off the heavy lenses of his eyeglasses, he stood, at port arms, "stood there like a fool," watching the barrel of his shotgun fill with water.

The suit was a blue cotton-poplin, forty-six regular, maybe $250 retail—"Dry Clean Only," it said. Burnside knew it was gone. It was five minutes before the prisoners were brought down, another ten before all were loaded. By then Burnside's pockets were filled with water, and the suit jacket's cuffs had begun their irreversible journey from Burnside's wrists to the middle of his forearms. Destination, size forty, short.

The suit was a total loss.

As one of the prisoners was hustled through the downpour, he shouted through sheets of rain:

"Burnside, what are you, crazy?"

Burnside, one of two deputies from his district, the other posted inside the building—as Burnside would later describe it, "the drier of the two positions"—gave an answer that was more than ample to explain things to every other deputy on the detail.

"No," Burnside replied. "I'm Brooklyn."

Overworked, understaffed, and perpetually out of style, the Eastern District of New York is notorious within the Marshals

Service. Its deputies handle more trouble before lunch every day than the average district sees in a month. The spiritual heart of the only American city that can claim over 2,000 homicides a year—two dozen on a summer weekend, twenty in a single day —Brooklyn is occluded by neighborhoods where the sound of gunfire is almost orchestral, a vital metropolitan community swollen by aneurysms of violence. Its broad, tree-shaded boulevards, some of its older and more venerable thoroughfares, like ancient vessels collapse here and there into dangerous free-fire zones.

Magnificent, ineffable, eternal, a source of centuries of civic pride, the borough, awash today in the workaday bloodshed endemic to some of the world's darker pockets of political insurrection, currently enjoys a reputation as the nation's answer to frontier Tombstone: *The town too tough to die.*

One good look at the action here—on the streets of Bedford-Stuyvesant, Brownsville, or East New York—would bring the Earps to their knees. Working three years as a deputy in the bad neighborhoods of Brooklyn, New York, is like working maybe fifteen years almost anywhere else in the country.

"We had the Ohio Seven come in here," Victor Oboyski reflects, "the United Freedom Front. They thought they were going to come in and be tough guys. Maybe in Akron, Ohio, yeah, they caused some trouble . . . but in New York, forget about it. We took them all down, I mean down on the ground . . . we knocked them down, cuffed them, and dragged them out of the courtroom. And we all went back to work laughing. This is no big deal for us. This is going on all the time. Want to get tough? We'll get tough. We handle tough guys all the time. This is one tough borough. New York's one tough city. Our guys have a battle just commuting to work. You know what I'm saying? If you're going to come to Brooklyn, and you think you're going to be a tough guy, you better bring lunch . . ."

November 10 fell on a Thursday in 1988, so Friday came a day early to Parker's.

At the waterfront saloon in Brooklyn Heights terrorized weekly by Mike Pizzi and his crew, deputies had gathered to celebrate a birthday. It was 7 P.M., the United States Marine Corps was 213 years old, and at the instigation of his chief, who was hosting the event, Ralph Burnside was drawing attention.

Standing at the bar, he and Pizzi were comparing tattoos.
Again.

And Burnside had his boss beat pants-down.

Burnside, a martial-arts instructor before he had joined the
Service, was a contemplative man given to a deep appreciation
of Oriental thought. His reverence for the ways of the East extended to the elaborate ornamentation of his lower torso—on the
upper hip flexure, on either side of his pelvic girdle, was a full-
color fine-line tattoo, each measuring four by ten inches and
representing six hours of intricate work with a hand-held seven-
point pencil.

Like that of many highly trained martial artists, Burnside's
body art was an expression of spiritual values—loyalty, strength,
and grace, dedication and fierceness in battle—in his case sym-
bolized by a dragon (emblematic of the celestial) on the right
side, a tiger (the terrestrial) on the left. An extremely personal
expression, it was artwork in the manifestation of which Burnside maintained a measure of dignity; it was not something he
was inclined to exhibit. Had anyone but the chief asked him to
do so, his answer would have been no.

Burnside's opinion of Pizzi was not one of those things he
disguised.

"He's one of the few people in the Service I would go to the
gates of hell with."

The best Pizzi, for his part, could do was a kewpie doll surrounded by three hearts, etched into the flesh of his right shoulder, and a U.S. Marine Corps bulldog (inspiration for all the
undressing) imprinted on the tricep below it. Each had been
applied in low-end, single-needle fashion: the kewpie doll, popular with a lot of the guys in his gang, when he was twelve years
old; the bulldog a few years later. A pretty lame statement by
artistic standards, the layout spoke eloquently to Pizzi's operational style.

"Keep things simple. The more elaborate the plan, the more
difficult it is to execute."

And Burnside knew this as well as anyone. It was a management philosophy he had seen translated consistently in his three
years on the job. Earlier, he had seen it translated in instructions
he had received from the chief on the conduct of a high-threat
prisoner move.

The instructions, in their way rather Zen, stand as a model of the principles of economy as applied to organizational leadership:

"Take the shotgun—we're in close enough—we don't need the AR-15."

. . . admittedly not applicable to every administrative situation.

Mike Pizzi is five-foot-ten, weighs 160 pounds, and his graying hair is as slick as a wet deck on a destroyer. He buys his clothes from Sears, Roebuck and Company, leans toward landscapes when he paints—"my middle name is Angelo"—and he has the best posture in the United States Marshals Service. He speaks fluent conversational Italian with the same forty-weight Brooklyn accent in which his punctilious English is immersed and to hear him explain why he wears his gun backward is to enter a world your friends have never been to.

"Well, really, I'm ambidextrous. I write right-handed, but I'm a natural left-hander, I play ball left-handed. I shoot left-handed . . . *better* . . . because I have difficulty blinking my left eye. At night I shoot right-handed."

At night he shoots right-handed.

"That's what the rubber bands are for."

The grip of Mike Pizzi's revolver is circled by elastic bands that appear to have no practical purpose. When he carries the revolver off-duty, he slides the bands toward the fore end of the grip, just below the hammer; off-duty he carries the piece *without* a holster, and the rubber prevents the gun from disappearing behind his waistband.

"It's an undercover trick. You think undercover cops wear holsters?"

When Pizzi carries the revolver in his waistband, he carries it forward on his *right* hip, grip facing rear, and draws it straight up and out, firing the gun right-handed. When he carries the revolver on-duty, he carries it in a regulation holster which he wears just behind his *left* hip. Both holster and gun face the rear —grip forward—as if positioned for a right-handed cross-draw. Swiveling his wrist and grabbing the gun palm-outward, he draws and fires with his left hand, so in reality he carries the gun backward. He gives no satisfactory explanation for this, though he does volunteer the following:

"It saves on the lining of the jacket."

Mike Pizzi, it can be safely assumed, is a man who gains advantage in a gunfight simply by *confusing* the opposition.

There is no record of his ever having been asked by the Service to give firearms training to others.

Pizzi entered the Marshals Service in June 1965 after four years in the United States Marine Corps and two years spent driving a truck. He was twenty-three years old at the time. Taking a $3,000 pay cut, he was sworn in, given a badge and a gun, and put to work in the Southern District of New York. Pizzi's formal deputy training, which the Service did not get around to giving him until sometime the following year, amounted to two weeks of instruction in prisoner handling and in the use of firearms (the latter presumably ignored) at the federal penitentiary in Atlanta, Georgia. Pizzi worked three years as a deputy in Manhattan before being transferred to Brooklyn.

"We had no radio equipment, no backup, no vests—we used wits, stealth, and cunning—we had no computers, no access to intelligence, all we had was what we could develop in the street. We worked day and night, we worked fugitives on our own initiative, usually before nine or after five."

Pizzi was assigned to Air Piracy in 1970 and within a year he was the deputy-in-charge, directing the screening of all departures out of New York, assigning deputies to selected flights. As a supervisor, he also was overseeing twelve WITSEC details, and had two men working warrants. (Supervising WITSEC details in the days of "resident security," when witnesses, as often as not, had to be protected in their own homes—"Find me places" was Pizzi's standing instructions to deputies—Pizzi remembers taking the entire top floor of the Kennedy Airport Holiday Inn. With government plates on all the cars parked out front, the details were anything but inconspicuous. "And we never lost anybody," he says.) Four years later, with the end of the Air Piracy Program and the formalization of WITSEC as a program conducted out of Washington, he was promoted to operations supervisor. He was made acting chief in 1975, and became chief deputy in 1977.

From the start of Pizzi's tenure as chief, all the lies they told about Brooklyn were true.

"We never asked for help or pity, never asked for anybody to give us a break, we never asked judges to reconsider orders, we took everything they threw at us and we did it. What we established in the eyes of the Service was that we were the toughest, strongest people they had on the job and in Brooklyn only the strong survive. We developed a loyalty on the part of our people, the loyalty to stay in the district. If you left, you looked back on Brooklyn with reverence. Eastern New York was the toughest district, and you carried the word throughout the country."

Not many districts, Gerri Doody observes, would have handed the Leacock warrant to a woman. When she brought him in, she says, "Mike was ecstatic. It was just pandemonium [in the office]. Anywhere else, they'd remember it for years. [But] it's hard to make an impression in Brooklyn." Usually, she points out, "When you have a top-fifteen, headquarters sends in a task force. Not in Brooklyn. In Brooklyn *you* are the task force. The [Special Achievement] award [I received] was a joke, because everybody in the place, at one time or another, worked on the case."

Ask Mike Pizzi where he comes by his management and leadership skills and he will give you the three-word answer that embodies everything about America he sees as noble.

"The Marine Corps."

Mike Pizzi had the bulldog tattooed to his arm *before* he joined the marines.

"You notice it has green eyes."

That Pizzi's own eyes are green is not their most compelling characteristic.

Ask Norman Mailer.

It was Mike Pizzi with whom the distinguished Mailer had the anonymous run-in that Mailer chronicles in his 1968 classic *The Armies of the Night*. And it was Pizzi's eyes that inspired Mailer to forgo the fistfight he was contemplating, at the moment of Pizzi's appearance, with one of his fellow prisoners, a neo-Nazi who, like the author, had been arrested by deputy marshals for demonstrating on the grounds of the Pentagon:

"A tall U.S. Marshal . . . now leaped into the truck and jumped between them . . . he had a long craggy face . . . and his eyes in Cinemascope would have blazed an audience off their seat for such gray-green flame could only have issued from a blowtorch. . . . he was one impressive piece of gathered wrath. . . . Speaking to [him] at this point would have been dangerous. . . . he was full of American rectitude and was fearless, and . . . savage as the exhaust left in the wake of a motorcycle club."

In his memorable screed on the visitation of Mike Pizzi—his "insane look . . . the Knight of God light in the flame of his eye" . . . it goes on for a couple of pages—Mailer, a veteran of the Second World War, goes so far as to speculate "whether the Marshal had once been in the Marine Corps."

Norman, it goes like this: Mike Pizzi *is* the Marine Corps.

In Pizzi's paneled office, on the first floor of Brooklyn's U.S. District Court, flanking his government-issue desk, are two standing flags, one the Stars and Stripes, the other the Marine Corps banner. On the wall behind the desk hangs a photograph of the first-among-equals in that assemblage of convicted felons injected into government service by President Ronald Reagan, Lieutenant Colonel Oliver North, autographed and inscribed: "Semper Fi." Interspersed among the Special Achievement Awards and other honors—Outstanding Performance Rating, Distinguished Service Award—bestowed on Pizzi by the Marshals Service and occupying frames adorning the walls of the office hang, among other things, a photograph of the flag-raising on Iwo Jima's Mount Suribachi, a mounted commemorative stamp set memorializing same, snapshots of Pizzi as a teenager on military duty overseas, and a large photograph of the legendary leatherneck general, Lewis "Chesty" Puller, whose resemblance to the Corps' canine mascot was uncanny.

And on November 10, Pizzi wore a Marine Corps necktie.

"The Marine Corps birthday," in Brooklyn, according to Vic Oboyski, "is bigger than Christmas. Dave [O'Flaherty] called from Florida: 'Happy Birthday, Chief.' "

Detailing the capture of Garnett Leacock, Gerri Doody remarks, "We were ready. The chief trained us. We still have training on Thursdays. But back when we had more time, we had practical exercises. He'd blow a whistle and we'd have to run, have all our gear ready, like in the army, and we'd have to stand there—we'd have so many seconds, and we'd be hysterical—gun, badge, flashlight. . . . We were ready for Leacock. If we had taken our time [going out the door] I don't know if he would have been there."

Mike Pizzi is an inveterate teacher, and on Thursday, *every* Thursday in Brooklyn, the young deputy is going to learn something new. Celebrating the birth of the Marine Corps that day, there was not a deputy in the district who had not learned first-hand how to fingerprint a suspect using a flashlight.

"You can use it to eliminate a suspect, not to identify him," Pizzi explains.

One's fingerprint classification (FPC) number is a series of numbers—a series of numbers and/or letters—twenty characters in all, two assigned to each digit. When a suspect's fingerprints are taken, the prints are individually classified and the series entered into the National Crime Information Center (NCIC) computer. The characteristics of each print, ulnars, radials, whorls, double loops, tented arches, etc., by which the prints are coded, are visible to the naked eye upon close examination of the hand itself. A good investigator, using nothing more than a flashlight, can get a broad reading on those characteristics and use the information to his advantage; an individual in custody, a suspected fugitive, can be eliminated as such on the scene.

"You can eliminate a guy over the phone," Pizzi submits, with nothing more than a working knowledge of the technique. "The first time that it happened to me, I was in the office alone and I had some other things going on, and I got a call from a cop in a local precinct. He told me he had a fugitive—an eight-year-old escape case out of California, the way it read on the printout."

The information had come by way of a hit in the NCIC computer, a search comparing name, sex, race, and date of birth.

"So I asked the cop to give me the printout, and I pulled it up on my machine, and on my machine it showed the guy was missing all of the fingers on his left hand, because the FPC has all X's for missing digits. But in the scars, marks, and tattoos column, it didn't say anything about a missing hand. So I called Tony Perez, who was a deputy in California at the time, I says, 'Tony, go get the records on this guy.' They had a big system of records . . . you had hundreds of warrants, and you really didn't know where shit was . . . he finally finds the folder, and I says, 'Tell me something. Is this guy's left hand missing?' So Perez says, 'How the fuck did you know that?' So I explained it to Perez. So he says, 'Shit, we should have put that in the alert, you know, the NCIC entry.' I call back to the cop. I says, 'Has the guy in front of you got his hand missing, or the fingers missing?' He said no, he's got all his fingers. I said let him walk, he's not my guy. He says, 'How can you tell that?' So I did the same thing with him. He says, 'Who the fuck are you, Charlie Chan?' "

Pizzi, who sees the process as a fairly routine exercise in police work, argues that no law-enforcement agencies really teach it.

"I have gone in the middle of the night to precincts, where cops who had been assigned to their BCI [Bureau of Criminal Identification] are actually working as detectives, and I have done that. And they want to stop the show, and they want me to show them how to do it."

Among those agencies that do not teach you anything about fingerprints is the United States Marshals Service. Only in Brooklyn is one expected to apply such knowledge to his daily work. And deputies in the district are not loath to brag about doing so. Least of all to each other.

"Hey, I'm going to tell you something," Oboyski says to the chief, "you would have been proud of us last night, Gerri and me, the detective job that we did. NYPD arrested a guy in Queens, some bullshit charge, okay, his name was like Larry Brown, or something like that, some common name, right. They get a hit on a D.C. warrant, they get a hit on, like, a Dennis Brown. Now, they come up with his rap sheet, similar height, similar weight, exact same DOB [date of birth], exact same last name. On his New York rap sheet, there's no FBI number, so we can't pull up a fingerprint classification. On the D.C. hit—we pull it up on the machine in the office—there's no FBI number and there's no fingerprint classification. Okay? What do you do?"

"That makes things a little difficult," grants Pizzi.

"Aha! Dick Tracy . . . Dick *Traski* . . ."

"I would have let him put my hand between his legs," says Pizzi, "to see if his *pulse* was beating *faster* when I asked him if he was the guy."

"You know what we did," Oboyski, the self-styled Traski, continues, "we called Metropolitan PD, got a hold of their identification unit, and got the NCIC fingerprint classification on the fugitive . . . *then,* I called Albany and got hold of DCJS [Department of Criminal Justice Services] and I got *their* identification section . . ."

"So you didn't have to go to Queens. You did it on the telephone."

"All on the phone. Gerri sat there like this . . ."

"Were they far apart?

"*Far* apart," Oboyski replies, "tons, one guy had an SR, a scar. So I called back to the ADA [assistant district attorney]. The

ADA doesn't believe me. He says, 'How can you do that over the phone?' I said, 'Because I know fingerprints don't lie and classifications don't lie. I checked with D.C. and I checked with Albany. It's not the same guy. As a matter of fact, if you want to be doubly sure, when the guy comes out, go to his right index finger and see if he has a scar through the middle of his finger. If he don't have a scar, he's not our guy. Our guy has a scar.' He goes, 'You guys are unbelievable.' "

It is Mike Pizzi's very *believability,* in fact, that makes him such a natural for the District Operations seminar at Glynco.

"Mike is considered a street guy, a street cop," Oboyski contends, "because of his life experience rather than his cop experience. He came off the streets of Brooklyn . . . a truck driver, the Marine Corps . . . he's a home-grown New Yorker, a self-made man."

The Glynco lecture typifies Pizzi's style:

"I heard a rumor," he will tell the students, "that the last time I came to this class, I took the manual and threw it in the garbage pail. I didn't do that. I wouldn't do it. It's too big to fit in the garbage pail. It's now in three volumes. Volume Three there is of the manual. . . . The manual is a guide, okay? There's numerous ways of doing something right. . . . Please don't say [when you get to your district] 'That's not the way it's done at the academy.' When you leave the academy, it's over . . ."

The Brooklyn chief has abiding respect for what transpires at Glynco, and what he offers students is really only an amplification on various techniques. There is one thing, however, that is taught at the academy (and at every police academy in the country) which carries as much practical weight as flat-earth theory for Mike Pizzi, and for his exception to it he has become legendary.

" . . . your famous *felony car stop.* . . . PUT YOUR LEFT HAND OUT THE WINDOW . . . PUT YOUR RIGHT HAND UP ON . . . AND DROP THE KEYS. . . . You try that in a major city, anywhere, you'll have people walkin' . . . you'll have people like this . . ."

And here Pizzi pantomimes the typical New Yorker, a carefree civilian, stepping into the line of fire, one of many, strolling back and forth between the police officer and the suspect . . . rubbernecking . . . asking questions . . . one pedestrian pausing to examine the gun, cocking his head as he peers down the barrel . . .

"... that 200-yard felony car stop. I guess on a rural highway in Tucumcari, New Mexico, it would work, [but] not around where I come from."

Pizzi, during his two-hour lecture, engages the students in street scenarios he considers typical. In the scenarios, Pizzi plays the part of the suspect and chooses a student on each occasion to play the arresting officer. For the first scenario, Pizzi always selects the best shooter in the class, arms him with an unloaded revolver, unloads his own, and in the course of the scenario—in which he gives the deputy the advantage; that is, the deputy has the drop on the suspect—quickly succeeds in shooting the deputy's character to death.

"You have to play by the rules," he explains, "and this bastard don't have to play by no rules at all. . . . You're talking, your lips are moving, you can't pull the trigger. . . . You're a decent human being, like every one of you people in this room, and you don't have it in you to do what this bastard can do. There are a lot of things a bad guy can do that you can't do [by law]. . . . We do not want to lose any of you. I would rather [see] half the goddamn prisoners in the institutions today [go free] than lose one of you."

The advantage a deputy gives away in any potential confrontation is essentially twofold. A criminal need not observe departmental guidelines governing the use of deadly force, he need not wait to be threatened with a gun before pulling the trigger; for a bad guy there is no such thing as a bad shoot. Nor does a suspect have to consider bystanders and passers-by, innocent civilians who happen to be in the line of fire or in the path of ricocheting lead.

When Tony Perez in 1988 arrested the treacherous Ricky Cravero, whose gang was thought to have been responsible for thirty-five torture-slayings and disappearances connected to drug trafficking in Florida's Dade and Broward counties—a 15 Most Wanted, he had been serving three consecutive life terms for multiple murders when he escaped from prison—Cravero told Perez that he and the members of his gang "always stayed in shape" with guns.

"He told me," Perez says, " 'We meet, the first thing we do is draw, and the faster man wins the bet.' Sometimes they'd shoot each other by accident . . . 'Sorry, man . . .' When they would run into a cop, he told me, 'We shoot twice and drop the gun.' Cravero and his crowd, it was a tactic. He said, 'We know cops won't shoot if you're unarmed.' "

What Mike Pizzi's scenarios reinforce is the inadvisability of working alone.

"The toughest thing in the world is to take a guy alone. Some of us are here only because the guy chose not to do us in."

Having said that, Pizzi will choose a second student from the class, and in a scenario similar to the first, in character, he will deliver an injury to the arresting officer as devastating in its own way as was the earlier lethal gunshot. While the student, having put the freeze on suspect Pizzi, recites instructions over the barrel of a gun—"hands where I can see them . . . do this, do that . . ."; the arresting officer is not to be fooled this time—Pizzi simply walks out the door of the classroom, closing the door behind him.

"Could happen," warns Pizzi, reentering the room to the uproar of laughter. "What's going to stop me. Guy walks away. Now you got a foot chase. You can't shoot the dude . . ."

Vic Oboyski, elaborating on the point that the scenario makes, acknowledges that "You get a lot of that in New York. Guy goes, 'Fuck you, I'm not putting my hands up.' What are you going to do, shoot him? 'I'm going. Bye.' And he walks away. You're standing there with your gun and your badge in your hand. What are you going to do with the guy? You have a lot of guys, you point a gun at them, they could care less, because they've had guns pointed at them their whole life. 'Hey, stick your gun. You think I'm afraid of you with your gun?' You're going to have to do something. You're going to have to put your gun away, you're going to have to put your badge away, you're going to have to roll your sleeves up, and get down with this guy. Because in this city, they don't really care. They look at you, 'Who cares, your gun and your badge? In New York everybody's got a gun and a badge.' "

"Sometimes, too much equipment can confuse you," Pizzi tells the students. "You got a radio, you got a gun, and you got a badge, and you got a slapper, and you got a flashlight . . . and you only got two hands. . . . You think you could put those handcuffs on me? You think, if I don't want you to put the handcuffs on me, you could put them on? I'm going to tell you now, you ain't going to put them on. . . . What are you going to do with the piece? You got a disadvantage. You got a piece on you and I don't. You got a disadvantage and I'll tell you why. You got to fight me one-handed. You think you could fight me with one hand? It's one hand now, 'cause you can't use the other one, and I got two free. Can you shoot me? No, I'm unarmed. I turn my back, you can't shoot me in the back. There's a lot of things you can't do. Now you got handcuffs in *this* hand . . . *now* you can't even push me off. If I don't listen to the command, you're dead. What makes you think the bad guy's going to listen to you? He ain't . . ."

Vic Oboyski tells the story of one New York City arrest he made in which he had pulled a car to the side of the street, jumped out of his own car, identified himself, and ordered the driver to step out. The driver hit the accelerator and tried to run Oboyski and his partner down.

"I shot the guy in the face, in the *head,* and he got out of the car *mad* at me. What am I going to do, shoot him again? He's unarmed. I shot him in the *head* and the only thing I did was piss him off. The guy wanted to tumble."

After the fight, the suspect refused the handkerchief Oboyski offered to stanch the blood leaking from the hole in his face.

At Camp Beauregard, the military base outside Pineville, Louisiana, where Special Operations Group headquarters is located and at which SOG conducts its training, the Marshals Service periodically conducts specialized courses, one of which, a survival course for the marshals themselves—the political appointees, many of whom have no background in police work—was attended by Mike Pizzi's boss, U.S. Marshal Charles Healey.

"A former homicide cop, very tough guy," Pizzi advises the class, "worked TPF in New York, the Tactical Patrol Force, worked riots, knows his way around the street. They're doing a felony car stop and they asked him to be a role player, and the role he's playing is, he decides he's going to be the brother of the guy who's handcuffed on the ground. He walks over, he says, 'Hey, what happened, this is my brother.' The marshal [playing the arresting officer] says, 'Stand back, man, he's under arrest, felony.' [Healey] says, 'What do you mean, arrest, felony, he's my brother, he works in a grocery store.' 'Stand back.' 'What are you telling me, stand back . . .' Now they go through this for about five minutes. He got the guy so excited . . . the marshal *shot* him. Here's an unarmed guy arguing in the street, and this guy *shot* him. And *then* tried to justify to the rest of them why he shot this guy: 'He didn't listen!' You can't shoot somebody for not *listening* . . ."

The confusion Charlie Healey employed on the untrained marshal, the same confusion Pizzi utilizes in the street scenarios, serves the experienced felon well. Even when not deployed as a tactic, it is characteristic of every emergency, and thus of every arrest.

"Since the last time I spoke here," Pizzi declaims, "that's just since the last class, two police officers in my city were murdered. . . . Many more officers have been shot, including a couple with their partners' weapons and their own weapons . . ."

The volatility of an arrest and the exploitability of confusion are why deputies do not work single-handed.

"We never work alone," Southern District warrants supervisor Frank Devlin insists. "We do not conduct interviews alone and we never arrest with two people . . . we always go out with at least three or four. We do our homework. We try to pick the location, the time. We want to *control* the situation."

Explaining the heavy security he has thrown at a typical prisoner move, Mike Pizzi will tell you, "We handle so many badasses, it's almost routine. We get it on all the time. We very rarely fight fair . . ."

As Vic Oboyski describes serving the typical warrant: "This ain't the O.K. Corral . . . I slap leather . . . there's none of that shit. We sneak up when you're sleeping and put a shotgun up your ass . . ."

"Fugitives," Frank Devlin says, "sleep late."

Oboyski remembers working a warrant one morning in Bedford-Stuyvesant:

"I'm holding my gun out: '*Wake up!*' There's, like, five people sleeping. I mean, I'm standing in the middle of their room. I came in through a window from the fire escape, screaming at the top of my lungs. '*Wake up!*' One guy looks up from the couch and goes . . . 'Can I help you?' Yeah, a six-foot-three white guy with a gun in his hand. . . . 'Yeah, I just thought I'd drop in and ask you people if you need any *reupholstering.*'"

Mike Pizzi affirms the merits of "a real show of force . . . intimidation . . ." Bud McPherson, when he talks about WITSEC's going high-profile, is talking about the same thing.

As SOG commander John Haynes explains tactical response: "A show of force is a tactic itself."

Vic Oboyski, after fifteen years on the job, attended Enforcement School at Glynco, a course in advanced training for journeyman deputies. Veteran instructor Bob Natzke, one day, was conducting a practical exercise:

"He goes like this," Oboyski recalls, "he says, 'Hit the door. And hit it the way you would do it on a regular hit.' I said, 'You really want us to do that?' 'Yeah.' 'Okay' . . . BOOM! BOOM! BOOM! . . . 'OPEN THE FUCKING DOOR!' Natzke busted out laughing. He says, 'No, no, no, you know what I mean.' I said, 'That's what I do.' I know the bad guy's in there? . . . 'OPEN THE FUCKING DOOR OR WE'LL KICK IT IN, YOU SON OF A BITCH!' . . . That's the psychological factor. I want the bad guy to think that the biggest monster that he can imagine is coming through that door. That's what I want him to think. You know [and here Oboyski assumes a falsetto], 'Excuse me, federal agents.' I don't want him to think, you know, like, some five-foot-one IRS agent's coming in. . . . I want him to think that King Kong is coming through that door . . . and is going to eat his gun and eat him and his kids and just leave an empty apartment."

"Things don't happen [out there] like [they do at the academy]," Mike Pizzi assures his Glynco students. Certainly they do not happen that way in New York. And Pizzi, the relentless teacher, sees to it that upon arrival in Brooklyn, young deputies hit the ground running.

"One of the first training aids I give: 'Here's the [telephone] number of Rikers Island. There's only 10,000 prisoners on Rikers Island. There's ten or twelve wardens. Each building has a different warden. Find this prisoner. . . . Now, the dude's in custody. That shouldn't be too difficult. . . . Find this prisoner.' The first hour, the deputy's sitting there, with the phone, like this . . . he still don't get anybody there to pick up the *phone* . . . they won't pick up the *phone* . . . !'"

In gauging Mike Pizzi's popularity throughout the United States Marshals Service, one cannot overlook the singular impact upon his superiors and fellow deputies of Pizzi's proven ability to piss off the FBI.

"I'd like to say we're all in this battle to fight crime and/or evil and the Red Peril together," Duke Smith concedes, "but you know that's not the real world."

To understand FBI agents, think of them not as policemen, but as lawyers and certified public accountants with gun permits. Trained to conduct fraud investigations, unsurpassed in their ability to follow paper trails, they are acknowledged experts at gathering evidence in a variety of white-collar crimes. In the early years of the Cold War, they managed to distinguish themselves in the field of counterespionage. (Recently they have drawn almost as much attention for their counterintelligence failures.) But much of the work for which the Bureau has always sought statutory authority is what might be considered traditional police work, and for that its employees are poorly trained. In truth, the only time FBI agents have ever made history as street cops is from ambush.

In its pursuit of bank robbers during the Great Depression, the FBI's principal success was in the field of public relations; the agency's gunning down of John Dillinger in July of 1934 helped establish a preeminence in the media that the Bureau has never relinquished. The Bureau's ascendancy in Washington can be attributed to J. Edgar Hoover's understanding of both the sophisticated and elemental uses of power—he held his job for forty-eight years—and to his preternatural gift for the manipulation of publicity.

As Marshals Service director Stanley Morris points out, "When the FBI made an arrest they got the credit, of course, but when we did, the story credited 'federal agents.' "

Effective application of the principles of self-promotion was not developed by the Marshals Service—not the only agency to find itself on the short end of that editorial proposition—until a little more than a decade ago. And its public-relations triumphs, as they mounted, cast "the sister agency" in an unflattering shadow.

Those triumphs accumulated while the FBI was politically hemorrhaging from wounds that were self-inflicted.

At a time when the Bureau should have been celebrating its operational successes—its victory over The Order, the violent and well-organized white-supremacist group it had so effectively worked to emasculate; its disclosure of widespread corruption in the Chicago court system, which led to the convictions of over sixty judges, lawyers, and law-enforcement officers; and its exposure of institutionalized bribery in the Pentagon procurement program, to name a few—it was instead applying its public-relations resources to damage control. Having lived down its complicity in the Watergate cover-up, having survived revelations of investigative excesses under Hoover, it was now coming to grips with major counterintelligence failures, including the conviction of one of its own agents for espionage; defending itself before a Senate intelligence committee against charges of systematic political harassment of U.S. citizens, FBI director William Sessions admitting to an "unnecessarily broad" investigation of CISPES, the Committee in Solidarity with the People of El Salvador; and facing substantiated claims of sexual and racial discrimination within its ranks, a federal court not only ruling that the agency responsible for enforcing the nation's civil-rights laws was in violation of them, but also finding that it had illegally retaliated against those agents who had brought the suit.

According to former federal prosecutor Larry Barcella, the Bureau's recent travails are, in fact, a consequence of positive changes within the agency.

"All the bad publicity is the result of more openness [at the FBI]," he suggests. "You never *knew* about this stuff under Hoover."

But bad publicity is only half the story. Good publicity today, in law enforcement, is generated on the street, and the FBI, which has grown gorged over the years on the fat of its jealously held status, is not in shape to win headlines there.

"I never see them in the ghetto, I never see them in the projects. No, you don't run into them out here," says one federal agent. "And when you do, there's like a hundred of them, they come out in force."

And they come accompanied by a television crew.

"They work against themselves," he explains. "They're dysfunctional, bureaucratized, rigid, bound up in procedure and image."

International Branch chief Larry Homenick, touting the speed and efficiency with which the Marshals Service hauls in fugitives, points to a paralysis in the FBI, a symptomatic impairment of initiative induced by a complex chain of command. Special agents, unlike deputies, in order to operate at all, first have to navigate their own bureaucracy, he says. While a deputy marshal, on his own, might close a case in a matter of days, his mechanism for doing so, Homenick suggests, is incompatible with procedure as observed by agents of the Bureau:

"We're hungry. In the Marshals Service you got to do it on

your own. On a fugitive case, we send two guys . . . they spend millions. They'd spend a week," he says, "giving it a *code name*."

And, if successful, adds Tony Perez, the Bureau's agents would inflate the statistics.

"On one case," he says, "they will close four cases—Miami, L.A., New York—all the offices that were [telephoned] on the warrant investigation."

The Bureau, famous for its lack of reciprocity with the press, notorious for its disdainful treatment of state and local police, is no less self-aggrandizing in its official dealings with the investigators of other federal agencies.

"The cooperation is all one way," one of those investigators reveals. "They show up with a notepad at your office. They share no information. They don't aid law enforcement, they hinder law enforcement."

The Bureau, in 1988, in servicing its image, actually attempted to sabotage Gerri Doody's arrest of 15 Most Wanted fugitive John Matthew Boston, whom she dragged back from Jamaica no more than a few months after she snatched Garnett Leacock in New York.

The FBI had learned that Director of the Marshals Service Stanley Morris was about to appear on network television's "America's Most Wanted" to announce the addition of Boston to the Service's 15 Most Wanted list. (FBI Director William Sessions, himself, had recently appeared on the program—"the biggest posse in American history," according to deputy Bob Leschorn—to add three people to the list of the FBI's 10 Most Wanted.)

In the advent of Morris's appearance, FBI agents began calling members of the fugitive's family, alerting them, and by extension Boston himself, to the fact that he was going to be featured on television. Hoping that he would give himself up to them (he was wanted by the FBI on a UFAP warrant, unauthorized flight to avoid [state] prosecution being a category of federal warrant over which the FBI maintained jurisdiction), the Bureau's agents worked at the same time to drive Boston further underground, undermining the value of any phone traps, pen registers, or surveillances the Marshals Service might have in force, effectively acting as accessories to his escape.

The FBI's help, in the end, was not enough for Boston—Gerri Doody collared him anyway.

The quintessential bureaucracy, the FBI is a case study in the methodology of the cancer cell—the growth of growth. Sustaining itself by feeding on an ever-expanding variety of programs, it differs from other law-enforcement agencies only in the degree of success it has enjoyed. When J. Edgar Hoover in the late 1960s turned down President Lyndon Johnson's offer of a share of the federal dope mandate, he was acting counter to established tradition, but he was not acting out of character.

Nothing, Hoover knew, was a greater threat to the rank-and-file than narcotics.

"He didn't want his apple-cheeked agents in their Brooks Brothers suits getting dirty," explains a deputy marshal.

Were he alive today, Hoover would see drug money corrupting not only federal agents but occupants of every job category in the criminal justice system, from parole officers to prosecutors, backroom functionaries to members of the bench; he would see that corruption taking hold of U.S. military personnel assigned to interdiction. And open to that same corruption he would see the FBI.

With the entrenchment of dope on the criminal scene and its feeding on the lion's share of the nation's law-enforcement budget—with drug enforcement, so accessible a source of self-serving political rhetoric, sucking up all the nation's headlines —the FBI has finally cut itself in.

"And they're not prepared," the deputy points out. "They can make mass conspiracy cases, but they can't do it like the DEA does. The DEA gets down in the street, and rolls around in the gutter with these guys. That's the only way you're gonna fight narcotics. You're not gonna fight narcotics with wiretaps, and putting a guy under surveillance for five years like the Bureau does. You have to get out there in the street."

And, he adds, not irrelevantly, the DEA delivers the drugs.

"The Bureau comes up with these multi-multi-conspiracy indictments, and they come up with one kilo of heroin. You have all these guys on trial, where's the drugs? There's no drugs."

Nor, in 1979, were there any fugitives. When President Jimmy Carter, that year, assigned responsibility for their capture to the Marshals Service, it was in part because the FBI for half a century had neglected to deliver on the mandate. Once the Marshals Service started generating headlines for succeeding where the FBI had failed, it was only a matter of time before the Bureau filed an official grievance.

The noisome complaint, quite audible by the end of 1987, was to escalate rather rapidly to a full-scale Justice Department turf war. The actual outbreak of hostilities in the official territorial battle between the nation's largest law-enforcement agency and its oldest—eventually resolved with compromises on both sides—came when newspapers, one morning that November, arrived at the FBI field office in New York with Mike Pizzi's picture all over them.

The FBI had not been ecstatic over Christopher Boyce. Edwin Wilson, very clearly, had been a humiliation. The agency had gone so far as to beef Tony Perez personally over a pair of escaped bank robbers named Terry Lee Conner and Joseph Dougherty. And now, finally, there was this.

As Duke Smith, in characteristically deadpan fashion, points out:

"Persico didn't please them."

10.

You Know Me Al

Victor Oboyski's approach to police work is probably best illustrated by a story Southern District chief Flip Lorenzoni tells about their days together as deputies in Manhattan. Lorenzoni and Oboyski were transporting two federal prisoners from New York to Pennsylvania. One, convicted of armed bank robbery, was to be driven to the maximum-security penitentiary at Lewisburg; the other, convicted of bribery, was to be dropped at the minimum-security Allenwood facility no more than fifteen miles from there.

The two felons, hooked to each other in the rear of the sedan, in leg irons, waist chains, and handcuffs, were also locked for much of the journey in aimless conversation, but it was not until the car arrived at Allenwood that the bank robber was suddenly put wise to the fact that his fellow prisoner was a justice of the New York State Supreme Court.

Stepping out at Allenwood, the irrepressible Oboyski, opening the rear door of the sedan, slapped the palm of his hand twice on the roof of the car and ceremoniously barked:

"All rise!"

As Lorenzoni saw it, the move was classic Oboyski.

"He loves his work," Lorenzoni insists. "He's *always* in a good mood."

A master of the conversational aside—"here we have a suspicious-looking vehicle . . . no, just your typical New York psychopath driving to work"—Victor Oboyski is one of those incidentally hilarious people who, on the job, tends to loosen his colleagues up with his running commentary on the passing scene.

"As a cop," he will readily tell you, "you take yourself too seriously and you got a problem."

Periodically heard counseling younger deputies to lighten up and relax, Oboyski, when he is not making fun of the activity around him, is making fun of himself.

Pursuing a convicted murderer once, on an international warrant, Oboyski followed leads into New York's Hassidic community, a society known for its distrust of outsiders, where the fugitive, professing to be a devout Jew, had found it convenient to go to ground. Oboyski spent much of his time on the case cultivating the cooperation of an elderly rabbi; his oral account of the investigation, in formal terms, comes down somewhere between the traditional Yiddish and the very loud Kabuki theater.

"You're a policeman?"

"I'm a deputy U.S. marshal."

"A marshal, what, a marshal?"

"A marshal. You know, like Matt Dillon. Matt Dillon, the Old West. 'Gunsmoke,' remember 'Gunsmoke'?"

"What, gunsmoke . . . who?"

"Deputy United States marshal, here . . ."

Oboyski handed over his badge and credentials. Respectfully, the old rabbi studied them. Then he handed them back. He patted Oboyski's shoulder:

"You're a deputy United States marshal . . . and a very good one, God bless you."

Not to be dismissed, Oboyski prevailed upon the old fellow. The two homicides eventually came up.

"This guy's wanted for murder."

"Did he kill a Jew?"

"Murder!"

The rabbi's index finger went up:

"Alleged."

During one of his many visits to the rabbi, Oboyski was called away on a warrant. He told the rabbi he would be right back. He returned five hours later to confront the old gentleman's wife. He apologized for being late.

"Five hours?"

Oboyski politely explained to the woman that police work was unpredictable.

"You can't call . . . ?"

"We have to arrest . . ."

". . . five hours, you couldn't find a telephone?"

The six-foot-three Oboyski, hanging his head, stood like a penitent schoolboy in the face of the dressing-down.

"I'll ask the rabbi if he can see you," said the wife.

Recounting the event, Oboyski grabs his earlobe and pantomimes being dragged by the tiny woman into her husband's office.

Addressing the rabbi, he said, "I'm sorry I'm late, but . . ."

"Five hours it's been. . . . You can't call? . . . What, you couldn't find a telephone?"

Victor Oboyski, a native of Ozone Park, Queens, entered the Marshals Service under the Veterans Readjustment Act in 1971 after one year of college and three years' experience as a military policeman with the United States Army in Germany. A deputy by day, Oboyski attended school at night, receiving his bachelor's and master's degrees—in police science and public administration, respectively—at New York's John Jay College.

Like others who came on the job the same year, Oboyski came on assigned to Air Piracy, the Marshals Service being charged with the establishment and maintenance of the now-familiar "sterile corridor" at the nation's airports.

"We didn't fly. That was Customs. Our job was ground detection. We didn't call [ourselves] sky marshals, we called [the program] Anti Air Piracy. We'd go from gate to gate. We developed the hijacker profile. The airlines would profile them, we would stop them. We came up with a lot of guns."

While the screening of airline passengers has become a fact of American life, the practice of actually putting armed agents on aircraft, Oboyski points out, was abandoned almost immediately.

"What are you going to do if a guy pulls a gun? Shoot him? You're on top of all that fuel at 30,000 feet. You can't let a round go off up there."

After working Air Piracy out of Brooklyn, Oboyski was assigned to New York's Southern District, putting in ten years there before recrossing the East River to answer to Pizzi. At district awards ceremonies in 1988, when he received his twenty-year pin (the Marshals Service credited Oboyski with three years for his military experience), his fellow deputies fondly presented him with an occupational aid—an army-surplus M72 rocket launcher, a sixty-six-millimeter light anti-tank weapon—in observance of his advancing years and his abiding affection for forced entry.

While his physical attributes bespeak the stereotypical, old-school deputy marshal, Victor Oboyski is modern law enforcement personified, clearly a renaissance door-kicker. He weighs 235, he will tell you, but only "when I'm not running." In 1980 and again in 1982, Oboyski ran the New York City Marathon, finishing on both occasions, his best time three hours and forty minutes.

A working deputy well in command of the traditional tools of his trade, Oboyski betrays an oceanic ignorance on the subject of guns, a field of study he finds emotionally and intellectually unrewarding. He can speak to none of the specifications of any of the weapons he so effectively uses; the rocket launcher completely mystified him, a reporter explained what it was.

Nor is Oboyski entirely atypical of the average working deputy. Few seem to know or care much about handguns beyond maintaining them and mastering the ability to fire them accurately. Rare in the Marshals Service is what is traditionally thought of as the gun freak, he who worships at the altar of the National Rifle Association or the local rod-and-gun club. There are stockbrokers, actors, and ad executives who can discuss more knowledgeably the subtle differences among various sidearms than can most of America's cops. The Service does have its aficionados, but the fact is that guns today are just too expensive for the average deputy to get interested in. They cannot *afford* the luxury of taking seriously such arcane discussions as those on the subject of "firepower." Of those who do, of course, each has a theory—semiauto versus revolver, ammunition capacity, caliber, etc.—and each thinks everyone else has a different theory. "I know everybody else . . . ," they begin, but the truth is that not everybody thinks anything. Everybody's idea of *traditional* theory is different.

Weapons in general Oboyski finds distasteful, and when he speaks of them at all, in any but a purely reportorial context, it is to make fun of civilization's preoccupation with them.

"Everybody in New York carries a gun," he says. "They all got identification." Reenacting events as he pictures their transpiring at the weapons checkpoint at the door of the U.S. Courthouse, he flashes an imaginary pistol permit:

" 'Colombo crime family.'

" 'Good morning, sir.'

" 'Soldier. Gambino family.'

" 'Come around.'

" 'Capo.'

" 'Capo? Right this way.' "

For all the noise he makes around the office and on the street, the fair-haired, green-eyed Oboyski is, underneath it all, rather genteel. He recoils at the possibility that he might actually go on the record as having used the word "fuck" in any of its variations. Apart from the horror of that, the only thing Victor Oboyski is truly afraid of is Mike Pizzi's dog.

Half shepherd, half Doberman, to the Pizzi family the dog is known as Rocky. Oboyski calls him Doctor Demento. Mike Pizzi had made the mistake of complaining one day to a visitor that Rocky, the affectionate animal that he was, made a singularly lousy guard dog. To his everlasting regret, Pizzi accepted the visitor's offer to help correct the problem. The visitor called Rocky over, reared back, and punched the pup right between the eyes almost fracturing the poor mongrel's skull. From that moment on, Rocky posed a certifiable threat to everyone in the neighborhood. A splendid guard dog, he was worthless as a housepet, but Pizzi continued to love him nevertheless.

Approaching the front door of Mike Pizzi's Bath Beach home, one can hear Rocky spoiling for a fight. And approaching the door in the company of Vic Oboyski is not something one is likely to forget. Following his chief up the steps to the house, Oboyski, armed and more dangerous-looking than anyone even in *that* neighborhood, will turn without shame to a younger deputy and tell him:

"You go first."

And this is a man who has crashed through reinforced doors to come up against working members of the Jamaican Shower Posse, an organization whose level of respect for officers of the

American constabulary is traditionally expressed in the greeting "Lock and load."

It is Oboyski's firmly held opinion that Rocky has it in for him personally:

"That dog wants some Polish meat. He wants to take a bite out of my kielbasa, there."

Included in the property seized under NASAF guidelines in the Eastern District of New York were several apartment buildings in Brooklyn and Queens that had become infested by cash-heavy street-level dealers in heroin and crack-cocaine. As part of their elaborate security measures—booby traps, electronic surveillance, reinforced doors, snipers on the roof—the occupants, to discourage intruders, had taken the additional precaution of putting pit bulls on the staircases.

"In Staten Island they had two pit bulls tied to the top of the stairs on a leash. They would turn off the lights to the hallway, so the cops couldn't see where they were going, and release the pit bulls down the stairs. Here you have the cops fleeing out of the building just to get away from the pit bulls. You can't shoot the dogs, because you can't see them. You hear them coming down the stairs . . ."

Animal-lover Mike Pizzi had gone so far as to purchase for the district a gun designed to fire tranquilizer darts—the same gun employed by the Emergency Services Unit of the New York City Police Department—for use upon entry during the seizures.

"We will subdue the animal and release him back into the wild," announces Oboyski, conjuring, complete with the French accent, a naturalist he calls Jacques-Pizzi Cousteau.

Oboyski himself is of that veterinary school which teaches that one feeds such animals double-ought buck. On one seizure he demonstrated his willing adherence to the principle.

"The dog's barking at everybody, a cop runs up, he's yelling, 'I got him, I got him.' He shoots the dog in the ass with the tranquilizer gun. So the dog starts running in *my* direction. I got the shotgun, I go . . . Ohhh . . . I'm going to kill him. The cop says, 'Don't worry, the dog's been shot.' The dog sees me, makes a right turn—one of the government cars has the door open—the dog hopped in the government car, sat down in the passenger seat. I slammed the door, right? So the boss goes like this: 'If *that* dog takes off with *that* car . . .'"

The dog passed out and was removed by Emergency Services.

. . .

"No matter *what* he does," says his former partner, Frank Devlin, "Vic makes people laugh."

Exiting that day at Allenwood, the first person to laugh was the judge.

The bank robber, however, did not find it funny.

"That dude a *judge?*" the bank robber asked.

Oboyski said that he was.

"*Shit,*" said the holdup man, indignant, "next I'll be ridin' with Richard Nixon!"

"Well, him," Oboyski said, "I think you'll recognize."

"Man, you people be lockin' up *everybody.*"

Oboyski could not argue with that.

Little did Oboyski realize at the time that one of the people he would be locking up in the course of his career was the most wanted organized-crime figure in America.

A warrant for the arrest of Alphonse Carmine Persico, under-boss of the Colombo crime family, the old Profaci family, in New York, who had been convicted on three counts of extortion, was issued on June 23, 1980, three days after his failure to appear for a pre-sentencing hearing in Brooklyn's U.S. District Court. "Allie Boy," whose criminal record dated back to 1949—assault, fraud, firearms violations, possession of stolen property, loan-sharking—and who had previously served seventeen years of a twenty-year sentence on a second-degree murder conviction, was facing, on each of the three counts, twenty years in prison and a fine of $10,000, when he defaulted on his $250,000 bond and vanished.

For the more than seven years that he was at large, Persico was the technical responsibility of New York's Eastern District where the arrest warrant had been issued, and in that time more than one task force answering to headquarters had been unsuccessful in locating him. Persico, placed on the 15 Most Wanted list in 1983, was not the typical fugitive. He had access to the protection and to the unlimited resources of the Colombo family, only a few of whose members had knowledge of his whereabouts; he could be assumed to have the help of organized-crime figures in whatever region he had relocated; and he did not follow any obvious wiseguy pattern: he did not run off to Florida, for example, only to show up at Hialeah, at the hundred-dollar window, flashing money.

Persico went underground and stayed there.

Over the years, thousands of investigative leads were developed, but nothing of substance materialized. In May 1987, a new task force was formed out of New York. Mike Pizzi, who had grown up in Bensonhurst, in the shadow of the Colombo family clubhouse at Seventy-sixth Street and Thirteenth Avenue—the Wimpy Boys Club run by Gregory Scarpa's crew—assigned the case to himself.

"The case was ours because it was failure-to-appear post conviction," Pizzi explains. "The FBI would have retained it had it been *pre-conviction*. That was under the first Memorandum of Understanding."

The FBI, putting Persico on its 10 Most Wanted list, claimed jurisdiction on the grounds that the warrant grew out of an organized-crime case.

"When he failed to appear that day, I sent [Inspector] Bob Leschorn out to look for him. From that point, it was Leschorn's case."

For three years Bob Leschorn worked the case reporting to Pizzi. With the establishment of the 15 Most Wanted list in 1983 and Persico's appearance thereon, and with weekly progress reports thus required by Washington, Leschorn found himself answerable not only to Pizzi but to headquarters as well, to the chief of the Enforcement Division directly. An untenable command structure, from Mike Pizzi's point of view, it was made impossible by Leschorn's promotion and transfer to headquarters in 1984. At that point, Pizzi prevailed upon Washington to let Leschorn take the case with him. For the next three years the investigation was run by Washington. In early 1987, with little to show for its efforts, headquarters invited Pizzi back in.

"I said, under one condition. No interference. Leschorn was reporting to two people, and it was unfair to him and it was unfair to the district. I said I'll take it, but no interference, and I'm telling you now, I'm going to run it my way. And I'm going to assign it to me."

Pizzi, over the next several months, was answerable, by agreement, only to one man in Washington, Chad Allan, the new deputy chief of the Enforcement Division. The investigation, backed by the weight of a district chief, was given the support of headquarters but without the day-to-day scrutiny that went with it. Chad Allan gave Pizzi room to operate.

"Whatever I asked for, I got. People, funding . . . no interfer-

ence . . . we asked, we got it. And he never asked me for anything."

Washington did ask for *one* thing.

"When they gave me the case back, they also asked me to sit
down with the FBI. One more time. So, we sat around a table
and we divided tasks. Same results. We gave them everything,
they gave us nothing."

The information upon which Pizzi proceeded was that developed over the years by Leschorn.

"It started out as an enormous task."

Going over all the case files, Pizzi's investigative team discovered its greatest problem to be not a lack of leads, but an over-
abundance of them. There was information putting Persico in
Europe, in Florida, and in Mexico; he was reported sighted in
Japan and Brazil on the same day. The truth was that no reliable
witness had seen him since the day before he was to have appeared for pre-sentencing in 1980.

"There was not one positive sighting on the guy, from anybody."

Speculation that Persico was dead, however, was nothing
more than that and ultimately could not be accepted. Of the
thousands of leads Pizzi inherited, the more encouraging led to
Connecticut.

"Connecticut came from sources on the street. Intelligence
sources . . . stoolies, tips . . . from locking up OC [organized
crime] guys and from talking to NYPD. The rumble was that he
was in Connecticut. We heard a rumor that one of the guys protecting him in Connecticut was one of his own people, a friend
of his, a very close, trusted soldier. We said, that's bullshit, the
guy's in jail, that doesn't make any sense. Dismissed. We went
and pulled the guy's jail records and learned that in his early
career he had taken a number of collars in Connecticut. We said,
maybe that's just a term, that 'protecting him' meant [simply]
under the umbrella or cloak of his protection."

The Colombo family's connection to Connecticut was impossible to dismiss in light of a discovery that many of its members,
when arrested, had been in possession of Connecticut driver's
licenses. That Allie Boy might actually be there was reinforced
by intelligence gathered by District of Connecticut deputies Art
Roderick and Don Donovan. In their search for another high-
profile Mob fugitive, Salvatore Caruana, reputed financier,

among other things, of a New England marijuana-smuggling operation, they had begun to uncover what appeared to be a kind of underground railroad for racketeers, statewide, centered around Hartford. It was Donovan who had called Pizzi with the rumor that Persico was being protected by his jailed associate; now he and Roderick were reporting that Caruana and Persico were rumored to be running around together.

"The rumble was that the Patriarca crew, who Caruana's hooked up with, was hiding these guys," Victor Oboyski recalls. "They had a system by which . . . just like the government has safe-houses, they would do the same thing . . . you go up there, you sign in . . ."

New England Mob operations were overseen by the Patriarca crime family in Providence, Rhode Island, and if Persico were in Connecticut, he was no doubt there with their knowledge.

"There were too many times that we heard Connecticut for it not to be pursued," Mike Pizzi explains. "We decided to resolve the Connecticut issue once and for all. We went into Connecticut and said we're not *leaving* Connecticut until we can say he's *not* there."

Before dispatching deputies to Hartford, however, Pizzi developed a rigorous investigative protocol.

"We conducted no interviews, *not one*, in the Persico case," he says.

With the exception of that—in fact, one interview was conducted, but not until the weekend of Persico's arrest—the investigation represented classic police work, a marriage of old-fashioned shoe leather and contemporary electronic software.

Pizzi proceeded upon the assumption that Persico, if he were in Connecticut, had obtained a driver's license there; he was looking for a man who had received his first license at the age of fifty, or thereabout, and who had done so after 1980. He was also looking for a man who had no credit history up to that point.

"If you had credit before 1980, you were not our guy."

Or if, before then, you had a telephone listed in your name.

Assuming Persico would choose a date of birth that was easy to remember, Pizzi took the month, day, and year of Persico's birth, December 6, 1929, opened it up one day in either direction, did the same with the month and year, and targeted his search upon people whose birthdays fell within those parameters. Allowing for two inches on either side of Persico's height, he sought a man between five-ten and six-two.

"We were looking for somebody with no background."

Somebody whose first name began with the letter "A."

Pizzi, no stranger to the fugitive's life history, knew that the word "Al," though it had faded over the years, was tattooed to Persico's fist. A cheap ink job, the tattoo was enough to limit the mobster's choices when it came to assuming an alias.

"I thought that somebody with 'Al' tattooed on his hand would at least have his first name begin with the letter 'A.' I didn't want to limit it to the name Al, because I thought it would narrow down our investigation. So we expanded the investigation to cover having the first name begin with the letter 'A.' "

Pizzi also targeted his search upon people whose last names, like the ethnocentric Persico's, ended in a vowel.

"Old habits die hard. Usually somebody would use a name he was comfortable with. Or at least somewhat comfortable with. Even if it contained the same letters. So we thought he would use the letter 'A' for his first name and at a minimum his last name would end in a vowel. Because he was of Italian extraction he would be comfortable with it."

Establishing these parameters, and taking bits of information gathered from sources over the years, Pizzi assembled a task force. As field supervisor, he assigned Victor Oboyski.

It was on the DMV computer in Hartford that Oboyski and the task force began their investigation, and as the information came back, Mike Pizzi was immediately confounded.

"Who in the world would have thought that thousands and thousands of people would have gotten their licenses after they were fifty years old. How many names came out of there? The fucking thing came in a box."

Persico, if he were in Connecticut, was not the only one, Pizzi discovered, to have moved there post-retirement. Of those drivers licensed in the state who had received their permits after 1980, fully 15,000 were over fifty years old. More than 7,000 fell within a ten-year age span of the fugitive.

Motor vehicle records represented only a fraction of the data base.

"Studying all the intelligence over the years," Vic Oboyski says, "we believed he had had a heart attack, we believed he'd been in a boating accident, that he'd been in a car accident, that he had been burned. We knew that he was an alcoholic. And that he drank scotch. Cutty Sark, we believed. All this information had been gathered through street people, little pieces, and we put them together. And a lot of things on his profile were true."

In fact, only that Persico had been burned was untrue. (That and the fact that the quart of scotch he drank every day happened to be Dewar's.) While the DMV records were being collected, Mike Pizzi put deputies to work simultaneously assembling others.

"We got guys checking ambulance runs. We also had guys checking with the Coast Guard. And we're looking for a common denominator. The computer wasn't doing the work for us. We had to develop a program ourselves and pump the information in. It was legwork. It was guys actually going through all of the accident reports, all of the ambulance runs, guys going through all the Coast Guard accident reports, *boxes* and *boxes* of files."

Art Roderick estimates that the task force sifted through 175,000 records.

Pizzi instructed his deputies to proceed upon the assumption that nobody could be trusted.

"You don't want anybody to know who you're zeroing in on. You want one record, you ask for ten. Find what you're looking for, you go right past the name. *Discipline*, that was the key. Whenever we got a lead or a fact, we had to sit on it. We had to stop, refrain from asking the question which could take us over the top, or at least save us lots of time. If we asked the wrong person, he was gone."

Not only would it turn out that Persico had been receiving assistance from a crime family other than his own, it would later be discovered that a former official of the Connecticut Department of Motor Vehicles had been a part of the conspiracy. The underground railroad that Pizzi's investigation ultimately exposed, the network of which the DMV official was alleged to be a part, had been operated by the Patriarca mob for close to a decade and had been used to shield high-ranking members of at least three organized-crime families.

So painstaking was the task force in disguising its target that, in compiling a list of all the liquor stores in the state of Connecticut that received regular shipments of Cutty Sark, deputies ran a background on the owner of each, looking for organized-crime connections before making a move to interview them.

"That's how careful we were," Oboyski explains.

In the end, in fact, the interviews were never conducted.

That the investigation could go south in a heartbeat was consistently reinforced by events. The night after deputies received information they had requested from the state liquor authority, for example, the official who had provided the information appeared on television:

"In handcuffs," Oboyski says. "He was being locked up for taking bribes."

It was Mike Pizzi's belief that in the past the investigation had suffered because too many leads had been abandoned, often in favor of others that appeared to be more promising.

"Every time they got a lead, they ran out on it. But that was not the way we were going to run this case. We were going to do this slow and methodical and leave nothing behind us. When we said clear, it was clear. If we had jumped on a lead, we would have left the state of Connecticut more than once. But we moved like a plodding Roman army, we weren't going any place until everything behind us was destroyed and devastated."

Sometimes the task force got lucky.

"In one subpoena, so that we wouldn't tip our hand when we went into a housing complex, we asked for all the records of all the people who had lived in the complex over a certain period of time. There were cartons and cartons and cartons, virtually a roomful of cartons. We got the subpoena as broad as we could possibly get it under the law. The first box we opened, we found the file."

The task force, assuming that Persico had had a heart attack, obtained records of over 10,000 ambulance runs alone. Sifting through these, and through vehicle and boating accident reports, they also compiled lists of dry cleaners, barbers, opticians, and subscribers to New York newspapers who were residents of Connecticut.

"Later we learned that we were right on target," Pizzi notes. "He had suffered a heart attack and was taken to one of the area hospitals. Once we had gotten to the hospitals, we were going to look for someone who didn't have hospitalization [insurance]. I mean this thing was going to go on *ad infinitum*. We started with a scope and we narrowed it down. We figured we could always expand outward if we started to strike out."

· · ·

Pizzi's list of 7,000 licensed drivers included 700 whose first names began with the letter "A" and whose last names ended in a vowel. Credit checks on each of them reduced the list to 150 people.

Twenty-six of them actually shared Persico's exact date of birth.

One of them was named Anthony Perri.

Anthony Perri had been issued a permit to operate a motor vehicle in August 1982. His application for the permit showed that he had been born in Middletown, Connecticut, and that he had attended Hartford High School. Payment to the DMV for the permit had been made in cash.

"We started checking."

The task force, disguising its target, sent a deputy into the high school with four names in addition to Perri's. While one deputy handled that, the others continued feeding data into the computers.

Hartford High School showed no record of Perri's attendance. The state Bureau of Vital Statistics had no record of his birth in Middletown or, for that matter, anywhere in Connecticut.

Pizzi was not about to abandon any other investigative leads, but the street cop in him was nobody's fool.

"It was our first, live, son-of-a-bitchin' clue."

It was now September and, with the hit on Perri, the Persico task force set up a command post in a Hartford hotel. Of the six deputies under Oboyski, three had fewer than two years on the job; one, Janet Doyle, out of Eastern Pennsylvania, was right out of the academy. The task force had been formed over a period of months, reaching full strength, Oboyski explains, just in time for the move to Hartford.

"We had had Artie Roderick and the kid from Pittsburgh [Deputy U.S. Marshal Dean Michael] up there. As time went by, we beefed it up a little more. We got the whole complement of people at the exact time that we hit on Perri. We had brought them in to do record searches. Now I had them doing investigating."

Each deputy took a room at the hotel. They rented cars, ran in their own telephone lines, put their own locks on the doors, set up a typewriter and a fax machine, and went to work.

To his application for a road test Anthony Perri had affixed a signature. Upon cursory examination, the signature displayed similarities to that of Alphonse Persico. Had the document offered up nothing more, Pizzi would have been encouraged. But on the application, Perri had also deposited a latent fingerprint. That was another matter altogether. Yet, as Mike Pizzi would later explain it:

"You can't just go with some dust on a piece of paper that's seven years old and expect to get a print. It has to be done with special chemicals. People who are experts can do it. So we took it to a friend in the NYPD and let him put some chemicals on it, without telling him who it was for or what it was about. He did it for us."

Pizzi responds to the obvious rhetorical question in the affirmative:

"Yes," he soberly agrees, "ordinarily you would go to the FBI."

Pizzi matched Perri's print to that of Persico's left index finger.

"When Anthony Perri shows, when we got the goddamn document from the motor vehicle bureau, the original, and finally match that fucking print on the back of the paper . . . I mean, we had the signature and that looked real good, but that's not a fingerprint . . ."

"There had never been a confirmed sighting of him," Vic Oboyski points out. "Up to that point everybody was telling us he was dead. They were laughing at us."

Pizzi called Chad Allan in Washington:

"Chad," Pizzi said, "he's alive."

Perri had taken his road test in a car registered to a man named Albert Longo. The task force pulled the records. Longo's signature also bore similarities to that of Alphonse Persico. A background investigation of Longo produced a profile similar to Perri's.

"Longo was a backup," Oboyski explains. "Longo was also Persico."

(In fact, Perri was the backup. Longo was the name under which Persico was living.)

Running title searches of all of Perri's and Longo's cars, deputies discovered that all had passed through wiseguy hands, before and after Persico had owned them.

"Some wiseguy's girlfriend would ultimately end up with the car. Artie Roderick would recognize the names. Artie was our biggest asset. He knew all the local wiseguys in Middletown,

Connecticut. He knew everybody up there who was not trust-worthy."

Art Roderick, a native of Provincetown, Massachusetts, had been on the job five years. In a district as small as Connecticut —it had no permanent warrants squad—his talents, which were ample, were never completely exploited; the Persico investiga-tion, if it did not bring him to the attention of Washington, cer-tainly raised the value of his stock there, and it was not long after the case was closed that Roderick was promoted to headquarters, where his talents could be exploited to the fullest.

"He shined like a diamond in that small district," Vic Oboyski maintains. "He helped us tremendously in the case. He steered us clear of the minefields, places where word might have leaked out . . . *marshals from New York* . . . that's all Allie Boy needed to hear. All he had to do was call a car service, plop the money down, fly to California, and that was it, we would have lost him."

Deputies charted all the addresses used by Perri and Longo both to obtain driver's licenses and to register their cars. Using yellow pins to signify Longo, green pins to signify Perri, they transferred the charts to a map, the pins forming a distinct cluster in the Hartford-Bloomfield area. The address most recently used was an address in suburban Bloomfield. It had been used by Persico as Albert Longo.

In 1985.

After that the task force lost him.

Meetings were held every night.

"We'd discuss everything in committee," Oboyski says. "Each team would explain to the other what it had done that day. I took notes. I would question them all. I would take input from every-body. We would reach a consensus on our next move. The chief and Dave [O'Flaherty] were getting subpoenas and everything else we needed and faxing them to Connecticut. We had no direct contact with headquarters."

Not only was the task force insulated by the district against interference from Washington, it was also sheltered by its own precautionary measures from the scrutiny of greater Hartford.

"We ate breakfast, lunch, and dinner together," Oboyski says. "We would drink together in the evening. We did not mention his name in the state of Connecticut until we got him. We never mentioned the word 'Persico.' We were all talking code, he was 'our guy,' or 'that other guy,' we were all talking like gangsters."

Deputies would later discover that one of the hotel bartenders had once moved Persico's furniture. Quite innocently as it turned out. But it was one of those coincidences that would infuse memories of the investigation with a gratifying measure of intrigue. Notable perhaps, yet no less circumstantial, was the name of the rental-car agency patronized by the Persico task force: "Healey. . . . Charlie's name was on the back of all the cars," Oboyski happily recalls, referring to the U.S. marshal for the Eastern District. Yet such pleasures notwithstanding, it is quite apparent that as November rolled around and the task force found itself anchored to the hotel, the collective mood was one of frustration. Oboyski did not unburden himself to the bartender. He took it out on Pink Floyd.

"Artie knows the guy who's head of security for Pink Floyd. They were staying at the hotel. They were playing at the Hartford Civic Center, which is attached to the hotel. I met two of the guys in the band. It was about two in the morning, we were all drinking . . ."

Oboyski, whose musical career had peaked some twenty-five years before, when his drum and bugle corps appeared on stage at Carnegie Hall, mentioned to one of the musicians that his, Oboyski's, mother had worked for the band Kiss.

"Oh, name-dropping, are we?" said the aging British rocker.

"I'm not name-dropping," Oboyski said.

His mother, he explained, had been bookkeeper/controller/accountant for Kiss, then worked for singer Diana Ross.

"Yeah, well, Kiss," began the Englishman, going on to dismiss the forgettable band, and by extension the genial Oboyski. . . . "What do *you* do?" he asked.

"Let me ask you something," Oboyski said. "Did you guys ever play in Carnegie Hall?"

"Carnegie Hall?"

"Yeah, it's the most famous concert hall we have in New York. You ever play there?"

"No."

"Well, I played in Carnegie Hall, buddy. Don't bullshit *me . . .*"

Oboyski, driving to Connecticut every Monday, was driving home every Saturday afternoon. As Thanksgiving approached, he and the task force began to grow desperate.

"We were under the impression that we were going to be severely cut after Thanksgiving, and we said we have to get this guy before then. Also we were worried about the agreement with the Bureau. There were negotiations going on at the time."

Oboyski's fears proved to be well-founded. Under the agreement finally reached with the FBI, the Marshals Service would be forced to yield the investigative prerogative in cases of organized crime. Under the new agreement—it was reached early the following year—Persico would have been off-limits.

On Monday, November 2, Oboyski arrived in Hartford only to tell his troops:

"We gotta dig in. We're only one or two pieces of information away from this guy."

"Yeah, Vic, like his address."

On Saturday, November 7, the task force conducted its first interview.

"Up until that point," Oboyski maintains, "we had not shown Allie Boy's photo anywhere. Or the photos of the bust."

The bust to which Oboyski refers is the plaster bust for which the investigation would ultimately become famous, a forensic sculpture that had been commissioned by Pizzi, a rendering of what Persico might have looked like seven years after his disappearance. A stunningly accurate likeness of what proved to be a rapidly aging Persico, the work of art, in the wake of the investigation, received an enviable share of press attention. The bust, or as it came to be perceived, THE BUST, photographs of which the task force had added to its collection of Persico's mug shots, was not sculptor Frank Bender's original.

"We went to Philadelphia, sat down with him," says Pizzi, "and told him it was unacceptable. We made him change it. The guy's nose was too short, his hair was too white, and his features weren't sharp enough. And the mustache. *We* actually put the mustache on him."

"Because one of the things about wiseguys," Oboyski explains, "is that they're always clean-shaven. No wiseguy walks around with a mustache . . ."

"No Mafia guys have mustaches, none of them, or beards," Pizzi says.

"And," Oboyski continues, "one of the first things a wiseguy does when he goes on the lam . . ."

"Grows a mustache," Pizzi says. "Grows a mustache or a beard."

The sculptor, Mike Pizzi will only too willingly remind you, did the second bust for free. Mike Pizzi is a man who appreciates a bargain:

"We went to rent the fax machine, and they loaned it to us, gave it to us for free. Wonderful company, Pitney-Bowes . . ."

And so . . .

"So we ended up with two busts. The bust that's in [the bicentennial exhibit sponsored by] the Smithsonian is not the bust that we felt was the best bust. The best bust is in Brooklyn."

The best bust.

Asked to estimate the bust's value to him as supervisor in the field and to measure its ultimate impact on the investigation, Victor Oboyski, upon due reflection, speaks for himself and no doubt his chief when he readily concedes the inevitable.

"The bust was meaningless," he replies.

Running a background on the Bloomfield house, Persico's last known address, Oboyski had established that its owner, over the period that Persico was in residence (the house had since been sold), was by occupation a salesman. The man sold pinball machines and was currently in Las Vegas doing so. Call Victor Oboyski prejudiced: he wrote off the former owner of the house as a source of information.

On Saturday, November 7, Oboyski took a chance on a neighborhood dentist.

"We didn't tell the dentist who we were looking for. We walked in, we said we're federal agents, we're interested in the people who live across the street."

Oboyski, of course, was not interested at all in the people who lived across the street. Once he received an answer, he asked:

"Who lived there before that?"

The dentist, unable to provide information on previous occupants of the house, directed Oboyski to neighbors who he said could. After running a quick check on them, Oboyski approached the neighbors in question.

"I'm there with the little redhead, Janet."

Oboyski and "the little redhead," Deputy United States Marshal Janet Doyle, made it only as far as the neighbors' front door.

"I interviewed the husband. He doesn't know much. He starts telling me, 'Well, I really don't know,' etcetera, 'let me ask my wife.' He wouldn't let me talk to his wife. He relayed the questions. He leaves, he comes back. This goes on three or four times. I said, well, thank you very much. I wanted to get into the house, but I could see that the old man was very hesitant. And I don't blame him. So I leave."

Oboyski left somewhat confused. The information he left with, while rather limited, was at the same time distressingly specific. The man who two years before had occupied the house in question, that which had been listed as Longo's address, had lived there with a woman, Oboyski had been told. A daughter would come and visit. Alphonse Persico had a daughter, but his wife's whereabouts had always been known. Oboyski was not encouraged by what he had learned, but Vic Oboyski was not done yet, either.

He and Janet Doyle went for a cup of coffee.

"I've found," Oboyski says, "in investigations . . . when I meet you for the first time, you're a little hesitant, we're establishing a relationship, back and forth, you're feeling me out. A half-hour later, if I come and see you and say, 'Oh, by the way . . . ,' we've already established something. You've seen me once, I'm not a stranger. You trust me now. A half-hour later, believe it or not, you'll give me more information. . . . It works. I'll talk to somebody, I'll drive away, an hour later I'll come back, 'Hey, how you doing?' . . . 'How are you?' . . . 'Oh, I'm still working, you know' . . . the people act like they know you. Well, they *do* know you. All of a sudden, they're a little more friendly."

It was not the luck of the draw that put Janet Doyle at the scene of the interview in the company of the strapping Oboyski.

"I'm a threatening guy, that's why, right away, I want to sit down. I'm a big guy, I look intimidating, so in order to get somebody to talk to me, I have to sit down, lean back, and joke and laugh and get over the intimidation end of it and get them talking to me. . . . It's good to have a female deputy if you're interviewing a female. I'll ask the question and the female will answer the female . . . won't even answer me. I'll ask the questions and she'll look right at the female marshal and answer her, like I'm not there. There's that bonding or whatever you want to call it that takes place between the two of them."

The two deputies finished their coffee. Now it was time to go back.

"Sir, look, I'm very sorry to have to bother you again, but it's *very* important that I talk to your wife. All I want to do is show her some photos. Would that be all right? Do you mind if I come in? I'll be in and out in two seconds."

He said his wife would come to the door.

"I open the album up."

The wife identified Alphonse Persico.

"That," she said, "looks similar to him."

She was pointing to one of the early photos. Oboyski, assuming that in 1985 Persico would have had some more age on him, had expected her to identify, if anything, the photo of the bust. He asked her to describe the man who had lived in the house as she remembered him.

"He had black hair, slicked back," she said, "and he had a big belly on him."

Oboyski immediately thought: the booze.

"Where do you think he was from?"

"I believe he came from New York."

And then she gave Oboyski the information that completely ruined his weekend.

"He was with a British gal."

An attractive blond woman with a British accent.

That really threw Oboyski. Where, he asked himself, did the British accent come from? Persico's wife, Oboyski was well aware, was a blond. But now he had a blond whose English was inflected. He asked how old the man's daughter was. A young girl, he was told. And that threw him even more. Persico's daughter was in her mid-thirties.

"Did she live with them?"

"No, she would just come and visit."

And that was it.

"I was kind of down, I'll tell you right now. I was depressed that whole weekend. I wasn't sure it was him. But even if it was, I didn't have a hell of a lot more to go on."

Oboyski had *nothing* to go on. Deputies, having scoured the local post office files, had already come up empty. Neither Longo nor Perri had received mail at the house, let alone left a forwarding address.

What really bothered Oboyski was the I.D.

"The old woman, when she looked at the bust photos, that's what hit me in the stomach, that didn't make me feel good, because she didn't pick out the bust photos, she picked out the old photo, the one taken in 1980."

Persico, an alcoholic, who had allegedly suffered a heart attack, a man on the run for five years, should have looked older, more haggard.

"I sent everyone out again."

Oboyski instructed his fellow deputies to search the post office records for the names of any and all people who had received mail at the address during the time Persico had lived there.

And then it happened.

"We come up with two names."

Both of the names belonged to women. One, a Veronica Rees, had given as a change of address a box number at the same post office, then canceled it. The address she had given when she subscribed to the P.O. box was fictitious.

On Monday, the 9th, the task force started looking for the women.

"Teddy [Brooklyn deputy Ted Gloo] comes up with a phone number on Veronica Rees. In Hartford. Roderick comes up with the DMV information on both women. Sure enough, they're a mother and daughter."

The records search showed that the addresses given by Rees's daughter for her driver's license, her automobile registration, and her telephone were all the same. Veronica Rees, herself, tall, trim, forty-two years old, had not been so straightforward.

"The daughter has everything going to one address. The mother has everything scattered—the car one place, the driver's license another, the phone still another. What do we go for? The phone, it has to be the most current."

The telephone was billed to a ground-floor garden apartment in a thirty-nine-unit, red brick building at 5 Highland Street, West Hartford.

"I gave Artie and his partner the album and sent them out. Joey and his partner [Brooklyn deputy Joey Orlando and District of Idaho deputy David Meyer] had to go get a tire changed. Teddy Gloo had to head back to Brooklyn; he was on his way to Washington to go through some passports. We were yanking passports under the names Longo and Perri. So I was left there with Janet, we were by the phone, I was in touch with Mike."

Mike Pizzi had made the decision to keep headquarters twenty-four hours behind. He had asked Chad Allan merely to be within reach within a reasonable amount of time. On Friday the 6th, after the task force had made the decision to show the photo spread for the first time, Pizzi had called Allan in Washington and said:

"I want to know where you're going to be twenty-four hours a day starting now."

"Before everyone went out," Oboyski recalls, "Artie turned to me and said, 'I got a good feeling about this.' I said, 'So do I. I like this.'"

Art Roderick, at 5 Highland Street, interviewed the building's superintendent. Roderick asked her who lived in the apartment.

"Well there was a woman living there," she said, "but she's gone."

The woman, the superintendent acknowledged, spoke with a British accent.

Roderick asked, "Who's living there now?"

"Just the guy's living there now."

"Who?"

"Al."

Roderick showed her the photo spread.

"That's Al," she said.

"Which one?"

"He looks like all of them."

Roderick called Oboyski at the command post.

"I think we got him," he told Oboyski.

"What have you got?"

"The name Al . . . the discoloration on the lip . . . the blond . . ."

"What does she think about the bust?"

"She says he looks like all of them."

"Sit tight."

The building superintendent had told Roderick that, though Al had been sick and had not gone out in a week, it was normal for somebody to pick him up in the evening and take him to dinner.

"If somebody picks him up," Oboyski told Roderick, "they're going to bring him home. Don't worry about it. Don't jump the gun."

Oboyski called Pizzi in New York.

"Chief, I think we got him."

Pizzi's reaction was apparent to no one, least of all Oboyski.

"I was so fucking pumped up I couldn't see straight," he would say later.

To Oboyski, he said, "What are you going to do?"

"We're going to go out and arrest him."

"What about surveillance?"

"Screw surveillance. I'm tired of surveillance. I'm tired of mincing around. We're going to go out and collar this guy."

"Call me immediately."

Oboyski's plan was to try a scam telephone call, to make sure the man identified as Al was at home.

"I'm not going to knock the door down," he would later explain, "because if he's not there, then we blew it. That's why I didn't want Artie to make a move. Slow. We had been so slow and methodical up to that point, we had to hold back."

"When he called me," Pizzi remembers, "I said, Victor, you're on the scene. If I could fly there right now . . . I'm going to try and get a helicopter, I'll fly there . . ."

But Mike Pizzi says he knew better than to try to make tactical decisions from New York:

"You have to balls it out and make the decision on the scene."

It was Oboyski's call from that point forward.

"Years and years and years of searching for this guy," Oboyski says, "and now: Here we go."

Pizzi, finding it difficult to control himself, called Chad Allan in Washington.

"I said, now I want to know where you're going to be *all* the time. I told him, we're going to break this thing. And he started laughing. After seven years of telling him you're going to get a guy. . . . He says, all right, I'm here, and I'm not moving."

Oboyski did not want to make his move without his other team.

"Now, I sit there and I'm waiting for the other two guys to show up. I'm trying to get them on the air. I can't get them on the air. Teddy's on his way back to New York, he hears me on the air, he hears me trying to get Joey Orlando and his partner, but he doesn't know why. I call up the Texaco station they're at. They're not there. I say, where are these guys? I'm pacing back and forth in the room now. I got Persico sitting in the apartment, I got Artie with this woman saying 'He looks like all of them,' I want the other team, I don't want to go there without the other team."

When Orlando and Meyer showed up, Oboyski split up the teams. He put Orlando with Janet Doyle, took David Meyer in his car, and told Roderick over the radio to meet him behind the apartment complex. He did not want to risk being seen rolling up in front of the building. He had Orlando pull up and park on the street and sit there with his arm around Doyle; acting as an innocent couple, the two deputies watched the apartment window. He had Roderick take him to the superintendent.

"Look again," he said, and opened up the photo spread.

"That's Al," she said again. "He looks like all of them."

That she had identified the bust, where the Bloomfield woman had not, suggested to Oboyski that Persico had deteriorated significantly in a matter of two years. He asked her if she thought he would be home. She said that he should be, explaining again that he had been sick all week.

"The super had no idea who he was," Oboyski says. "All she knew was she had a whole bunch of deputy marshals there who were coming out of their skin. We were trying to act as calm as possible. But this is November 9th. This thing's going to end Thanksgiving. We were coming to the end of the road, as far as I was concerned."

Oboyski, discovering that workmen had been in the apartment the previous week to repair the bathroom ceiling, instructed the superintendent to call the apartment and get the man she knew as Al on the phone, to ask him if it were okay if the workmen returned to do some touch-up. He sent Roderick and Michael downstairs to stand outside the apartment door with their radios turned low.

The superintendent made the call.

Alphonse Persico answered the phone.

"When I heard that Brooklyn accent," Victor Oboyski says in his own, "I knew it was him."

"Yeah, no problem," had come the reply to the superintendent's request. "It's okay, don't worry about it."

"Right away I get Artie. I give him the word. Joey, outside, picks it up on the radio, they get out of the car. We're all going in together. And we want to get in quick."

At 5 P.M., with a passkey provided by the superintendent, the task force, guns drawn, entered the Highland Street apartment.

"I put the key in the door, turn it, boom, I give it a knock, the door swings open. . . . He's standing in the kitchen."

Alphonse Persico, underweight and old beyond his years, a victim of heart disease and cirrhosis of the liver, wearing a

T-shirt and house slippers, his trousers unbuttoned, $1,000 in his pocket, was standing over the stove with a wooden spoon in his hand, stirring a marinara sauce he had prepared that day and was about to serve himself for dinner. The table was set for one.

"Hey, Al, how ya doin'?"

"Who are you?"

"We're with the U.S. marshals, Al, you're under arrest."

"Okay, anything you say, just tell me what you want me to do, no problem," he said.

Oboyski told him to put down the spoon.

When in 1981 Christopher Boyce was arrested, in the city of Port Angeles, Washington, he was parked at a drive-in restaurant, enjoying a late evening meal at the Port Angeles Pit Stop. And it was Deputy U.S. Marshal Dave Neff, through the open window of an Oldsmobile, who shouted the memorable command against which all others would thenceforth be measured. His finger on the trigger of a pistol trained on Christopher Boyce's left ear, Dave Neff barked out: "Drop the hamburger."

"I was just so happy to see him," Oboyski says of Alphonse Persico.

Persico put down the spoon. They cuffed the mobster, frisked him, walked him, and sat him down in a chair.

"Joey, read him his rights."

Persico was alone in the apartment. One team had quickly swept through, careful not to disturb any fingerprint evidence that might be used in a prosecution for harboring; the racketeer, on the run for over seven years, had not managed to remain free on his own. In the pocket of a jacket hanging near the door deputies found an additional $6,000.

"The woman was gone. He beat her up. There was broken furniture and everything in the apartment. She was gone, he was living alone."

Using a handkerchief, Oboyski picked up the telephone. He dialed New York, said:

"Give me the chief."

When the phone in Mike Pizzi's office rang, Pizzi was standing about four feet away. Dave O'Flaherty had been trying to get him a helicopter. Pizzi had tried, but had been unable, to sit. He was having trouble controlling himself. O'Flaherty handed Pizzi the receiver. Pizzi took it and immediately spoke:

"Tell me something good."

And Oboyski spoke the words his chief had been waiting over seven years to hear.

"We just put the irons on him," Oboyski reported. "Alphonse Carmine Persico is in custody."

Oboyski in Connecticut could hear the pandemonium in the office as the news was passed around.

Pizzi says: "I wanted to take my gun out and fire a shot into the ceiling."

11

True Detective

"Are you sure?" Chad Allan said.

"Do you have a fucking bottle of whiskey?"

"Yeah."

"Well start drinking it, 'cause he's in," Mike Pizzi said.

He was Alphonse Persico, and he was seated, cuffed, in the back of Victor Oboyski's rental car, on his way to the lockup in Hartford. Oboyski, who was known on occasion to spell his name with an O-apostrophe to call attention to the Irish in him—he was a New York cop, after all—and who had been blessed with what was known on his mother's side of the family, rather charmingly, as "the gift of gab," had engaged the killer in casual conversation.

"Allie, did you ever think we'd get you?"

"I figured you'd get me someday," Persico replied politely. "I figured somebody would have to drop a dime."

Oboyski, somewhat frightfully, spun around in the front passenger seat and fixed the gangster with a glare:

"If you knew what we went through to get you, you wouldn't believe it!" Oboyski said. "I wish somebody *had* dropped a dime, because I'm sick of Connecticut. Probably the only good food in the whole state is in your kitchen right now."

"The sauce is still there," Persico told him. "You want to go back, you can help yourself."

Persico had calmed down quickly in the aftermath of his arrest. His body language, almost immediately, had begun to feature a special vocabulary. Deputies knew it well. Having spent seventeen years on the inside, Persico had become, in Mike Pizzi's estimation, firmly and quite understandably institutionalized.

"These are not people who give you trouble. These are not people who smart-ass or smart-talk you. This was a fairly likable guy. He was *always* a gentleman. Very polite. The Persicos, from our perspective, were always likable people, always joking, always pleasant. I don't know how they would be from the other side—you're a storekeeper and you're being made to pay them off—but always in a pleasant frame of mind, always pleasant speaking. All of the heat that we took trying to get him, of course, made us more aggravated. But it was never out of an intense dislike, like [one might feel for] a Leacock, that we went after this guy. We dealt with this case professionally and we dealt with it ethically. We didn't use the old tactics of breaking the family's balls, of going there on the holidays, unless we had a reason to believe he was there. We felt good about the way we conducted ourselves. Right through the investigation."

Persico's gentlemanly conduct, sincere as it may have been, had not been enough to forestall his investigation by West Hartford police chief Francis Reynolds, who had been introduced to Persico, as Longo, by an innocent Veronica Rees, a respected businesswoman in the community with whom Reynolds had enjoyed a longtime acquaintance. Chief Reynolds, upon meeting Longo, for reasons he cannot articulate, had experienced a subtle hammering of the street cop in his blood, and as a result had instructed subordinates to ask the FBI to check him out. The FBI had reported back that the putative Longo was clean. Reynolds, unsatisfied, would go as far on one occasion as to lift a cocktail glass from Longo's table in a local restaurant. He had been in the process of having the prints run when deputies went through Persico's door.

On the afternoon of Persico's arrest, the Service's enforcement chief, Louis McKinney, telephoned his counterpart in the FBI.

"We're taking Persico off the 15 Most Wanted list," he said.

"That's good," came the agent's reply, "because he's dead, and it doesn't pay to have him on there so long."

"No, no, no," McKinney responded. "We're taking him off because he's in custody."

"Shit was really flying," Mike Pizzi would later report. "There was no way to deal with them on this case. All the crazy stories you heard throughout the years, about how they could be so damn uncooperative . . . it was true in this case. It was disgusting. They never shared anything with us."

For Mike Pizzi, the obligatory FBI beef—one is the same as another and they are as predictable as the weather—is just one more entry in the daily log. (If anything perplexes him, it is where the FBI comes by all the spare time required to file official grievances.) Pizzi, as a district chief, has more important things to worry about. In the districts, according to Duke Smith, priorities tend to set themselves: assignments frequently unfold there like triage in the emergency room at Bellevue and, even on a slow day, the chief deputy may as well be wearing a lab coat.

Says Smith, "You might get a phone call that says, 'Hey, we got a collateral lead for you, we've got a top-fifteen guy, we think, in a hotel down the street.' And you've got five trials you're trying to work, and you've got to haul five prisoners to the West Coast, and two of your guys are off on special assignment working witness security, and three guys are ducking out the door during lunchtime trying to catch a fugitive and. . . . 'Wait. Time out. We've got to go over here and do this.' Or you'll get this seizure, you have to go up and arrest a boat. You'll get a court order . . . a 3,000-megaton ship with Norwegian registration is leaving the harbor . . . it just left and you got a seizure order. You jump down and get the Coast Guard, they have you fly out in a helicopter, you land on the deck—maybe you take a boat—and say, 'Captain, the ship's mine. Take her back.' . . . You never know what you're going to have to do."

Smith sees the deputy marshal, in the diversity of his responsibilities, as the glue that holds the criminal justice system together.

"If all the judges didn't come to work tomorrow, the system would still function. Prisoners would still get transported, people would get arrested. If the U.S. attorneys didn't show up tomorrow, some cases wouldn't get prosecuted; if the FBI agents didn't show up, the investigations wouldn't go on. But if all the marshals in the country had a blue sick day tomorrow, the whole system would shut down. Because we're the hub of all this activity. And it stretches you thin. You show up every day, and you don't know what the hell you're going to do next."

There is a respectable body of American opinion that adheres to the proposition that the fast alchemy of federal government, that venerable experiment to the somewhat orderly conduct of which the Marshals Service is dedicated, is a 200-year-old monstrosity, an overcooked hypothesis that never should have been let out of the laboratory. And such a reckoning, one is obliged to admit, is not without its logical constants. The federal government, face it, rarely serves as anything like your pal. In the absence of such assignments as, say, the avenging of Pearl Harbor, or the taking of miserable dudes like Garnett Leacock off the street, government, in general, as any taxpaying citizen will tell you, is there chiefly to make your life hell. The argument can be made that, when it works at all, government is inefficient. And if you do not think that is true of the criminal justice system, in particular, you need only go so far as to debrief the chronic felon. He will tell you, unequivocally, that the arithmetic is very much on his side. While the feds over the years have proved adept at terrifying the innocent, more stunning is their inadequacy to the task of bringing the guilty to justice.

It is not that they do not try.

"We got about six hundred warrants on file," in the Southern District of New York alone, Frank Devlin volunteers, "six hundred bad guys out there, wanted by us. We get forty in a month, new ones, on top of that. And we make about forty arrests a month. We're never going to catch up."

It is with such staggering numbers as these that the Marshals Service's FIST operations were specifically designed to deal.

FIST.

Ask Duke Smith:

"In government, you can't have anything successful unless you have an acronym."

An acronym is more than a series of letters, an acronym is a word, and by definition must be pronounced as such to qualify for the job. FBI is not an acronym, for example. Nor is ATF. Those are abbreviations. BOP, a legitimate word in its own right and easily pronounceable as one, strictly speaking is not an acronym. It does not enjoy the currency to qualify, not among deputy marshals, anyway. Rarely is the Bureau of Prisons referred to by anyone in the Service as "bop." Deputies call it "the B.O.P."

Acronyms as employed by the federal government fall into two general categories, the incidental and the contrived. To find an acronym that has come into government use in a wholly incidental fashion, look no further than Glynco, Georgia, and the Federal Law Enforcement Training Center there. Deputy marshals call the academy "fletsy." Some feds refer to it as "flettick." The name of the former naval air station on which the academy is situated is, itself, an acronym, and a more natural one—Glynco is a contraction of Glynn County, an acronym formed by combining not simply the initial letters but larger parts of the relevant words, the way *radio detection and ranging*, betimes, coughed up the insuppressible *radar*.

Only the federal government could find a word in an abbreviation like FLETC, yet in its doing so there is a demonstrable innocence. The name, after all, preceded the acronym. More symptomatic of the government's infatuation with acronyms are those that are fully contrived. These are words that so severely convolve the language as to render the expressions behind them utterly stupefying, and there is nothing innocent about their invention.

Probably the most tortured expression recently to enter what we like to think of as English is that which underlies the word *RICO*. The federal RICO statutes, as most Americans know, are those under which any citizen, no matter what his field of endeavor, may be prosecuted as a gangster. One look at what RICO stands for and it is clear that the acronym came first. That most Americans cannot tell you what it stands for, or, without a little practice, repeat the expression once they are told, speaks to the sinister nature of the word.

RICO stands for Racketeer Influenced Corrupt Organizations. Try it. Even if you put a hyphen where one belongs, between the first and second words, and insert the necessary comma between the second and third—there is adjectival purpose at work here, to be sure—the syntax is bewildering, so sophisticated as to find parallels only in formal Latin grammar, and only loosely at that, in certain adverbial constructions like, maybe, the ablative absolute.

This contorted expression exists only because the word *RICO* has to stand for something. Initially targeted against the Italian rackets—the Outfit, the Mob, the Syndicate, the Mafia, La Cosa Nostra—the RICO statutes were named in satisfaction of the acronym itself, which was engineered to bear the colorful, rather Hollywood freight of what is in essence an ethnic slur. The word *FIST*, absent the racism, came about in much the same way. Designed to strike a blow against those fugitives from justice whose resident population in the United States of America on any given day is just about half that of the state of Montana, the Special Enforcement Operations conducted by the Marshals Service under the acronym FIST might just as well have been conducted under, say, STATS, or PUBLICITY, for all the difference it makes; the Service would just as easily have conjured an expression to back the word up, one easily as mellifluous as Fugitive Investigative Strike Team.

(There is more than one way to clear a warrant. A significant collateral benefit of the operations was represented by those warrants "administratively cleared," those for fugitives whose cases were nol-prossed, who were found to be deceased, already incarcerated, arrested on other warrants or in other jurisdictions, or who were "not amenable to prosecution for other reasons." The Marshals Service now purges files on a regular basis in an ongoing reduction of the warrant backlog.)

Of prime importance in the neology of FIST was that the operations sell on page one. And the Marshals Service, to that end, etched its FIST operations with a cachet that made them irresistible to newsmen. Mike Pizzi and deputies like him, with the resources of Washington behind them, took a traditionally ugly and very dangerous business and opened it up like a three-ring circus; they took a time-honored theme, the classic criminal manhunt, and played it like rock and roll.

Says Pizzi, "All of us who work fugitive cases know how dangerous it is to have to go into somebody's house, especially by force. It's a very, very difficult thing. You never know what you're going to experience. It's a very emotional time, it's very upsetting, and sometimes people react in such a way that you have to use more force than you want to. It's dangerous and it's sometimes heart-wrenching, because there are kids in the house, and nobody wants to see Daddy or Mommy leaving in handcuffs. You try to avoid that when you can, if at all possible."

"Going in with guns out, throwing handcuffs on the father, dragging him out—that's going to terrorize a child, you can't do that," agrees Southern District warrants chief Frank Devlin. "When we know there are kids around, we don't take guns out. Also, a bullet would go right through the walls of one of those [tenement] apartments."

"Going into somebody's home," Pizzi says, "is probably the least desirable way to make an arrest, less even than a felony car stop, which is a very dangerous thing to do. You want as many of the odds in your favor as possible. And there comes the concept of a sting operation. It's a relatively safe, inexpensive way to arrest people."

The Atlantic City Bus Tour engineered by Mike Pizzi in the summer of 1985, which netted more felons than had ever been taken down in any single operation of its kind, was typical of the sting operations routinely conducted by the Marshals Service. It came at the culmination of a FIST operation run out of the Eastern District of New York with the blessing but not the participation of Washington. The mini-FIST, as such regional operations had come to be called, had been instigated by Pizzi himself, and over the course of that spring had resulted in the arrest by his deputies and officers of the New York City Police Department of over 300 fugitives through conventional, investigative means—working informants, following leads, breaking down doors, good old-fashioned police work.

In the sting itself, which was conducted in cooperation with the NYPD's Brooklyn Warrants Squad, headed by Lieutenant John Incontrera, and in which state and local fugitives were also targeted, Pizzi would oversee the arrest of twenty-one fugitives —sixteen men, five women—in a single day, in a space of four hours, in fact. The combined task force would arrest only felons, people wanted for assault, armed robbery, armed burglary, felony narcotics violations, and other serious offenses; it would do so at a quarter of the cost of the typical arrest; and it would do so without recourse to the unpredictable use of a lot of muscle.

The heavy lifting came in the creation of the scam.

"There are two post offices," Pizzi explains. "There's the regular United States Post Office and there's an underground post office." Going through the first, he says, an investigator gains access to the second. "Generally speaking, if you want to get a piece of mail to somebody, by sending to the last-known or best address you will get the mail to the person you want to get it to."

On this assumption, a thousand fugitives were notified by mail that they had won a free trip to the Sands Hotel and Casino in Atlantic City, New Jersey, along with $100 in bonus money, $50 of it in cash. The one-page circular, designed, printed, and mailed by the task force, contained a telephone number at which the winners were to respond to a Miss Bridewell, employed by a fictitious tour company, who would schedule appointments for them to claim their prizes.

"We anticipated that out of the thousand we would get about 2 percent. If our estimates were correct, based on our past experiences, we would manage to arrest about twenty people. But the response was kind of overwhelming. We had maybe sixty or seventy respond."

Miss Bridewell, named, in Pizzi's characteristically mischievous fashion, for the sixteenth-century City of London house of correction and portrayed by secretary Frances Nespoli—at the scene of the bust the role was essayed by that extraordinary leading lady of the American stage, the irrepressible Gerri Doody—scheduled appointments for the morning of July 20, bus departures beginning at eight from Hansen Place in downtown Brooklyn.

"We tried to stagger the appointments," Pizzi says. "We tried to limit it, as best we could, to what at the time we thought might be as many as six or seven an hour. In the end we came up with exactly what we had originally estimated, the original 2 percent, because out of the sixty-five or so responses, a lot were from people other than those we wanted—from relatives and immediate-family members, the wrong person in any event."

Each winner was assigned a lucky number. It was derived from the number of the actual file folder in which the fugitive's warrant was kept. A registration table was set up on Hansen Place, at which Gerri Doody, wearing a hidden transmitter, would greet the individual respondents and read the lucky numbers aloud. Task-force members aboard the tour bus, parked half a block away, receiving the transmission, would pull the corresponding folders and, training binoculars on the respondents through the blacked-out glass of the rear window, would I.D. each against the mug shot of the fugitive sought. Impostors were turned away, either at the point of arrival itself, or, if closer observation were required, as they were walked from there to the door of the bus.

"There were six or seven people on the bus anticipating the

fugitive's getting on. One deputy acted as the driver. The final escort, standing outside the doorway [of the bus], was a New York City cop."

Walking fugitives between the registration table and the bus was Dave O'Flaherty. Pizzi, Vic Oboyski, and deputy Bob Meltzer posed as a Con Edison crew working on a manhole nearby. There was an NYPD cop standing in a flower shop across the street; one, posing as a tourist, standing at the entrance to the Long Island Rail Road station, not far away; two more, dressed as telephone repairmen, working on a booth at the far corner of the block. In addition to all the pedestrian heat, there were two chase cars on the scene. In all, there were probably forty cops assigned to the operation.

The location had been selected for a reason.

"It's a very popular area, and it's kind of a busy area. And we selected it on purpose. When you are in a busy area, there are lots of invisible people. The setup was perfect. Hansen Place in Brooklyn, under the big clock that you see there . . ."

The big clock Pizzi refers to is the clock on Brooklyn's landmark Williamsburgh Savings Bank building. A further advantage to the location, he notes, was its access to a variety of public transportation.

Of those clever fugitives who cased the setup before approaching the registration table, only to flee because they grew suspicious, three were apprehended by one or another of the teams working surveillance. The bright green fliers the fugitives carried worked to give them away.

For added authenticity, each fugitive was invited to bring a companion along on the tour, a wife, husband, girlfriend, or boyfriend, as the case might be. That companion, for obvious reasons, had to be admitted to the bus with the fugitive.

"We would have them sit down, keep them under observation until we rendered the fugitive safe, and then we'd escort them off the bus and out of the area. The people who asked for a lift, we would put them in a car and take them to the nearest subway station or bus. The people who refused a lift, we asked them to walk in the opposite direction, away from the registration table. Some people were alerting others, and that may have caused us some problems. We may have wound up with more than twenty-one."

One respondent, who had been turned away, was discovered

on a subway platform not far away, alerting the general public to what he had determined was a bogus bus tour. He was arrested. Those people actually admitted to the bus, innocent companions of the fugitives, more typically expressed absolute shock. More than one was led away staggering.

As the fugitive was admitted to the bus, he or she was greeted with a handshake by its driver, deputy Tony McHale. McHale's grip was unusually firm. Members of the task force, weapons drawn, immediately immobilized the fugitive—grabbed him, cuffed him, searched him, and sat him down—and the felon was under arrest before he knew what hit him.

The entire operation was recorded on videotape, the fugitives, only too happy to be interviewed for what they were told was a promotional video, volunteering endorsements of Gem Tours, the nonexistent company under whose name the task force was operating, smiling and delivering themselves of accolades as they were ushered onto the bus. In the midst of all the histrionics—O'Flaherty, in his green Gem Tours T-shirt, really threw himself into his role as on-camera master of ceremonies—Pizzi's greatest difficulty was in keeping the task force cautious. The business at hand, he knew well, was no joke, it was fraught with potential danger. Criminals to begin with, many of the fugitives, as it happened, were seriously shaken by their arrests and, had members of the task force not been alert, they or innocent bystanders might very easily have been hurt.

The bus, making periodic trips to a prison van parked about ten blocks away, dropped fugitives off in groups of five or six, returning each time to Hansen Place to welcome a new handful of suckers. One late arrival, eager to catch the bus as it was pulling away for the last time, came running alongside, waving his flier, pleading to be let aboard. McHale, at the wheel, pulled the bus to a stop, opened the door, reached out a helping hand, and hauled the man inside. When six unpleasant passengers instantly put guns in his face, the prizewinner wet his pants.

The most violent confrontation of the day was with one of the many impostors who showed up. Looking forward to a free day at the gaming tables, he was being held at the door of the bus for more accurate identification when the city cop holding him there noticed a gun. Catching the prearranged signal, several deputies jumped the professed fugitive, threw him to the ground, and disarmed him. It was the only firearm recovered that day. Inevitably, it was returned. The man carrying it was in fact a corrections officer, a guard at Rikers Island, who, having intercepted the mail of the felon he was impersonating, had figured he was entitled to a trip.

Five months later, in Washington, D.C., a similar operation was run out of headquarters. Conceived by District of Columbia chief deputy Toby Roche, orchestrated by the Enforcement Division, and overseen by Bob Leschorn, the sting drew national attention. Three thousand fugitives were notified by mail that they had won free tickets to a Washington Redskins–Cincinnati Bengals football game as well as the chance at a grand prize, an all-expenses-paid trip to the upcoming Super Bowl in New Orleans. Winners were invited to collect their tickets at a "free brunch" to be held at the city's convention center on the morning of December 15. In the midst of the festivities, a total of 166 officers, drawn from the Marshals Service and the city's Metropolitan Police Department—some dressed as ushers, custodial personnel, and caterers; one in phony buckskin and a ceremonial headdress; another, as mascot, costumed as an oversized chicken; and those in black tie posing as employees of the fictitious sponsor of the event, Flagship International Sports Television (FIST) Inc.—arrested 96 fugitives *en masse*. In terms of sheer numbers, the sting was unsurpassed.

Among the differences between the Brooklyn sting and that conducted by headquarters was the participation in the latter of the Service's Special Operations Group.

"We handle our own muscle," Mike Pizzi says of the Eastern District, relative to the use of SOG, and he is content, it seems, to leave it at that.

Ralph Burnside explains it differently.

"If SOG were assigned to Brooklyn, the chief would have them working down in the pen, guarding prisoners . . . [just to] keep them out of everybody's way."

Mike Pizzi, clearly not moved to infatuation with SOG, is not so ready to dismiss the group out of hand—or to do so on the record, at any rate—but he does acknowledge the existence of an understanding.

"We don't need 'em," he asserts, and admits that "headquarters knows better than to ask."

It is unlikely that SOG deputies would be utilized by any of the district chiefs to effect arrests in an operation orchestrated along the lines of the Brooklyn bus-tour scam; the Flagship sting, by contrast, was choreographed in such a way as to make necessary the collar of all ninety-six fugitives at once. Where SOG's absence is notable in the Eastern District is on large-scale seizures and fugitive sweeps, on the more-than-occasional WITSEC detail, and on numerous high-threat prosecutions, those operations that would invite a tactical presence almost anywhere else in the country.

"We handle our own details, our own problems," says Pizzi, pointing out, with reference to the trial of the United Freedom Front, for example, that "we had plenty of muscle on the street every time we moved them."

According to Ralph Burnside, the scarcity of SOG details in Brooklyn is attributable to more than an understandable aversion on Pizzi's part to the brandishing of submachine guns on the pedestrian-choked streets of New York; it speaks to a fundamental inconsistency in the operational styles of the Brooklyn chief and the Service's paramilitary wing. SOG, in the words of its commander, John Haynes, takes its strength from "regimentation and discipline . . . willing obedience to command," while Pizzi, according to Burnside, "encourages individualism. There is no mold to fit in Brooklyn, you are encouraged to be your own best self."

Pizzi, who underwent SOG training in 1972, says that "a lot of good guys didn't make it," and admits that he "got a bad taste for it" back then (Pizzi was asked to leave on the day before graduation), but his stance, as a chief, on the subject certainly takes reinforcement from the fact that a lot of good men and women do not make it through SOG training now. One of those who did not complete training is Ralph Burnside, and Pizzi's avowed position on the matter of SOG assignments in his district is his way of making people like Burnside understand that to do so is no measure of a deputy's value.

Organized under then-director Wayne B. Colburn in 1971, the Special Operations Group today conducts its four-week training on the 15,000 acres of Camp Beauregard, a National Guard installation situated on the Red River outside Pineville, Louisiana. There, a permanent staff of thirteen answers to SOG commander John Haynes, who reports through a chief in Washington to the

Associate Director for Operations. Of the thirteen staff members, three are civilians, their duties solely clerical. The other ten are deputy marshals, and when they are not acting as instructors, they serve as the group's first-response team, the only deputies in the Marshals Service who work SOG missions exclusively.

"When there are no classes," Haynes says, "they're making arrests."

In addition to training its own deputies, the Special Operations Group regularly offers training to the police organizations of foreign governments. Under Marshals Service contract with the State Department, SOG has provided advanced instruction in counterinsurgency, hostage negotiations, fugitive tracking, interrogation, officer survival, personal security, and judicial security to police from Mexico, Colombia, Bolivia, Ecuador, Honduras, Costa Rica, Czechoslovakia, Poland, Hungary, Italy, Greece, Turkey, and the Philippines. The program conducted at Camp Beauregard is one of several sponsored by State's Anti-Terrorism Assistance Division.

A tool available to each of the several Marshals Service divisions, the Special Operations Group takes its manpower from some 125 SOG-qualified personnel dispersed throughout the rank-and-file, working deputies called as needed from districts around the country from what Haynes refers to as their "collateral duties," that is, their district assignments—serving process, securing the courts, working warrants, conducting seizures—which are in fact their principal duties, answerable as they are, as all deputies are, to marshals and district chiefs, SOG being the collateral mission.

SOG offers no special pay or rewards and is strictly volunteer. That 40 percent of those who occupy positions of leadership in the Service—inspectors, supervisors, chiefs, etc.—have passed through Special Operations speaks both to the cachet of having belonged and to the raw ambition inherent in those who apply.

SOG training by bureaucratic design, similar to such programs as Airborne and Ranger training, through which the U.S. Army puts many of its career people, by improving skills and encouraging leadership, contributes a leavening to the overall professionalism of the agency.

Training, Haynes argues, is accessible to every deputy in the Service.

"The door," he says, "is open to everyone. We're not elitist.

The standards are not that tough. They're fair. We don't ever want to be thought of as something everybody can't belong to."

The door may be open to everyone, but swings both ways, and fast. Out of an average-sized class of about sixty, half can be expected to wash out.

"We don't give a written test, they're tested every day, every hour, mentally and physically. A written test don't mean shit. I want to see you do what you got to do."

What you have got to do first, to be accepted for instruction, is shoot 70 percent with a pistol on the Marshals Service course of fire. That is *before* you apply. A current firearms qualification sheet—a deputy's "333"—must be presented upon application. You must requalify at Beauregard within three days of your arrival. To graduate, you must qualify on the more difficult SOG course of fire, you must qualify at 90 percent, 270 out of 300, and you must qualify at that level on every weapon SOG uses. On top of which you must survive a month of rigorous paramilitary field training, conducted in a disciplinary atmosphere similar to that of Marine Corps boot camp—drill and command, marching to chow, regular inspections, punitive push-ups, routine verbal assault, full Parris Island.

The training itself is in traditional SWAT, special weapons and tactics; deputies undergo exercises in tactical property entry, wilderness survival, hand-to-hand combat, they are trained in rappeling—required to free-rappel from the skids of helicopters coming in at ninety feet—they are put through combat trials and officer survival drills under stress conditions undreamed of even in the Maze at Glynco, and, outside WITSEC, they are the only Marshals Service personnel to qualify on automatic weapons.

"Pistol for us is a secondary weapon," says Haynes. "We go operational, a deputy's going to have shotgun or a rifle or a machine gun in his hands . . . Colt SMG, an MP5 . . . WITSEC uses the Uzi. SOG uses counter-sniper weapons that the Marshals Service [otherwise] doesn't use, a .308 or .30-06 scoped rifle. Right now we use the [.223-caliber Ruger] Mini 14 as our long gun."

But proficiency with all weapons, including a sidearm, is that without which there is no assignment.

"You have to shoot 90 percent or you don't go on the mission."

SOG deputies are expected to maintain the shooting standard between details.

"We tell them right from the get-go, this is not a military unit. We are first and foremost civilian police officers. Tactics is tactics, and it comes from the military. We study tactics from a military standpoint. We call them a task force instead of a platoon. We call them a team instead of a squad . . ."

Special Operations training, though it once did, no longer incorporates paratroop jump school.

"The basic philosophy is to locate, isolate, contain, and control. The LICC principle. Making an entry is the last thing you want to do. Make 'em come out, that's their turf in there. If you locate 'em, isolate 'em, contain 'em, and control 'em, you only got three things they can do. Surrender, fight, or flee. That's the only three options any human being's got in any situation. But once we contain you, you can't get away; once you see you're outnumbered, you don't want to fight. That only leaves you the option of surrendering. And that's the theory we work under in the Marshals Service."

It is the theory, in fact, under which successful SWAT teams everywhere operate. Haynes calls it "team-concept firepower," and it is the civilian variation on the theme of military fire control. But where the latter is orchestrated to inflict casualties, the former is arrayed to discourage them. A show of force, as Haynes points out, is a tactic itself, and the measure of any SWAT team's success is its ability to *neutralize* confrontation. More often than not such response teams bring suspects in alive. On the nation's better police forces, such work is open only to professionals, cowboys need not apply. In contradistinction to their portrayal in the various popular-entertainment media, few are those SWAT team engagements that actually end in fatality, and almost never do they result in the carnage with which they are so frequently associated. By the very nature of their training, and given the speed and efficiency with which they operate, successful police paramilitary units will characteristically complete their missions without ever firing a shot.

John Haynes, recruited by the Marshals Service in 1971 after eleven and a half years in the Marine Corps, first went on the job in his native Oklahoma. A graduate of the SOG class of 1972, he was made an instructor shortly thereafter. He has been with SOG ever since. He became the unit's commander in 1986 at the age of forty-three, and hopes, he says, to be the first deputy U.S. marshal to retire out of Special Operations.

His brown hair and mustache going to gray, the trim Haynes, pushing fifty, takes justifiable pride in his ability to keep up with his recruits. As with any able leader, few are those things that he asks them to do that he is not willing to do himself. But, while allowing that there is no age limit on admittance to SOG training, he does acknowledge the existence of certain physical parameters by which enthusiasm, even his own, is inevitably constrained.

In the shadow of the school's rappeling tower, eyeing a water moccasin as it courses the bayou, Haynes, around a mouthful of Skoal long-cut—"We all chew tobacco," says his second-in-command Louis Stagg—will grant the power of the simple passage of time:

"You can have all the heart and desire in the world," Haynes reflects, quoting the unit's first commander, William Whitworth, "but if your feet won't carry your ass, you ain't going to make it."

The cottonmouth will vanish, Haynes will smile, and the next day he will be the first man out the door of the helicopter.

SOG, Haynes concedes, has its image problems within the Marshals Service; it was not until 1985 that the unit was truly integrated into the agency.

"It used to be elitist, under Whitworth," Haynes admits. "He wanted it that way. But not anymore. They learned their lesson. [The unit was] looked down upon."

In 1985 SOG went from serving Justice Department political needs to serving Marshals Service operational needs, from reporting to the agency's director to reporting to its associate director, Howard Safir, who felt the unit was underutilized.

"He wanted them to do a lot of the stuff that they're doing now, not just AG [attorney general] stuff," Haynes explains.

SOG today participates regularly in a variety of district operations, backing up local deputies in sensitive prosecutions, high-threat prisoner moves, fugitive operations, and large-scale property seizures, and with the current plethora of major dope trials has become something of a handmaiden to WITSEC.

On WITSEC details, SOG very often works low-profile.

"Most court assignments, SOG wears civvies," Haynes points out. "A response team, hidden in the building, will be wearing black"—what Bud McPherson calls their Ninja outfits, the field gear that became standard SOG issue in 1985—that they might be "recognized as tactical officers" in the event of a confrontation.

Haynes says he seeks diversity in his deputies and grants that he has been fortunate in being able to draw from a large pool of talent and experience.

"Somebody's been an electrician, somebody's been a plumber, somebody's been a truck driver. I've got pilots, I've got ship's pilots, I've got communications specialists from the military, or wherever they were, somebody who did encryption in the military, somebody who did this or did that . . ."

No longer, he notes, does a deputy need a year on the job to apply for Special Operations training.

"I can take them right out of Glynco. Why make them wait?"

And he says he is getting a "new breed" of deputy.

"A lot of them are single. They've gone to college, remained single, and are just coming into the job."

There are character traits that Haynes identifies as typical of the SOG recruit: "You just about have to put a bit in their mouth. You won't see any of these guys backin' up. They're all hard-chargers . . . they're all strong-willed people." And it is instructive to look at those qualities against the backdrop of police work in general. For there is a very good argument to be made for the fact that they are merely an exaggeration of the attributes of the average American cop.

The well-adjusted human, from infancy, is programmed to recoil from danger—to avoid it, and, failing that, to flee. Policemen are programmed by training to run in its direction. Their fitness reports, like those of firemen, reflect their ability and their eagerness to do so. Theirs is a career, characteristically, that thrives on confrontation. And their willingness to initiate it. According to Victor Oboyski, it has always been that way.

". . . a cop banging his nightstick, 'Gimme the corner, gimme the corner!' You have to assert your authority. 'It's *my* corner now.' "

Cops are physical people. The image of the typical officer is that of a man with a gun in his hand. The impression, of course, is a false one; most cops spend their entire careers without ever drawing their weapons. In truth, what street cops, both men and women, spend most of their time doing is fighting. Putting their hands on people. Wrestling, mixing it up, getting in people's faces, throwing their weight around.

"In our profession, you're meeting the worst people, the dregs of society—and you're meeting *good* people at their worst."

People do not call the police when things are going well at home.

Police work is all about muscle, a perpetual ass-kicking contest, and where size and gender offer advantages, they inevitably give way to attitude, to a force of personality not otherwise rewarded. A successful cop is a self-confident cop, a self-confident individual. Everywhere a cop goes, he manifests a sense of turf, his (or her) *own* turf. On the street you learn to read it. Cops wear it like an off-duty uniform. On or off the job, cops are always reading the street, they are the ones making eye contact. Ask any denizen of the urban jungle. Only two kinds of people stare at other people out there: psychotics and police. The day you see a cop backing up is the day he starts looking for work.

Apparent fearlessness in a cop, a display of fearlessness genuine or not, is an instrument of survival.

"Just like an animal can sense fear, you get these street people," says Vic Oboyski, "guys that've been arrested ten, twenty times, you know, for gun collars and what-not, they can sense fear. They can look in your eye, or they can actually *feel* it, like an animal can, they can *tell* you're afraid. Once they know you're afraid, that's it, you're on the defensive."

As a veteran, Vic Oboyski has learned how to turn the authority on quick. With reference to Mike Pizzi's semiannual shenanigans in the classroom down at Glynco, Oboyski is quick to point out:

"If I had Mike pulling that shit with me, I'd crack him. I'd hit him in the head, I'd knock him down. BING. 'Now, what are you gonna do?' If I'm arresting a guy, and the guy starts acting a little funny, he's on the ground, he's going. Before he even gets to, like, 'Oh, excuse me,' BOOM, he's going down. If he acts cool and everything, fine, you know, I'll treat him like a gentleman. But I ain't gonna play with him. Everyone wonders why cops throw guys against the wall. That's the initial I'm-not-gonna-play-with-you routine. You got to take the high ground. You got to be aggressive, right away."

Oboyski's size simply makes it easier for him. But what makes a cop a cop, male or female, is the ability to turn on the aggression convincingly regardless of his or her size. (Women in the Special Operations Group, at least a random sample, actually seem to fall into that category that dress designers call petite.)

"A guy your size handling a guy like me, you got to show me right away that you're not going to take no shit. You got to feel me out. The first time you shove me, push me against the wall, and I don't do anything, well, then you know point-blank you got the high ground. But if I'm going to fight, you might as well get the first push in, get the first shove, and get me off balance. You don't do it to agitate the person . . . but if the guy's going, 'Hey, man, what's the problem,' blah, blah, and he starts all this shuckin' and jivin', well you got to put him down right away."

A cop, making an arrest, wants a suspect in handcuffs before the suspect has time to think. One reason is the gun. The gun belongs to the cop only as long as he or she is at a distance from the offender. Once a cop closes in, the gun belongs to whoever gets his hands on it. When an arrest attempt results in a fight, the cop more often than not is fighting for his life. And that is why such struggles are characteristically so ugly to watch.

Duke Smith says, "I had a rule when I was a cop in Miami. A guy fights me, he goes to the hospital."

"One of those things you always see," says Oboyski, "cops have a guy against the wall . . . 'Face the wall.' The guy's turning around. 'Don't look at me . . . Don't be lookin' at me, man . . . I don't like you lookin' at me . . . Get your face over there, Jack, don't put your face in my face.' You know? You do that to take the high ground. And you don't want him checking you out . . . looking where your gun is, what you're doing, where you're standing. If he can't see you—even though he's got peripheral vision, he can't really tell where you are—he's at a disadvantage. . . . When the chief does his little routine with the kids down there, they're not really sure, you know? You can do that with academy kids. But in the real world he would have got cracked."

Marvin Mack says that after making an entry, a deputy wants to see hands:

"You get some of these guys, they keep moving. 'Hey, don't move. Stay over there, get on the floor, get down.' You got to talk to them with a demanding voice, let them know you're not fucking around . . . you got to be on them, they got to know. These guys are thinking and scheming, and you don't know *what* they got and *where* . . . under a chair, under the seat of a couch, in a corner . . . you want to see hands and you want to get them into cuffs. 'Don't do nothing, you just do what I tell you . . .' "

Coming on strong for a cop is a weapon like any other. Coming on strong at the wrong time, Victor Oboyski acknowledges, can escalate what would otherwise be a relatively peaceful confrontation. Being an effective cop is all about knowing when to turn it on and when *not* to. There are times when, handled properly, everything goes down smoothly, and others when, as one big-city cop puts it, you "have to take control of it and start screaming and motherfucking people."

Times, unfortunately, tend to favor the latter.

"They don't fear cops now," Oboyski says, cruising the mean streets of Brooklyn. "A cop now is just an obstacle. . . . People here don't fear jail. You and I do. They don't."

Retired Customs investigator Bill Hughes waxes almost nostalgic when speaking about the bad guys in whose faces he flashed his badge.

"The game was a lot different then. When the jig was up . . . when you put that government tin on them, they knew you meant business," he says. "The old-timers thought the feds were bulletproof."

Bad guys today, he acknowledges, are far less likely to go quietly and far more likely to go the limit.

"Now, they kill the feds."

"Everybody comes out of Glynco with a three-fifty-seven. I give them another one," John Haynes says. "A four-inch sidearm. All my people carry a four-inch weapon, a Smith and Wesson six-forty-five, a forty-five-caliber weapon. Backin' up FIST operations, we were getting real heavy into making entries, and I wanted something heavier. I gave 'em forty-fives."

As a secondary weapon.

What John Haynes refers to as "making entries" is about as rough as it gets for cops.

Car stops can be dangerous, domestic-disturbance calls are a genuine nightmare—one of those comes over the radio and the rosary beads always come out—but for sheer balls-to-the-wall behavior, nothing is more unnatural than to walk up to a door, knowing nothing about what is behind it, and to start swinging at it with a sledgehammer.

Outside the Marshals Service, the real thrill-seekers work narcotics.

"Drugs and guns, guns and drugs, they always go together," Vic Oboyski says.

In 1987 the United States Marshals Service's FIST operations

—those that SOG was backing up—went the way of the seventy-eight long-playing record album. That was the year FIST became WANT. Warrant Apprehension Narcotics Team. With the advent of WANT (conducted in collaboration with the DEA and local authorities and under which the Service for the first time pursued pre-arraignment fugitives), the agency's Special Enforcement Operations, its famous fugitive sweeps, suddenly took on a new rhythm, a switch in emphasis as audible to the unassisted ear as that heralded by the release some thirty years earlier of Bill Haley's "Rock Around the Clock."

For deputy United States marshals, the arrest of bank robbers, rapists, and racketeers had officially entered the realm of the classics.

Number one with a bullet was dope.

The nation's "war" on dope.

(A questionable construct at best when you figure that better than half the nation is *on* dope.)

And while the agency, through its fugitive and NASAF mandates, arrayed its forces on the domestic front—WANT was nothing more than the public-relations arm of the incursion—there were selected deputies who carried the battle deep into enemy territory.

Same war, different theater.

★ ★ ★ ★

The Glory and the Dream

12.

Brothers in Arms

"He thought we were going to kill him. . . . They put him through the fence, we grabbed him . . . he was still blindfolded, handcuffed behind his back. . . . Down he goes, down on the deck . . . and you can smell the adrenaline. . . . 'Please don't kill me, I'll tell you anything you want to know, don't kill me, I got a family' . . . and at that fucking moment I felt great, I felt that Mrs. Camarena, bless her heart, her kids, and everyone . . . at that moment that son of a bitch paid . . . at least, through his mind the thought crossed, 'They're going to fucking blow me away,' and he knew that it was payback. . . . Obviously, it didn't happen, but that guilty fucking conscience of this dog, at least for that little bit of time, I felt like a million dollars . . . that minute, maybe three, that he was down there, that made it all worthwhile for me."

The arrest of René Martín Verdugo on January 24, 1986, was the first of what would become known in the months that followed—when they were eventually exposed to international scrutiny and acknowledged privately for what they were by certain members of the Marshals Service—as "Tony's black bag jobs."

"What it is," says Deputy U.S. Marshal Tony Perez, "is you

convince the people on the other side to do the right thing. And they do it. Most of the time. But if you tell them to cross t's and dot i's—if you gotta do it diplomatically and through diplomatic channels—it doesn't get done. And I'm not saying what I did was right, I'm saying what I did was effective and it was not illegal. I got a clean heart."

Arrests such as Verdugo's, essayed at the outer limits of the agency's statutory authority, are the utmost manifestation of the deputy U.S. marshal as "the long arm of the law." An expression of the Service's federal fugitive mandate only in its most ruthless interpretation, such operations entered the realm of inevitability only when law enforcement became personal.

On Thursday, February 7, 1985, U.S. DEA agent Enrique "Kiki" Camarena, thirty-seven, was abducted by five men outside his agency's offices at the United States consulate in Guadalajara, Mexico. A month later, on March 6, Camarena's mutilated body and that of Alfredo Zavala, a local pilot Camarena had occasionally employed, were discovered seventy miles away, across the Jalisco border, buried behind a ranch in the neighboring state of Michoacán. There was speculation that Zavala had been buried alive; Camarena had been beaten to death. Both men had been tortured before being murdered, Camarena for perhaps thirty hours.

The search for Camarena, the investigation of his death, and the obstruction of both revealed a sustained, systematic conspiracy between some of Mexico's most successful traffickers in cocaine and marijuana—Félix Gallardo, Rafael Caro Quintero, and Ernesto Fonseca Carrillo—and the officials and former officials of several of its government agencies. Not until three years after Camarena's murder were the first U.S. indictments in the case unsealed.

Eventually nineteen foreign nationals, all but one of them Mexican, would be indicted in the United States, among them the former head of Mexico's federal police and the former Mexican INTERPOL director. Also indicted was Dr. Humberto Alvarez Machain, forty-two, a Guadalajara gynecologist alleged to have kept Camarena alive that he might sustain the amount of torture necessary to extract information from him.

The success of U.S. agents in bringing the indictments, realized in the face of White House and State Department efforts to suppress the investigation, was bitter fruit, nurtured by nothing more than a passion on the part of Camarena's fellow officers to make his murderers pay. To this day, it is questionable whether all will ever be made to do so. DEA agents, in exacting but a taste of revenge, relied heavily on back-channel maneuvering. They did it without the help of President Ronald Reagan, and they did it in spite of his secretary of state. And when they had gone as far as they themselves could go, they turned to the only man they knew who could take it one step further.

They turned to Tony Perez.

I been chased by cops all my life. If I was out on the street today, and Tony Perez was after me, I'd surrender.
—Jimmy Fratianno.

What Jimmy Fratianno saw in Tony Perez, he probably saw in his eyes. Dark, flickering, firm of purpose, the kind of eyes some women associate with the bedroom, they are the kind of eyes some men associate with the ring. They look like they give off heat. And Tony Perez looks like a guy who sleeps with them open.

If your house were on fire, you could call Tony Perez, and if he said he would be there to handle it, you could roll over and go back to sleep.

Soft-spoken, well-spoken, sometimes shy, with dark, curly hair and a mustache to match, Perez is strung together like a prize-fighter, something like a fast light-heavyweight. A master of the poetry of American street slang, he comports himself with the kind of cheerful dignity that Cubans seem to display in abundance, the Hispanic that colors his speech not in the accent so much as the cadence. When he talks it is almost like you can scan it. He is as quick with a smile as he is on the draw, and the good humor he brings to his work is infectious.

Straightforward, stand-up, forever young, Perez is the kind of guy who gives cops a good name, and he is the heart and soul of the U.S. Marshals Service.

"Good man, good kid, and he was from the first day," according to Bud McPherson, who was present when Fratianno expressed his opinion. "He was fresh out of the marines, and he had a degree of maturity that was far beyond his young age at the time."

José Antonio Pérez escaped from Fidel Castro's Cuba on May 1, 1965. He arrived in the United States of America in a fourteen-foot rowboat with an uncle, after eight nights and seven days at sea. He was not yet fifteen years old, and like many Americans who earn their citizenship the hard way, he was quick to identify not only its rights and privileges but its duties.

There was more than one star in his future.

Before he was sworn as a deputy marshal, Perez, honoring those duties one late afternoon, near An Hoa, South Vietnam, drew attention to himself as a U.S. Marine Corps platoon sergeant, "holding some folks back while the better part of our platoon got the hell out and got some reinforcements." Of the "folks" in question, a force of enemy riflemen who had overrun his unit, Perez concedes, "there were a lot." Perez held his position "for two or three hours . . . me and a guy named Petersen, all e's, a black guy with red hair . . . green eyes . . . he was my A-gunner, I had the machine gun, the M60 . . . he was my assistant gunner. All he kept saying was, 'Tony, the motherfuckers are getting closer to us.' "

The two escaped under cover of darkness, each pausing only to pick up the Bronze Star for heroism.

With a Bronze Star, a Navy Achievement Medal, and a Purple Heart, Perez, returning from Southeast Asia—he had served nine months in-country before gaining his American citizenship —entered the Marshals Service through the Veterans Readjustment Act's Project Transition. At the Marine Corps' Camp Pendleton, in Oceanside, California, he attended the six-month academy run by the Los Angeles Police Department, was recruited by the Service in January 1972, and assigned to its Los Angeles office. In 1973 Perez "got going on warrants," and it was not long before he developed a reputation as a bodysnatcher.

"He's like flypaper," says deputy Larry Homenick, chief of the Service's International Branch, and Perez's former partner in L.A. warrants. The two, who are best friends, have known each other "from the get-go." It was Perez in 1973 who, coming to Homenick's rescue, patiently taught him—as Homenick's baffled fugitive looked on—how to say "Put up your hands" in Spanish.

The Marshals Service fugitive mandate extends to several categories of warrants. The highest priority is given to escape warrants, those issued for the arrest of fugitives who have escaped from federal confinement, from state confinement if they owe federal time, or from the custody of federal officers, including agents of the FBI. Christopher Boyce and Garnett Leacock were arrested on such warrants. Alphonse Persico, by contrast, was sought for failure to appear. (The Marshals Service works no FBI failure-to-appear warrants that are pre-conviction; those are retained by the Bureau.) Parole and probation violators represent the majority of federal fugitives, and the priority assigned to their capture varies from case to case; John Matthew Boston, a 15 Most Wanted fugitive, released after serving fourteen years of a twenty-year bank robbery sentence, was arrested by Gerri Doody for violating his federal parole—one of its conditions being that he not commit murder. The Marshals Service works all international warrants, those issued for the capture of fugitives wanted by the law-enforcement agencies of foreign governments; the International Operations Branch maintains liaison with INTERPOL, the State Department, and the CIA, and also coordinates the investigation of U.S. fugitives thought to be abroad. And, finally, the Service, as it always has been, is responsible for executing the warrants of the various federal agencies not invested with power of arrest.

Fugitives over which the FBI maintains authority are those whose cases concern organized crime, terrorism, and national security. The FBI also executes all UFAP warrants, those for unlawful (interstate) flight to avoid prosecution (UFAC, if to avoid confinement), which are issued for state, not federal, fugitives, though rarely does the Bureau make such arrests in cases which require investigation. It was their UFAP warrant on Boston by which FBI agents justified their request that the fugitive surrender himself to them. Accepting UFAP cases from state authorities, but usually only when they are submitted along with the fugitives' whereabouts, FBI agents will take credit for such arrests, but are reluctant to run down leads.

Tony Perez, as chief of Major Case Investigations, oversees the Marshals Service 15 Most Wanted program, under the purview of which fall fugitive cases selected not only for their complexity but for their high visibility as well. The 15 Most Wanted list functions primarily to support a public-relations effort, and its blueprint was stolen by the Marshals Service in toto from the FBI.

The figurative notion of the Public Enemy, having adapted over the years, does not trace its origin to the 10 Most Wanted list, but the construct, in its modern form, started walking upright there. Such lists as the FBI's, from more shapely beginnings, have evolved in a predictable fashion, their features having been bureaucratically distorted to give prominence to crimefighting success. Essential, then, to one's placement thereon is the likelihood of eventual capture. Fugitive financier Robert Vesco, for example, is not a 15 Most Wanted, though he tops the Marshals Service's wish list.

To make the Marshals Service's 15 Most Wanted list a fugitive must be a Class-One violator. Misdemeanor warrants carry no weight. National media exposure is not essential, but its power cannot be ignored. Garnett Leacock made the list in spite of his relative obscurity because he met other qualifications. He was considered armed and dangerous and he was wanted for a crime of violence. He also was wanted for escape. But it took Leacock almost eight months to make the list, and his lack of star quality was partly responsible. Violence, of course, invites star quality, they can be made to go hand in hand, yet there are avenues to criminal celebrity that stop short of a tendency to cut throats. One of them is big-time drugs. But however you make the list, the paperwork your case generates will cross the desk of Tony Perez.

"It takes more discipline to stay out than to get out," says Perez, an expert on the psychology of the fugitive. "There's pussy, there's drugs, there's booze. Pillow talk's a motherfucker, man."

And confidential informants (CIs) are as indispensable to deputies like Tony Perez as they were to Pat Garrett over a century ago.

"There's no case where everyone is stand-up and solid. There's always someone that you can break down. I can tell you who is a good cop and who is a fuck-off in the business, I can tell you who is a lazy deputy marshal and who is a smart, hard-working deputy marshal, by [the measure of his] informants."

It is an article of faith among cops; as one veteran officer puts it: "You get a detective with good informants, he's gonna be the best detective."

Deputy marshals, however, must develop separate informants for every case they work. Rare is that instance of the standing informant that a police detective might have.

"Most of your ongoing informants are professional criminals," Brooklyn's Vic Oboyski explains, and while "you can always go back to a CI, if you treat him right," the typical deputy's experience with an informant, Oboyski concedes, is more often "a one-shot deal."

"It's more a reward situation," suggests Perez. "Tell me where the guy is, and I'll give you money. Or I'll do something for you. Bottom line. One transaction, it's over."

And a cop never gives up his informants . . .

"It's like having a girlfriend," says Oboyski. "A girlfriend trusts you, she relies on you."

. . . ever.

"If you give up your informants, you get them killed."

There are some in the U.S. Marshals Service who claim Tony Perez goes too far.

"My biggest problem, the criticism," he says, "is that I care too much for these folks. Not only do I employ them to do a certain thing, I care about them. If I tell them I'm going to do something . . . sometimes I go out of my way too much."

In 1984, working a FIST operation in Los Angeles, Perez and his partner, LAPD officer Manny Mata, chiefly by developing informants, arrested thirteen homicide suspects in under six weeks, an extraordinary achievement by any measure. The informants, like the suspects, were Cuban.

"Mariel Boat Lift people . . . these were criminals themselves. There's nothing we can do to these people, we can't *threaten* them, they've been in worse jails . . . they've eaten that rice and beans for years . . . put them in jail here, shit, they got nothing to worry about. The way we deal with them is with the truth. Their sense of values, of human life, it's different. . . . *'This guy crossed the other guy, he looked at his woman wrong'* . . . You don't do that shit to a Cuban . . . *'He had it [murder] coming, he was an asshole anyway.'* . . . We spent time with them, that is, talking their talk, walking their walk, convincing them this is the only way to go, not the right way or the wrong way as they see things, it's the *only* way. . . . Manny and I slept in a fucking station wagon for days on end because we told one guy, 'You are very important to us, without you we can't break this case, and that's a fact.' He was very scared to give us any information, because he was going to get bumped off if word ever got out . . . and only *he* knew this guy's movements. . . . We promised him we would 'cool off' the information to the point that the guy would never know it had come from him . . . three days sleeping in the station wagon to cover the fucking guy . . . MacArthur

Park, the worst of places, but I kept my word. . . . *Fuck it, let's take him.* No. It's respect. Word gets out, you can deal with Tony, Tony's stand-up, you can deal with Manny, Manny's stand-up."

But there is more to capturing fugitives than the cultivation of confidential informants.

"You anticipate what the fugitive is going to do," Perez explains. "You get out all your leads . . . 'I want to leave this guy two or three places to go. I'm going to burn eight' . . . Or maybe you're going to burn them all, leave him one, but then you run a risk."

"It's like hunting an animal," Vic Oboyski believes. "What you do is you lay traps. You try and push him out of where you think he is and lay traps to where you think he's going to go."

"You know in your heart when you've done it all," Perez says.

"You go through an investigation," Oboyski volunteers, "it can take anywhere from a month to two months, to three, four, five years, to seven years like Persico . . . you're doing paperwork, you're interviewing people, you're like an insurance salesman. You're trying to sell yourself, you're trying to do this, you're trying to do that, you're trying to convince people what a nice guy you are, or what a tough guy you are. Sometimes you're like Charles Bronson, another time you're like Pee Wee Herman, you keep changing your personality. But finally when you go through that door, then you're a U.S. marshal. You know: 'Now, this is it.' You've stepped off your horse, you're kicking the barn door down, and now you're going in. That's it, no more Mr. Nice Guy. That thirty seconds, or that minute and a half, is like when you're a cop."

Most fugitives, Gerri Doody reveals, are a disappointment.

"You build up this image, and then when you actually see them face-to-face, it's not what you had in mind."

"I figured Leacock would be this big vicious animal, and he'd be growling and spitting at us," states Oboyski. "He turned out to be a little piece of shit."

"Looking at a plain, flat photo. . . . It's different if you've seen them before," Gerri Doody says. "But the image you put in your mind is whatever *you* create."

"You think they're cunning, you think they're smart," says Oboyski, "because they have to be to elude *us*, right? You always give the criminal more credit than he's due. . . . Sometimes when we start to think we're so smart, we have to remind ourselves that we're not, it's only that they're dumber than we are."

The variety of fugitives abroad in the land is limited only by the imagination brought to bear upon the contemplation of their number. All one can predict about them is their unpredictability. And there is no yardstick by which to measure the level of desperation any one of them might sustain at the prospect of returning to prison.

Perez and Homenick, in 1981, radically diminished the resale value of a rural dwelling in San Bernardino, California, in their attempt to arrest a parole violator.

As Homenick explains, "I sneak up beside the house, look in the window, and I see the guy looking out at me. He bolts. I say, 'Tony, he's in the house.' Tony says, 'United States marshals, open the door.' "

In addition to the fugitive, there were three women in the house, and they proved to be uncooperative, though their response to Perez was straightforward enough:

" 'Fuck you. . . . Go pound sand up your ass,' something like that, you know, the usual answer," as Perez recollects.

"Tony goes to kick the door in, his foot goes right through the door, literally."

"I get my foot out . . ."

"The girls, now, are tickling Tony's feet . . ."

"I'm going, 'Higher, oh, higher! . . .' "

"We crash the door, it ends up inside the house," says Homenick. "It's laying on the floor now, completely shattered."

"We're in, and Gus is going, 'Where is this mother*fucker*?' "

One of L.A. Warrants' better fugitive hunters, Gus was Perez's two-year-old German shepherd.

"The girls clam up. We sit 'em on the couch. We do a quick check of the house. Nothing. Then we do a room-by-room. The place is one story with an attic. Tony pulls a piece of furniture away from the wall in the living room. There's a hole in the wall with paper stuffed inside it. We think maybe he went in there. Tony starts pulling, and the wall collapses, it falls right into the living room. Now we're getting hyped. A guy hiding like this doesn't want to go to jail. You start getting concerned. In the bedroom, I hit the light switch in the closet, I hear something, I look up. There's an access to the attic, and the fugitive is looking down at me. I grabbed my gun, said freeze . . . he was gone."

Though Homenick and Perez threatened the fugitive with their sending Gus up into the attic in pursuit of him, the threat was an idle one. They could not ignore the possibility that the fugitive was carrying a gun and would simply shoot the dog.

"Guy wouldn't say a word," says Homenick. "No acknowledgment at all. I found a crutch in the closet, and I started hitting the ceiling with it, to see if I could feel his weight. The crutch went right through the roof . . . the ceiling . . . right through the floor of the attic."

After Homenick, to no avail, effectively destroyed the bedroom ceiling, he and Perez notified headquarters. They had decided that the only way to dislodge the fugitive, safely, was to tear-gas him, and because they were sixty miles from Los Angeles, that meant calling in the local authorities.

After a near-fatal comedy of errors outside the house, in which Homenick, wearing civilian clothes, flirted with the possibility of being shotgunned by a uniformed sheriff's deputy—in the middle of the hostilities Perez appeared . . . "There's a second one, he's got a canine," said the local man into his radio, before ordering Perez to freeze . . . Perez simply responded, "Fuck you," and walked back into the house—after that and after Homenick, crawling around the yard in the dark, finally retrieved the service revolver he had been forced to drop before being allowed to identify himself, the obvious became apparent: shooting tear gas into a house so old would very likely set it on fire, it or what was left of it after Perez and Homenick had walked through.

"I'm tired of fucking around," said Perez. "Let's get him."

And so the two men stopped fucking around.

"Tony puts a baseball cap on a broom handle . . ."

"I saw it in a movie . . ."

"He puts it up through the attic access and moves it back and forth."

In a real no-fucking-around kind of way.

"Guy doesn't shoot," says Perez.

He probably thought Perez was fucking around.

"So now we got to come up with another plan."

Sound reasoning on Homenick's part.

"Not a *peep* out of this guy!" Perez says.

"We hoist a mirror up . . ."

Now they were *really* not fucking around.

". . . we can't find him, it's dark . . ."

The two deputies exchanged a look, one they had shared many times in the past:

"Want to do it?"

"Yeah, let's do it."

"One by one, inch by inch," says Homenick, "we slowly creep up into the attic, as low as we can. We worm our way up there and start looking around. Finally, we pick him up with the flashlight. He's all the way at the other end of the attic, lying between the rafters. We start to move toward him, covering each other. The sheriff wants to come up with the shotgun. He comes up, there are three of us now. We're stepping rafter to rafter . . ."

And Homenick missed a step.

"I slip off the rafter, I catch it, I'm hanging into the kitchen. . . ."

At the expense of the kitchen ceiling and, after that, of little more than his dignity.

"Now, the front door's completely dismantled, the living room wall is down, the bedroom ceiling's full of holes from the crutch, and there's a hole in the kitchen ceiling . . ."

And the deputy sheriff—a big man, carrying the shotgun—losing his balance after lifting Homenick to his feet, went right through the ceiling of the living room.

"Coming down on the women . . ."

Call it The House that Fought Back.

The fugitive had yet to speak. Finally doing so, he claimed to be hurt. He was unable, he said, to move. The deputies, seeing no reason at that point to elevate the level of communication, in the mood, in fact, to give the man a taste of what they had just given the house, did not insist that he stand; hooking him up, they dragged him out, hauling him across the rafters as they would a sack of durable produce.

"Bump, bump, bump. . . . We put him in the car. . . . What happens? Gus licks him in the face. That pissed Tony off so bad . . . it was the ultimate indignity."

Few are the figures of speech to pour forth from the crucible of American slang that test as positive for pure, unalloyed truth as does the expression "doing time." Time, and specifically the killing of it, define prison life as blue defines the sky. Monotony and tedium, relieved by periodic eruptions of homicide, color life on the inside as thoroughly as they tend to saturate modern marriage or the typical weekend at sea, and convicts seem to spend all of their time, all of that which is purposeful, in one of two noticeable endeavors. Both are mechanisms for survival. One, the most common, is weight lifting—it yields the heaving, triangular, don't-mess-with-me upper torso that cops on the street invariably identify as a "joint body." The other is planning escapes.

A walking tour of any of the nation's maximum-security prisons would render a visitor astonished at the frequency with which the security of those institutions is breached; but only until one stops to consider that an inmate, so inclined, has nothing more to do with his time, hour upon hour, week upon week, month upon month, year upon year, than plan his unauthorized departure therefrom. As an expression of dissatisfaction with prison life, escape is a hard one to beat. In terms of flat-out sincerity, it pretty much speaks for itself.

One escapee was clearly not kidding when he told Tony Perez, "I'm not going back."

"An Argentinian . . . he was in for dope, I think. He escaped from Terminal Island. Place is notorious for that shit, they got everybody going over the fence. I staked out his girlfriend's house, a Cuban girl . . . it was all Cubans in that area . . . my brother owned a restaurant down the street . . .

"It was early in the morning and I was working with a new deputy, Margie, I was breaking her in. The fugitive was into restoring cars, rebuilding cars from the forties and fifties, which is a way of life in southern California. . . . At dawn, a big '48 Caddy comes down the street, real slow, real cool, like even that early in the morning everybody is watching . . . he and his girlfriend . . . he matches the photo. . . . She gets out of the car and goes into the house, he stays and messes around with the car which gives me more time to approach. . . . He's down doing something under the car, he looks up and sees me and Margie coming . . ."

"What do you want?"

"I'm Tony Perez, we gotta talk."

"What about?"

"And by that time, he's moving . . . and I'm moving . . . we're walking very slowly around the Cadillac. . . . Margie covers the apartment house, to make sure no one comes out, and right now it's a very fucked-up situation, because the man continues to walk and you see rabbit in him."

"I'm not going back to Terminal Island, man."

"Well, this is not the time or place to talk about that. Let's resolve the thing here. There's nothing I or you can do about it, I'm here, we gotta go."

"I'm not going."

And it went back and forth like that for a while.

"Well, I take out my shit," says Perez.

At the appearance of Perez's revolver, the fugitive just shook his head:

"You better shoot me and kill me, because I ain't going, I'm serious."

"So, now I put the gun back, because it ain't doing anything. By this time the girlfriend comes out, and it's getting heated behind me. . . . *'Get back in the house.'* . . . *'Bitch.'* . . . *'No, you're a bitch'* . . . and they started *that*. Margie did good. Now, it's getting out to a foot race around the car, he's going a little faster, and I stop and go around the other way, and he stops and . . . it's getting ridiculous . . . only two or three minutes but it seems like an eternity. Lights are going on now . . . he's hollering, 'I'm not going back, you have to kill me!' . . . all the neighbors are coming to life . . . I make one of those TV jumps over the car, and I grab some hair but he gets away. I don't know where Margie is at this particular moment . . . somewhere, though, I can hear it, and she's got her hands full with this bitch. . . .

"Now the guy is *in* the apartment . . . he *slams* the screen door and I go *through* the screen door. And his teenage stepson is blocking my way . . . seventeen- or eighteen-year-old Cuban boy, who's pretty hefty. . . . *'Leave my dad alone'* . . . *'Out of my way, boy'* . . . No cooperation . . . so a handful of face and push him back . . . and these kids that are working out, a seventeen-year-old can kick your *ass*. . . . I hear the back door slam, now he [the fugitive] is *out* of the apartment. . . . Now this *teenager*, I had to do a little corrective counseling before I left the house. . . . *Out* I go, over the fence . . . 'cause I hear a dog . . . you know: one fence, a dog, the typical shit. . . . Now, this would never have happened . . . he goes *through* my brother's restaurant. . . . He goes in the front door of my brother's restaurant, out the back . . . I'm going in and out, too . . . a small restaurant, the cook's inside, he's cleaning up . . . 'Hi, Rubio,' 'Hi, Tony,' as I'm going through . . . and the *cook* gives chase with a fucking ladle or something in his hand . . . *he* has to do something. . . . So now I've got me a fucking *posse*. . . .

"We fucking chase the guy, and now I'm pissed, because now he's making me *work*. . . . He's under a bush and a dogcatcher spots him. . . . *'Hey, Officer, he's over there'* . . .

"Well . . . he's under arrest. I find Margie and off we go. End of story. Two days later the guy hung himself in Terminal Island. They called me in the middle of the night. Margie busted up crying when she heard. The man was not bullshitting when he said he wasn't going back. I will never forget his face. He said, 'I ain't going, I'm serious'—with Argentinians there is a singing rhythm to their conversation, more so than the Mexicans, who also sing when they speak—'I ain't going,' he said. He wasn't bullshitting. I think he was in for dope."

Working a warrant, Tony Perez says, a deputy marshal must bring a firm sense of purpose to every interview he conducts.

"By the time you knock on the door, you should pretty well have your shit together; you should know what you want to come away with."

There is no such thing as a routine visit.

"We have to go into people's houses. Sometimes the guy is there. We don't know. We don't call ahead to say we're coming to interview you about a fugitive, we don't have people come downtown to talk."

"We got a call once," says Larry Homenick, "a fugitive turned himself in to his parole officer, who called us. We weren't even looking for him, we just got the call. Tony and I went over to the P.O.'s office to pick him up."

The parole officer introduced them:

"Well, Bill, these two men are U.S. marshals, and they're here to take you in on that warrant."

Homenick asked the fugitive to step over to the desk and empty his pockets. It was a moment Homenick says he will never forget.

"He pulled out a gun . . . a toy gun . . . we didn't know it was a toy. And my heart stopped. If it had been real and he had fired it, we'd have both been dead. I remember seeing it, it's like slow motion, I was in no position to do anything. After that I never said to anybody, 'Empty your pockets.' *I* empty their pockets. If I ever learned anything about complacency, it was then."

Tony Perez has worked warrants with several partners. In Los Angeles, there was Kato Banks—"smart, tough, former marine, stand-up motherfucker, street smart, loves to fight, never seen a pair of hands like him, very loyal son of a bitch, very refined, drives a Mercedes and all that kind of stuff"—who once arrived late, Perez recalls, to play softball against the LAPD, out of uniform but not out of style. "We all got sweatshirts and shit, and here shows Kato in a three-piece suit, with a glove. 'I'm ready to go, I'm dressed, Coach, send me in.' He goes out there in center field, and bigger than shit, my man is grabbing everything that goes out that way. And hitting. He does it all. And *looking* good. I said, 'Kato, what is this shit?' He says, 'Tony, I got to look good *all* the time.' " But of only one of his many partners over the years does Tony Perez carry photographs.

"I'm acting chief, I'm pulling up to my house, I get a call on the radio, *shots fired, call right away.* I'm in Inglewood, I gotta drive to Stanton, forty miles away . . .

"Me and Gus."

As partners go, Gus was clearly the first among equals. And Perez remembers the incident in question as Gus's finest hour.

"What happened . . . we had the girlfriend of this fugitive in pocket, she was going to help us [apprehend him] . . . '*He's coming, be here,*' she said, and all that, you know. He put the fear of God in her. I say fine, all in a day's work, I go home, I have a team assigned to it. . . . They had this restaurant covered and the guy did come . . . but it got ugly."

The fugitive arrived at the restaurant at the wheel of a stolen pickup. The girlfriend was to approach him slowly.

"He pulled her by the hair *into* the pickup—now we got ourselves a chase. Compounded by one of our *hot dog fucking deputy marshals* who emptied his fucking nine-millimeter at this fleeing pickup truck, with the informant-slash-hostage inside the truck . . . there's apartment buildings in the line of fire . . ."

The local police arrived first:

"What the fuck are you doing? Is this the way you marshals do business?"

By the time Perez appeared on the scene, local SWAT had taken over.

"The shooting team comes up, they got paramedics there, they got K-9 units there. . . . I get there and I see my people all in a line, sitting on the sidewalk, watching the show. I ask Kato what happened, he tells me . . . Kato is livid . . . I almost choked this fucking guy with the gun . . ."

The pickup had been abandoned a mile away from the shooting, in a residential cul-de-sac, to the right of which stood a tract of suburban dwellings. Straight ahead, beyond a fence, was a trailer park.

Perez talked to the SWAT commander, who said:

"You can't be in here, you'll be in the kill zone. We think he's in one of these houses. We can't take the risk."

"With all due respect," Perez told him, "he's putting as much distance between us as possible, right now. He's running, he's not in a house. He's moving as we speak."

Perez could read the cop's mind.

". . . federal assholes, come shooting up the town. . . ."

Finally convincing the SWAT commander to allow his deputies to work, Perez let Gus sniff the truck.

"Gus alerted on the fence . . . it's nighttime, it's dark . . . Gus looks at the fence and goes rigid."

Deputies discovered a purse near the fence. The woman, they realized, was still working with them. But there were countless trailers in the compound.

"I pile every swinging dick into the station wagon, six or seven of them, and circle the park to the entrance on the opposite side. Gus has the wind in his face. I line up the guys—I pulled this one out of my ass—'Follow Gus,' I say. 'Don't get out in front, don't lag behind, don't play with yourselves, let's go.' I want to know where everyone is in case we got to shoot . . ."

Physically punctuating the narrative, Perez suddenly snaps his fingers.

"*One* minute . . . Gus picks up the scent. I get an erection. I know I can win . . ."

Instantaneously, the dog froze on one of several new trailers parked on the sales lot.

"I pull my shit out:

" '*You! Open the door slow.*'

"Bigger than shit, that door opens slowly.

" '*Let the woman go.*'

"He lets her go, slowly, down onto the deck . . ."

And then the man made a mistake.

"I told him, 'Whatever you do, your hands are always behind you. I want to see your hands. And move *slowly*.' "

He jumped.

"And before he hit the deck, he had two bites in his ass. Gus is trained [to allow] no sudden movements. . . . He's in the air, Gus is in the air . . ."

The arrest was followed by a parade.

"I put this motherfucker . . . I walked him about a mile . . . with the headlights of the station wagon behind us, Gus between me and him, 'You're gonna walk real slow to where you see a group of policemen . . .' I did it more for the dog than anything else, to make him feel proud, because they know that shit, they know when they're in control. And I'm glad he got a bite, because it's like a lot of foreplay and no sex. He earned that fucking bite. I wouldn't have sicced him on the man, but it all worked out just fine . . . *found* him, *bit* him, now *walked* him . . . slowly . . . Gus right behind him with his nose in his asshole, nudgin' him. And me behind that. The SWAT commander, when he saw that. . . ."

Tony Perez is one of those deputies who is reluctant to hang his citations, and it is the speculation of some of his colleagues that there are very few offices in Washington with the wall space to display them, anyway. With questions on the part of his superiors as to whether he was "management material," Perez, following his assignment to headquarters in 1984, went about earning Marshals Service promotions with a diminishing ceiling in the bureaucracy. To put him back out in the districts, his bosses would have had to make him a chief, and because they were reluctant to do so, and because he was so downright talented, they essentially invented a job, Major Case Investigations, into which to promote him in 1988.

The accuracy of the assessment of Perez's management abilities is open to serious question. What is not is his admitted reluctance to entirely give up the street. A warrants man—"probably the best warrants man in the Service," it is said—who loves nothing more than the hunt, Perez grants that for a man of his age and achievement there is a certain propriety, a meaningful challenge, in "flying this fucking desk." Still, he is a man who grows wistful. Walking the streets of Washington, acknowledging that working surveillance eventually catches up with a man—"It's tough . . . the waiting and waiting"—he will pause to stare up at a lighted window, and, lost in thought, he will quietly confide, almost as though speaking to himself, "But there's nothing like that hard-on that you get when you know that the asshole is in there."

In January of 1986, Perez was an inspector, a regional manager, in Enforcement Operations at headquarters, and René Martín Verdugo was just one of the several thousand assholes on whom the Marshals Service was holding paper. Outstanding against Verdugo was a routine felony dope warrant issued in San Diego by the U.S. Court for the Southern District of California. Insulated by money, enjoying the unofficial protection of the government of his native Mexico, Verdugo was virtually untouchable, immune to capture by the United States, into which he now was moving marijuana by the ton as a Caro Quintero lieutenant.

When an FBI forensics team in 1985 recovered from the scene of Kiki Camarena's interrogation and murder a hair sample belonging to Verdugo, indictments in the Camarena case were still a good three years away; a grand jury had yet to be empaneled when shortly after the evidence was recovered Tony Perez, in the Mexican resort town of San Felipe, on the Baja California peninsula, brought to Verdugo's attention the matter of his outstanding San Diego warrant.

Perez had received the call from the DEA on December 17.

"I had the pleasure of meeting Mrs. Camarena, she was there in the task-force room when I went to DEA headquarters. DEA had called me and said, 'Hey, Tony, come over, let's talk.' I met the woman there, I met the guys who were running the show."

Their opening line was innocuous enough:

"We want to see if you can do something for us."

"I'm thinking, why doesn't DEA do this? Why don't they avenge their own thing?"

The Drug Enforcement Administration, in the wake of Camarena's abduction, was having serious problems operating in Mexico. They had already coughed up a lot of international trouble and as much stateside bureaucratic trouble as they could handle.

"We're just not going to be effective," Perez was told by the agents in the room that day.

Perez looked at Mika Camarena, he says, and "I knew it was for real."

As Perez saw it, it went way beyond dope.

"Just a guy sending dope over here, it's like . . . at some point, although you see the tragedies and all, at some point it's like a fucking guy importing shoes, or luggage, more than anything it's become a business, where tons of coke are grabbed every day and it seems like one load is bigger than the next, and the next, and all that shit. . . . But *this* . . . I could touch *people* . . . I can touch Mrs. Camarena, whose husband was tortured and killed for trying to do the right thing in a place I knew very well."

Perez, whose stepmother and stepbrother are Mexican, identifies Cuba and Mexico as "very tight, very close culturally"; the DEA knew Perez was no stranger to Mexico, that for him the country harbored no mysteries.

Perez says, "I promised nothing."

His first move was the obvious one.

"I went to Mr. Safir."

The DEA's request of Perez, when all the delicate language was peeled away, was essentially for the kidnapping of Verdugo. Even if handled lawfully—and for that adverb it would be a stretch—it would be one of those operations that, if it received any attention at all, would redound to the discredit of everyone. The request, however heartfelt, however appealing to the instinct of the cop in everyone, was a request in which any bureaucrat, in any response short of summary denial, would see nothing but wholesale disaster. It was a request that arrived at Marshals Service headquarters with little more than love on its side.

And Howard Safir, a cop the size of whose ego is exceeded only by the size of his balls, immediately said yes.

When Howard Safir favors the world with a smile, he does so with such apparent difficulty that to see it happen is almost heartbreaking. On the operational side of the Marshals Service, good humor does not bleed from the top. So painfully uncomfortable in the presence of others, at the same time so driven by ambition, Howard Safir makes it effectively impossible for others to relax in his company.

To think of Tony Perez as enormously fond of Safir would probably be a mistake. Perez does not dislike him, but his respect for the man, like everyone's, is polluted by such apprehension as to make camaraderie unimaginable. Safir, admired for his leadership, commands a deference that falls short of affection. In the rank-and-file he inspires a mix of sincere admiration and flat-out fear.

"Up here [at headquarters] credibility is everything. If you don't have it, you're fucked. Mr. Safir will back you all the way, he'll let you follow incredible hunches. If you get results. But the man takes no prisoners if you fuck up."

Perez is one of the few people at headquarters, on the opera-

tions side, who is not one of "Howard's people." Many have
been promoted to positions of leadership there, some in the face
of a demonstrated inability to perform, simply because they are
loyal to Safir. Perez is there for the simple reason that he is
overqualified to put anywhere else.

Loyalty to Howard Safir, the sheer instrumental value of it at
Marshals Service headquarters, is expressed nowhere more
clearly than in the presence there of deputies like . . . well, like
John Pascucci. An Enforcement Division inspector, answerable
only to Safir, Pascucci handles special assignments for the associate director, and the best anyone can say of him is that "He is
our leading candidate for charm school." That is how he is described *officially;* those are the words of the Service's Office of
Congressional and Public Affairs. An articulate spokesman for
the Service, a man of considerable intelligence—there is no one
in the Service more cooperative with the press—John Pascucci
is a man whose accomplishments, whatever they may be, are
entirely overshadowed by personal endorsements typified by
that offered by a deputy marshal in Brooklyn: "Getting close to
John Pascucci is like getting close to a rattlesnake." That he is
Howard Safir's rattlesnake accounts for Pascucci's longevity.
John Pascucci's days, however, it is generally agreed, are numbered; like several deputies deemed to have been promoted
beyond their competence—his is not called into question as
forcefully as is his congeniality—Pascucci flourishes in the nar-
rowing shadow of Safir's imminent retirement.

The Marshals Service without Howard Safir will be an agency
the lineaments of which have been dramatically altered. His
departure, however, as has his leadership, provokes feelings that
are invariably mixed.

"The Service," according to one chief, whose experience pre-
dates Safir's arrival, "needed a tough and tense boss. Howard's
the ultimate survivor. He's going to be hard to beat. The man
never gets tired. [And] he has the intelligence and the demeanor
to go along with his working habits. He's a good boss and a good
leader." But, notwithstanding his enormous respect for Safir, the
chief's remarks, almost predictably, betray a familiar subtext:
"I'll never jump back from the guy."

In the words of one of the Service's senior people:

"I just hope that when Howard hangs it up, he feels good
about what he contributed to the agency, because he *is* the person [responsible for its revitalization]. He's a great leader, a good

manager, [but he may have] missed the opportunity to be a great man."

Only in Witness Security is praise for Safir unequivocal.

"Howard Safir is the guy who took us out of the dark ages," Bud McPherson asserts. "We knew how to get there, but no one else would do it for us. [He arrived, and] things started to change almost immediately. In forty years in the military or paramilitary, I have never met a manager who comes close to Howard Safir. Everything he touched turned to gold."

If as Joseph Conrad suggests in the imperishable pages of *Lord Jim,* "You shall judge of a man by his foes as well as by his friends," let it be said of Howard Safir that numbered among his enemies are Edwin P. Wilson, Christopher Boyce, Alphonse Persico, and Josef Mengele, and thousands of garden-variety scumbags on the order of Garnett Leacock.

And, yes, René Verdugo.

On January 13, 1986, four weeks after meeting Kiki Camarena's widow at Drug Enforcement Administration headquarters in Washington, Tony Perez and three other deputy marshals traveled to Calexico, California, to talk to the DEA's resident agent-in-charge, and from there crossed to the Sonora, Mexico, side of the border, into neighboring Mexicali, where René Verdugo lived.

"I went down to Mexico . . . *we* actually went in and did the work as far as looking [for Verdugo]. We went in, spotted the guy, we knew his comings and goings—it would have been easy for us to grab the son of a bitch, put him in the car, bring him across the border, and lie . . ."

Instead, Perez enlisted the aid of members of Sonora's judicial police.

"We got six officers there to help us out."

Which was really the germ of the operation.

"It's really human relations, we talk to people, we convince them to do the right thing. No heavy compromises, no heavy demands on these folks, just one-on-one. . . . I go to a police organization in another country, go to someone in command, I tell them this is what I need, I'd like to have this man back. The moment we start pointing fingers at Mexico, Colombia, start saying, 'You're all corrupt, your cops are corrupt, you're all into this and that,' the moment we start doing that, we're finished. Because we are a part of that fucking corruption. . . . It's a one-way relationship, because I cannot get a Colombian citizen, put him in the trunk of my car, and drive him to Miami where there'll be a Colombian aircraft waiting. . . . 'You ask, ask, ask and never give,' they say, 'and when you do give, you give us the finger. . . .' And we say, 'You people are corrupt, you are fucked . . .'

"After we go through all that, you cut through it, you come to the *man*, heart-to-heart, cop-to-cop. If you do it right, their sense of authority rises. If you do it wrong, they got to come out. I fucked up the lives of six people, I feel I did. . . . I'm the one who has to deal with the fact that all of them are now in the U.S. Some of them may or may not have jobs, now . . . most are depressed. . . . This is a new life, a new start in a foreign country. They were happy, they were established, they had their careers and all that, and now they don't . . ."

What they have is Bud McPherson. All six had to be put in the Witness Security Program, they and their families relocated.

"We got six officers there to help us out, and they took a good ten days of watching him, and waiting, and finally he went to San Felipe, to a party. Laughing and joking . . . he left the party to get some more beer, and he was under surveillance, of course. . . . We said: 'Do it now.' And we grabbed him . . . *they* did . . . out of a party . . . they grabbed him, took him to the car, and they went over."

Over the border.

"It was his daughter's party, or someone very close to him in the family, maybe a birthday party. . . . He owned the house in San Felipe. He had houses everywhere. He was a very well-to-do man. San Felipe was like his beach house."

Up to the moment of his capture, Perez says, Verdugo, like any man in his position, saw no reason to be uncooperative.

"Any Mexican who is powerful, he will let you approach . . . *'Yeah, what do you need?'* The last thing on his mind is that you are going to grab him . . . *'Yeah, I will talk to your commandante later, you are dismissed now, thanks for the message.'*"

Or something to that effect.

"But fuck that. . . .

"Once they were close enough, just two Mexican males, plain clothes . . . with a rental car from here, I gave them a car to do the thing . . . said they were judicial police—a fact; they were at the time—*'We'd like to see you, like to talk to you a little bit . . .'* Down on the station wagon floor . . . and off they went. . . . Instead of taking him to their station, they made the choice of bringing him to the border, to the Americans, they did the right thing. . . ."

It was no typical evening drive along the Baja. Verdugo's wife and his Mexican lawyer were on the telephone within minutes of his abduction. Perez is understandably vague on some of the details of the caper, but it is apparent that there was a certain urgency in the timing of the actual snatch.

"We grabbed him there . . . his friends saw it. He broke away from a group. It had to be done there. We suspect one of those people called . . . and roadblocks were set up. . . . There were police barricades already set up . . . it was like a sixty-mile drive . . . and you talk about eluding those fucking roadblocks . . . your asshole puckers. And it wasn't no fucking freeway, either . . . you had to do certain things to get away from these folks . . ."

Perez and the three other deputies, Mike Carnivale, Ernie Tautimes, and David Mendoza—the core of what some in the Service call Tony's Tigers—had been joined in Mexico by then International Branch chief Don Ferrarone. In Calexico, Perez had rented three vehicles for the caper, a sedan, a station wagon, and a van. On the run for the border, Verdugo went into the station wagon with the six Mexican police officers. Running up front, at the wheel of the van, was Perez with Tautimes and Ferrarone. Mendoza and Carnivale brought up the rear.

"We had to get off the main road in a couple of instances, actually go *off* the road and get into the desert, and drive around [the roadblocks] that way. . . . I let [the Mexicans] take the lead after a while, because these guys knew where they were going. . . . Now I was in the middle, and the tail car, the chase car, continued to be Mike and David. . . . We were running without lights and were going eighty miles an hour, *off* the road, across the desert, and it worked, these people knew exactly what they were doing."

It took about an hour to make the run.

"I remember it was dark. Son of a bitch. It was not dark when we picked him up. There was a moon, it was pretty good. It was like a movie in slow motion, the way everything happened."

Perez says he experienced no sense of danger as such, save that inspired by the speed at which he and the others were traveling. Apprehension at what might befall him at the hands of Mexican authorities—what had befallen Camarena—was not uppermost in his mind, he says, though he welcomed the element of safety in the fact that he was traveling with police.

"Once you're in a situation like this, you just roll with the punches. There's no way to . . . it crossed our minds collectively, and we talked about it, but when we shook hands over here with DEA at headquarters, the deal was done. We never dwelled on that kind of stuff."

They made the border at twenty past six. The niceties of Customs and Immigration were bypassed. Five miles west of Calexico, Perez, at an unmanned crossing, climbed the fence to receive Verdugo.

"They put him through the fence, the Mexicans pushed him through, we grabbed him, we put him on the ground. . . . We laid him down, and there were no sounds whatsoever, because I made it clear, I didn't want anyone speaking English, Spanish . . . Chinese . . . nothing. *'Don't say a* fucking *word throughout this whole thing, because people are going to get killed behind this arrest if he recognizes that Mexicans were involved. . . .'* "

One of the more problematic considerations governing Mexican participation evokes understatement on the part of Perez.

"Their sense of how this stuff ought to work is a little bit different than ours as Americans. . . ."

A little bit, indeed. Perez was forced to speak to the issue.

" 'This is your country, these are your people. Your system is what it is. But we're working together now, and I can't have one bruise on this guy. No bruises, no cuts . . . treat him as if he were the president of the country, with all the honors . . . no slapping, no hurting no one. . . . That's one of the things, that's part of the contract here. . . . Whatever you do, don't give me a bruised spot . . .' And he didn't have a bruise on him. We undressed him, we took photos . . .

"Things started getting worse and worse for them. Because as word got out that he had been abducted, and it was believed to have been by police, they started making inquiries. This man was a man of means. So a lot of pressure was put on the officials there, and they started closing in on these people. And that's when the guy I coordinated with, he said, 'Tony, you got to get us out.' They're in the Witness Security Program . . . thirty-two of them . . . their families had to come out, too. . . . They fire-bombed their houses, took their fucking businesses over, and like that . . ."

13.

Government Work

The reverberations, political and legal, of Verdugo's recovery from Mexico (Perez eventually received a letter of clearance from the assistant U.S. attorney in the case) would compare rather anemically to those that emanated from the "return" from Tegucigalpa two years later of another international fugitive.

The April 1988 arrest of Honduran cocaine billionaire Juan Ramón Matta Ballesteros, which made headlines all over the world, was engineered by one of the few people capable of pulling it off only to tell the truth about doing so, the illustrious José López, in the words of Tony Perez, "all heart, all balls, and no paperwork," and, by consensus, among his superiors at headquarters, the biggest troublemaker in the United States Marshals Service.

"He's like an elephant in a circus act," Perez explains not altogether affectionately, "and I'm the guy following him around with the shovel."

When López went after Matta, the fallout was especially heavy.

"I went after him because I was *told* to go after him, because he was a fugitive like anybody else."

*Any*body else, José?

. . .

Juan Ramón Matta Ballesteros, forty-two, a Honduran native, had first entered the United States illegally at the age of sixteen. Using forged passports and twenty-four known aliases, he would continue to do so (he was deported five times) for the duration of his criminal career, much of which he spent on the streets of New York, self-employed as a pickpocket. At one point, upon his arrival, Matta was actually invited to stay; in 1967, convicted of illegal entry (passport and visa fraud) he was sentenced to five years in prison. In 1971, having served three and a half years of that sentence and presumably longing for home, he strolled away, during a church service, from the minimum-security Federal Prison Camp at Florida's Eglin Air Force Base.

For the next several years, Matta's record shows, he continued to work as a petty thief, both in the United States and in the land of his birth, a small-time, itinerant scumbag, who, had he heard of Horatio Alger, was unequipped to appreciate his prose and whose prospects, if any, were hardly of a kind to be inspirational to others. In 1988, when he was arrested by José López on the seventeen-year-old escape warrant that had been issued upon his departure from Eglin, Matta, still unable to read or write, in tribute to some remarkably primitive chemistry, was the largest private employer in the republic of Honduras, second only to the national government.

The primitive chemistry in question, of course, was the chemistry of cocaine.

Shortly before his capture, Matta, whose net worth was estimated to be in the billions, in a news conference called by his Tegucigalpa attorney assured the American press that the figure was exaggerated and insisted that his income, while admittedly substantial, derived from cattle ranching, construction, and trade in tobacco, spice, and coffee.

Which was not entirely untrue.

"He owned," according to José López, "the biggest cattle farm, the biggest tobacco factory, he owned every business he could legally buy. He would go out, and he would not twist anybody's arms, and if you had a business up for sale, he would buy it, fair price. He was doing a lot of charity for people. Wednesday mornings, there were lines in front of his house . . . he would send people to Houston for open heart surgery, give wheat shares to the people, he was building schools, he was like a Robin Hood down there."

Independent of the cash handouts on Wednesday mornings,

Matta, who built more than one school and funded the construction of a hospital, employed over 800 people on his tobacco and dairy farms, all of which won him the instant loyalty of Honduras's desperately poor.

As further evidence of his legitimacy, Matta cited the income derived from his holdings of residential real estate.

"Five houses leased by the U.S. embassy were owned by Matta Ballesteros," says López, "including one safe-house for the [Central Intelligence] Agency."

Four federal indictments unsealed in 1985, in Phoenix, Los Angeles, and San Diego, identified the source of the wealth that enabled Matta to reach the position he occupied. By then, the indictments maintained, Matta, using remote Arizona landing strips and safe-houses in southern California, was moving over the border and onto the streets of the United States about thirty tons of coke a year.

("More'n you and I make six weeks combined, buddy," quips Duke Smith, in a rough estimate of its value.)

"He was buying *pasta* [cocaine paste] in Colombia and refining it in Honduras," says López. "He was shipping cocaine through Puerto Castillo to Miami. He was not part of the cartel. The cartel and Matta were equal."

And Matta was equally untouchable. His extradition to the United States was prohibited by the Constitution of Honduras; by a 1909 extradition treaty between the two countries; and by a 1939 extradition treaty to which both countries are signatories. More than that, however, Matta maintained intimate ties with senior officers in the Honduran military. And though Honduras had had a civilian government since 1981, its military, as the nation's principal beneficiary of U.S. aid, was where true power in the country reposed.

As one European diplomat pointed out, "The U.S. does not have a policy toward Honduras, it has a policy *from* Honduras, directed at Nicaragua and El Salvador."

Subordinating Honduras's needs to the larger policy goals it had elsewhere in Central America, the Reagan administration, weeks before Matta's arrest, had ordered 3,200 U.S. troops into Honduras to support Nicaraguan counterrevolutionaries, who from base camps secured there were seeking to restore the pro-American dictatorship overthrown by the Sandinistas in 1979. The reciprocity Reagan showed toward members of the military in Honduras was in keeping with the established practice of previous presidential administrations, part of a time-honored tradition whereby the White House graciously facilitated Third World dope traffic into the United States while the Justice Department officially deplored it.

It was a policy that first drew attention during the American adventure in Southeast Asia, when the Central Intelligence Agency, in support of anti-Communist warlords there, was flying the heroin they processed out of the Golden Triangle—bringing tons of smack to market in the States (where the Justice Department was jailing marijuana smokers) in the name of national security. It was not long thereafter that the same agency, on the same authority, began to move Contra coke. Similar forces are at work today all over the Middle East; until recently a thriving market in hashish had its correlative in the security of American interests in Lebanon. International scrutiny was lately brought to bear on drug corruption in the White House upon President George Bush's inevitable betrayal of the nation's former partner-in-crime, Panamanian general Manuel Noriega.

It was such vectors of political depravity that José López confronted in Honduras. There was nothing serendipitous about the fact that the DEA office in Tegucigalpa had been closed in 1983. But as with Panama, it was U.S. domestic politics that finally made a morally bankrupt foreign policy, or at least the appearance of one, untenable.

Matta, as it happened, was moving much of his cocaine through Mexico. One of his associates was Félix Gallardo. The 1985 indictments charged Matta with conspiracy to smuggle cocaine, possession with intent to distribute, and engaging in a continuing criminal enterprise. He was also wanted for escape, his 1971 flight from Eglin. Yet, even given all that, the U.S. government did not give a damn about him. In the eyes of the Reagan administration, in the eyes of those members of the executive branch who were actually aware of his existence, Matta was perceived as an ally.

But Matta was wanted for something else. Something that breathlessly transcended the charges outlined in the indictments against him. He was wanted for questioning by the DEA; he was wanted for questioning as a material witness in the murder of Enrique Camarena.

Matta was believed, said the DEA, to be involved in "the planning and direction of it." He was believed, in fact, to have ordered the killing, he and his confederate, Félix Gallardo.

Call him the *former* cocaine billionaire.

José López got the call.

José López, tall, balding, bespectacled, Puerto Rican, and pushing fifty, alters the fair complexion of the Marshals Service like a beauty mark on a movie star—an affliction that confers depth of character, one to which her celebrity is harnessed and to which she has become quite attached, but an affliction nevertheless, constantly drawing attention to itself, impossible to ignore—and the Marshals Service wakes up every morning asking itself: "I wonder if I should have it removed?"

Proud, loud, and uncontrollable—the temperature of his blood will heat the room—López is incapable of disguising his feelings. Upon even the most cursory acquaintance, one is left with the general impression that if José López unbuttoned his shirt, his heart would probably fall out. He comes on like a force of nature. His eyes, liquid and inconsolable, serve to give him away even at rest, and when he cranks it up, which is most of the time, he looks like a man who is drowning.

Victor Oboyski's impersonation of him is exhausting to watch: *" 'You know how many men I have killed with this gun . . .?!!' "*

Where everyone else circumnavigates John Pascucci as one would the neighborhood pit bull, López gets right in his face, unsolicited, with death threats. Find a fight, says Tony Perez, and "López would be right there, you know he'd be kicking ass. He does have a big set of balls." Perez's opinion of López is amplified by the esteem and affection held for López by his polar opposite in the Marshals Service, consummate team player and quintessential company man Mike Pizzi, their friendship going back several years to a Latin American operation on which the two collaborated.

But friends and enemies of López—they exist in equal number—however they come down, all agree on one thing:

José López was Juan Matta's worst nightmare come true.

A week after Camarena's abduction in 1985, Mexican authorities delayed a raid on the Mexico City apartment to which Matta had been traced, giving him time to escape. Matta showed up in Cartagena, Colombia, where two and a half months later he was arrested. Charged in the drug-related murders of thirteen people in Colombia and scheduled for extradition to the United States, he was held in Bogotá's La Picota prison, where the first plan to spring him was foiled by warden Alcides Arismendi. Matta's benefactors in that escape attempt were his associates in Colombia's Medellín cocaine cartel, and it was at their hands that Arismendi was summarily murdered, gunned down in his car as he sat in a Bogotá traffic jam. It was they who supplied the estimated $2 million, subsequently distributed among guards and supervisors at the prison, with which Matta eventually bribed his way out. He returned to Honduras in 1986, surrendered there on a decade-old murder charge, was held briefly and released.

José López set out after Matta in the winter of 1987.

"It was a year and seven days from the day I got to Honduras to the day we got him out."

López's task was essentially the same as that faced by Tony Perez: to find someone in a position of authority and to convince him "to do the right thing." López, however, was required to operate at a much higher level, and the obstacles he faced were more sinister. After all, Ronald Reagan and Juan Matta were, for all practical purposes, colleagues; given their relationship to the Honduran military, the two were essentially in the same business. Contra resupply efforts were hard-wired to the engine of Matta's coke, and up to the end it was questionable whether the U.S. president would allow the cord to be cut. It was essential, at any rate, that deniability be built into the operation. Extraditing Honduran-born citizens was forbidden by that country's Constitution, and cooperation on the part of the government there, were it willing to cooperate at all, had to be concealed, it was decided, at all costs.

The official story would ultimately assume three variations, the last one approximating the truth. In support of the original lie, López's participation was essential.

José López, as U.S. marshal for Puerto Rico (1970–1984), had developed high-level political connections there and in the Dominican Republic. It was through these connections that he had made possible the arrest of Edwin Wilson in 1982. (Wilson, in a con orchestrated by the Marshals Service, had been lured to Santo Domingo from Libya, only to be expelled to the United States by the Dominican government.) In Puerto Rico López had been tight with the Dominican vice consul and, through a Puerto Rican brigadier general, he was introduced to the chief of the Dominican army.

"These people are not only business partners, they are personal friends [of mine]. The relationship between Brigadier Jensen and myself goes back to his father and my father."

The Dominican Republic was indispensable to the original plan to snatch Matta. From Honduras Matta would be flown secretly to Santo Domingo, and from there he would be officially expelled, just as Wilson had been.

Matta was not in hiding, he was living openly in Tegucigalpa. López was in Honduras a year not because he was unable to find him; nor did it take Matta long to spot López. It was Matta's awareness of the surveillance, and what he claimed were four American attempts to kidnap him, that had prompted Matta and his lawyer to go before the American press two months before he was captured.

"He had informants," says López. "[He had knowledge] of surveillance by the DEA. But he could never figure out who was Commandante Gavilan."

The task force included four other deputy marshals (Terry Curry, Roberto Escobar, Maria Escribano, and Rafael Pagan), all of whom had code names. López, the fictitious Honduran "Commandante," over the year that the task force was in existence, made twenty-seven trips between Honduras and Washington, with side visits to the Dominican Republic.

"The operation was so complicated, we were moving from place to place every other day. We had three or four hotel rooms in our names. At the same time we were living in a safe-house provided by the embassy. We were showing up in bars and public places wearing flight jackets with insignias: American Embassy Flying Group, Tegucigalpa."

Only two high-ranking Honduran authorities, a police official and a military official, knew López's real name.

"In some ways they were cooperating, in others they were in Matta's favor."

It was a wavering on their part, combined with vacillation in Washington, that prolonged the operation. What finally turned the tide at the White House was what news analysts eventually interpreted as "mounting concern" there over corruption and drug trafficking in the Honduran military. The mounting concern was, in fact, over press reports about the corruption, specifically reports in the *New York Times* and the *Washington Post* in February 1988.

Two months later López made his move.

"Three days before his arrest, Matta was in San Pedro Sula, at a very famous hotel [not far from] there, the Tela Mar Hotel. It was the first time in a year I had seen him together with a woman who was not his wife and he was having a hell of a time. He got up from his table, went to [his] room. . . . we went to the swimming pool that was right in front of that room and we waited there for two hours. After two hours I told my people, 'Hey, he's having a party, let's go back to Tegucigalpa and put a surveillance on his house. Sooner or later, he'll have to come back.' He got to his house Sunday, late at night, drunk, slept the whole day Monday, went jogging on Tuesday. We took him."

López took him.

In the case of René Verdugo, López explains:

"See, Tony did what is proper to do in a country like this. Mexicans made the arrest. They do the dirty work, but you have to coach them. [In Honduras] I was actually the one who had to do it. If they [the Hondurans] had done it for me, Matta would have been dead. Because their main concern was not expelling Matta from the country, it was [in] expelling Matta . . . what Matta might say about [them]. . . . We got to kill him [they decided, because] dead people don't talk."

In the course of saving Matta's life, López watched Version 1 of the official story collapse and made it effectively impossible for Version 2 to stand up under international scrutiny. And to this day, he is the only man in Washington who cops to the inconsistencies in Version 3.

As Tony Perez points out, with respect to his exoneration in the arrest of Verdugo: "As long as you don't put your hands on the person, as long as you don't make the actual arrest, you can defend yourself just about from anything coming out of that arrest. They did it, they put him in the car, they brought him to the fence, and once in the United States, I do with him what I got to do."

U.S. courts have held apprehensions such as Verdugo's to be legal. The U.S. Supreme Court has recently ruled that Fourth Amendment search-and-seizure restrictions do not apply in such cases; Supreme Court rulings, over the years, have held that it does not matter how international fugitives end up in U.S. courtrooms so long as the arrests do not involve torture that "shocks the conscience" of the court.

"When I came back from the Matta operation," José López says, "the first guy I saw at headquarters was [Howard Safir's special assistant] Ralph Zurita, and he told me he had an investigation going because Matta claimed that he was hit two times with a cattle prod. I told him he wasn't hit with a cattle prod. *Maybe* he had been hit with . . . what do you call that shit . . . ?"

A stun gun.

". . . with a stun gun.

"He says, 'What stun gun? Because I have a big investigation going.'

"I said: 'Motherfucker, with the same stun gun that you *gave* me.' "

Matta was returning from his daily run, at about 5:30 A.M., his bodyguards cruising in a car beside him, when a force of Honduran military police launched an airborne raid on his lavishly appointed Tegucigalpa home. (Estimates of the number of troops in the assault force range between 60 and 120.) He had stopped at his lawyer's house for a customary cup of coffee, where he received a call from his sister, advising him of the raid. Matta's lawyer, telling him that there was nothing to fear, that he was guilty of no crimes in Honduras, instructed him to return home, which he did.

More stunning, almost certainly, than what might have happened at that point is what Matta must have reflected upon very shortly thereafter: not more than twenty-two hours would elapse between the moment Matta returned from his morning run in Honduras, to confront helicopters in his Tegucigalpa garden, and his lockdown in maximum security at Marion. He was still in his jogging outfit when he took up residence in Illinois. They had not even served breakfast yet. Some twenty years before, Juan Ramón Matta Ballesteros, sentenced to do time at Eglin, had been dealt with rather efficiently by the nation's deputy marshals. But "the stunned Matta," as he was described by an American newsmagazine upon his return to the country, had never seen anything like *this*.

On the drive between Matta's house and the U.S. air base at Palmerola, his American attorney claims, Matta was "beaten on his head, back, and arms, and severely burned by double-pronged electric stun guns." The Marshals Service, at the time, denied the use of stun guns as "preposterous." In his official history of the Service, written under its auspices, Frederick S.

Calhoun says Matta resisted Honduran officers' "efforts to get him into the marshals' rental car. As the deputies watched, Matta kicked and punched."

Jóse López, volunteering nothing, does not cop to being a spectator.

Calhoun continues: "[Matta] knocked one of the Hondurans to the ground before other officers overwhelmed him. As Matta, who feared he was on his way to his execution, struggled, the Hondurans put a hood over his head and pushed him to the floorboard of the marshals' car. . . . Two Honduran officers scrambled into the back with Matta. . . . Commander Gavilan and another deputy followed in a second car. . . . No one spoke —except Matta. He offered $1 million cash if they would release him. . . . he raised his offer to $2 million, then $3 million. During the forty-minute car ride, he upped the price several more times, finally promising $20 million in cash if only they would let him go. . . . When they reached the airport . . . Matta repeated his offer of $20 million cash, no waiting."

According to Calhoun, López, whom the author never identifies by name—referring to him only as Gavilan—reported the bribe offers to Howard Safir:

" 'Boss . . . he was getting close.' "

Version 1 of the official story fell apart almost immediately.

"There were some people in Honduras who saw us taking him out," says López, in what may be the understatement of the operation. "The whole scam was to have Matta brought to Santo Domingo and for the Dominicans to tell the world that he was found *there* and that he was expelled because he didn't have a passport. . . . We owe the Dominican government—they allowed us to land our plane there, send it from there to Honduras with a Dominican crew to pick him up, return to Santo Domingo, and lie to the fucking world that he was expelled from there because he was *found* in Santo Domingo."

In Santo Domingo, no one denies, Matta was placed on a U.S. commercial carrier bound for Puerto Rico. When the plane entered U.S. airspace, he was formally arrested on the Eglin escape warrant. He was flown, again on a commercial airliner, to New York's John F. Kennedy Airport, and from there, on a Marshals Service jet, to Marion.

Variation Number 2 of the story, immediately embraced by everyone involved, was that the Hondurans had arrested Matta and turned him over to the Americans; Version 3, officially denied, was that the Americans had actually put the cuffs on him. Either spin on the final scenario was sufficient to explain what happened next.

On Thursday, two days after what Marshals Service director Stanley Morris called the "creative arrest," some 1,500 students at Tegucigalpa's National Autonomous University, shouting "Matta, *Sí!* Gringos, *No!*," stormed the U.S. embassy, setting fire to a seven-story annex. Two hours elapsed between the time of the students' arrival at the building—at which point they commenced torching cars out front—and that of firefighters and riot police, the latter of whom occupy headquarters on a hill overlooking the compound. At least four protesters were killed and a fourteen-year-old Honduran girl burned to death in the riot. The following day, a thousand demonstrators marched on the National Assembly building and Honduran president José Azcona Hoyo declared a two-week state of emergency.

It was left to Attorney General Edwin Meese, speaking a day later at a news conference in Ecuador, and citing "the tremendous power of narcotics traffickers," to opine that it was they who had orchestrated the riots.

In fact, the outbust had been several years in the making, its spontaneity the result of the systematic cannibalizing of Honduras by Meese's appetitive boss, who, long before, in the course of a Latin American feeding frenzy, had bought up the country's leadership, subordinating the destiny of the people there to the destiny of the very narcotics traffickers who were financing his foreign policy. The "tremendous power" of their dope, by way of the more accessible avenue of infestation, had gone to work not on the student body of Tegucigalpa but on the addled head of the most dysfunctional American family ever to occupy the White House.

For his sins the nation would condemn the president to the torture, out of office, of the continued company of that family, whose reciprocal loathing will one day be matched, no doubt, by the derision in which he is held by history. His brother-in-arms, Juan Matta, would hardly be inclined to show sympathy. Convicted on trafficking charges, Matta received consecutive sentences in 1990 of 150 years and 75 years, respectively. Six months later, acquitted of murder, he was convicted of racketeering, kidnapping, and conspiracy in the death of Enrique Camarena and sentenced to three concurrent life terms for that.

He got three years for the escape from Eglin.

. . .

If you want to know how the politics of dope poisons national priorities in America, ask your local fisherman, nostalgic for the days when the U.S. Coast Guard had a search-and-rescue budget: when uniformed sailors and chopper pilots, fighting force-ten gales, risked their lives to pull the drowning out of twenty-five-foot seas, to lift doomed men off the decks of sinking trawlers, descending with all hands beneath the icy waters off Nantucket.

It is those same brave officers who are paid now to notch the prows of their cutters with quaint pictures of marijuana leaves, to steam the ocean in search of dope, leaving fishermen to go down with their vessels.

You know . . . the Coast Guard? It is that branch of the United States armed forces whose personnel can be seen today being dragged off to federal prison, half a dozen at a time, for drug trafficking.

Of those diseases associated with dope, none is as infectious, none is as thoroughly contaminating, as the money. The billions in revenue that dope generates today has suborned more people in the criminal justice system than was imaginable a decade ago. The indictment of police officers in South Florida on narcotics and murder charges is now not even enough to lead the local news broadcasts there. Neither is it uncommon in federal drug prosecutions to see lawyers indicted with their clients, nor are members of the bench immune. No man's price is so high that the dope market cannot support it. There is an entire army of the bought-off out there, and once bought off, they are bought off forever. And for everything.

If there is one endeavor that currently generates more questionable cash than drugs, it is the White House "war" on drugs. Dope is a growth industry not only for those who traffic in it—dope is a growth industry for cops.

As any law-enforcement bureaucrat will tell you: "That's where the money is."

There are now more people behind bars in the United States than live in the state of Hawaii—and in each of eleven other states. In 1989, for the first time in the nation's history, there were more than a million people incarcerated in its jails and prisons. On the first day of 1990 there were 1,032,000 men and women being held in state and federal custody, a population that more than doubled in fewer than ten years.

Nationally, some four million people are currently under one or another form of correctional supervision—in prison, in jail, on probation, or on parole. Many facilities are operating at over 200 percent of their capacities. In many jurisdictions, the typical probation or parole officer has more than 200 offenders to supervise.

The Bureau of Prisons—the federal system, alone—is currently holding close to 60,000 prisoners, operating at 162 percent capacity.

And half of them are in for dope.

By the time of its bicentennial, well over 50 percent of the Marshals Service's resources were expended on activities related to drug enforcement: pursuing fugitives on drug-related warrants; securing the trials of traffickers; protecting witnesses in those trials; seizing, maintaining, and disposing of assets forfeited in drug cases; and transporting prisoners incarcerated for drug offenses.

Due to a chronic lack of jail space, deputy marshals, daily, transport prisoners by motor vehicle between court appearances and correctional facilities hundreds of miles apart. Deputies in San Francisco have housed their prisoners in Los Angeles, a full day's drive away; for deputies servicing trials in Boston, New York, and Washington, a four-hour drive in each direction, pickup and return, is not at all unusual. The closest facility to house Rhode Island prisoners can be a two-hour trip to Hartford, Connecticut, or a three-and-a-half-hour drive to Danbury. It is common in the Western District of Missouri for deputies transporting prisoners to be on the road at 4 A.M. and return home at midnight; overnight bed space is such a problem and the prisoner load so heavy that the district now has only one deputy working warrants, down from three deputies six years ago, and that despite the fact that the warrant load has increased. Deputies in Philadelphia all know the distance to the detention facility in Alderson, West Virginia—800 miles round-trip. In the Northern District of New York, thirteen deputy marshals, working sixteen-hour shifts, must cover 32,000 square miles, producing prisoners for court appearances in six locations across the area. For the Western District of Texas—which on a single occasion, in thirty-four jails spread across thirty-one counties, has had 800 prisoners in custody—reducing prisoner transportation by a thousand miles a week would be the equivalent of adding two new deputies to the staff.

With 15,000 prisoners in custody on an average day (in 1990 prisoners were produced for court appearances more than 400,000 times), it is dope, no doubt, for better or worse, that will carry the Marshals Service into the twenty-first century.

A nation, specifically its cops and courts, concentrates its resources on drug enforcement at the heavy expense of protecting its citizens from rampant crimes of violence—homicide, armed robbery, sexual assault—but in the United States the first fatality in a politically motivated war on drug use is the nation's Constitution and the individual rights it guarantees. The U.S. citizen's freedom from "unreasonable searches and seizures" conflicts directly with modern drug-enforcement techniques, an inconvenience that has led to something of a dope exception to the Bill of Rights.

In a country founded upon the principle that your rights are not what the government gives you, but what the government cannot take away, the Supreme Court has upheld, among other violations of the traditional notion of liberty, government license to stop, detain, and question people on the basis of nothing more than "suspect profiles"; conduct warrantless searches of motor vehicles and closed containers within them; make warrantless seizures of cash; and obtain search warrants on the basis of the uncorroborated word of undisclosed informants.

(New Jersey authorities deny "racial targeting" on the state's highways, but studies corroborate the fact that driving the New Jersey Turnpike approximates running the gauntlet for black and Hispanic motorists, that warrantless searches of motor vehicles are more often than not conducted on the basis of race alone. While blacks account for 40 percent of drug and weapons arrests statewide, they account for 76 percent of such arrests on the turnpike. And they account for only 7 percent of the traffic on it. While statistics show that whites sell most of the nation's cocaine and account for 80 percent of its consumers, it is blacks and other minorities nationwide, in part because of the overt nature of inner-city drug activity, who bear the larger burden of the unchecked law-enforcement crackdown.)

The public's apparent willingness to surrender personal freedom, to cede greater police power to government, in the name of a crackdown on drug use, has led to that empowerment's liberal seepage into general law-enforcement application. Today, not only will they CCE you for drugs, they are very likely to RICO your ass for sex and rock and roll.

"The problem with the RICO statute," says New York civil rights lawyer Ronald Kuby, "is that it takes the focus away from the specific culpability of the individual, which has been the cornerstone of Anglo-American jurisprudence at least since the signing of the Magna Carta. Individuals do things wrong and individuals are punished for what they do wrong. What the RICO statute does is it shifts the notion of culpability to the idea of an enterprise. And anything [involving] more than one person can be [considered] an enterprise. It doesn't have to have a fixed membership [and] it doesn't have to have fixed boundaries. If you are part of an enterprise, whether it's two people or twenty people or a labor union, and some of those people in the enterprise are committing illegal acts on behalf of the enterprise, you can be held accountable."

Its principal danger from Kuby's perspective is with respect to political organizations.

"Frequently in this country, you have organizations, loose affiliations of people, who believe generally in one specific cause or a specific set of principles. 'U.S. Out of El Salvador.' 'Free Puerto Rico.' Within that organization there is a tremendous amount of diversity in terms of how people want to implement their policies, what they say and what they do. And the danger is if any members of that organization arguably do anything illegal . . . the FBI under RICO then justifies an investigation into each and every person affiliated with that group. . . . You have a RICO investigation of enormous scope. . . . That's what you had in the CISPES investigation and that's what you had in a lot of other investigations."

And while the practice helps boost agency conviction rates—with convictions of people only peripherally involved or of people who may not themselves have had any intent to commit a crime at all—its chief purpose is to broaden the scope of what would otherwise be a justifiedly narrow investigation.

"Let's say Joe belongs to CISPES and Joe is a violent individual. Under traditional notions, you can investigate Joe. Make sure Joe isn't planting any bombs. Make sure Joe isn't making any death threats. Once you look at Joe, though, in terms of the enterprise, you can investigate each and every member and affiliate of that organization with an eye to alleging that the whole organization, because of Joe, may or may not be a criminal enterprise. It gives you a tremendous investigative and intelligence-gathering scope."

The statute was written by G. Robert Blakey, a former law professor of Kuby's at Cornell.

"He has had consistently mixed feelings about its application," says Kuby, "but generally has refused, for the most part, to come out and condemn it. . . . In 1970, when it was proposed, its purpose was very narrow. Its original purpose was to go after organized crime. [There] you have Mafia dons who maintain several layers of insulation from the people who actually do the dirty work, so what you're left with is prosecuting button men, basically, trying to get them to turn on their bosses, which is very hard to do . . . you're left with prosecuting only the small fish. And RICO gave [the government] a tool to hook the big fish into the small fish."

RICO, as wielded by the government, has both criminal and civil applications; in civil procedure the government moves for forfeiture under the statute.

"But the principal criticisms I'm familiar with," Kuby says, "[concern] the use by *private* parties of civil RICO. . . . It provides a private cause of action to individuals to pursue a civil suit. . . . You really only have to prove two predicate acts." Kuby uses the example of an automobile dealership which has misrepresented the car it has sold you and then claims falsely to have repaired it. "Instead of simply going into small-claims court and suing them, you file a RICO action. . . . And lots of businesses have been vexed, and I won't say rightly or wrongly, by private litigants who decide to give themselves the same latitude that the federal government gives itself, which is to call anything, really anything in the world, a racketeering enterprise."

Charges of engaging in a Continuing Criminal Enterprise grow out of a different statute. CCE, says Kuby, is a punishment statute, a sentencing tool, not an investigative tool.

"CCE is primarily used to multiply punishments. . . . RICO provides the investigative apparatus and the substantive offense, and CCE provides for mind-bogglingly long sentences for an activity which the actor, him- or herself, may consider relatively trivial—not that society should. If you're in New York State and you sell a couple of vials of crack, you know that's a B felony, you can expect to plead it down to a C felony, you may end up doing a few months, at most you'll end up doing a year. Once they hook you in through RICO and CCE, you're looking at twenty, thirty, forty, fifty, a hundred years, basically for the same conduct. Because, again, the focus is not on the culpability of the actor, the focus is on the culpability of the enterprise."

Kuby says that in all of this, he finds the Marshals Service largely blameless.

"They didn't pass the statute, they didn't draft it, they weren't the judges who enlarged it, they're not the prosecutors who are constantly seeking a larger scope, and they're not the FBI which is primarily in charge of the investigations."

Kuby's problems with members of the Marshals Service, which are ample and undisguised, grow out of their conduct, or, as he sees it, their misconduct, with respect to political defendants.

"What I fault the marshals for is the overblown security I've had to face in numerous trials that prejudices [a jury's view of] defendants, often creates physical confrontations, creates an armed-camp atmosphere. . . . In political cases they consistently exaggerate the threat, [which] deprives defendants of a right to a fair trial, right to counsel, right to assist in their own defense. . . . They're the ones responsible for courtroom security . . . [and] that is their only concern. . . . They're not concerned with protecting a defendant's right to counsel, a defendant's right to a fair trial, a defendant's right to anything else. Their job is to make sure that under no circumstances is there going to be a threat posed in the courtroom. And they are unfortunately given wide discretion in doing that, because judges are reluctant to interfere with security measures. As a result, you quite often have the judge, whose responsibility it is to protect the defendant's rights, abdicating that responsibility and placing it with people whose first, second, fifth, tenth, and hundredth concern is making sure there's no problem in court."

Kuby cites as particularly prejudicial the court-security protocol he faced in a celebrated extradition trial of Sikh nationalists he was defending in New Jersey.

"When the magistrate and the prosecutor started receiving death threats, the prosecutor was ushered everywhere, including Oklahoma, surrounded by a phalanx of marshals. Our clients were brought into court in chains and shackles and remained [that way] all through the hearings. . . . Marshals were on the roof, marshals had a bomb disposal unit, marshals surrounded everything. Marshals treated our clients as though they [our clients] had authored the threats, and [treated] us [defense counsel] as though we were the ones who had smuggled [the threats] out of prison. And it was only a month later—after the hearings, of course—that the FBI got around to discovering that it was the special assistant prosecutor herself who had authored the threats. And she then checked herself into the loony bin. But that kind of exaggerated response . . ."

Not only does it prejudice a jury, Kuby says, but it creates practical problems that prevent defendants from assisting in their own defense.

"I had to get a *habeas corpus* petition because my client's wrists were not just handcuffed together, they were chained to his waist, and he couldn't, for example, pick up a document. And these people were utterly innocent of these threats. I had to file a *habeas corpus* petition to get a couple of links added to his chain. Because [deputy marshals] are charged with courtroom security, and because of their ideological hostility to political defendants—they are the ones who have custody of these people —the situation is ripe for abuse. Many, many, many defendants have suffered very outrageously at the hands of the marshals."

When Mike Pizzi and his deputies, before dragging them out of the courtroom in Brooklyn, took members of the self-styled United Freedom Front down, "down on the ground," in the words of Vic Oboyski, they did so using electric stun guns.

"I personally stun-gunned Levasseur, Manning, and Williams," Mike Pizzi volunteers with a certain measure of pride.

He argues that he did so only after the defendants played tough, and says he was ordered to remove them from the courtroom by the judge. Ron Kuby, who does not deny that his clients were tough guys, remembers the incident this way:

"[In Ohio] Ray Levasseur [had] made a statement. There was no physical confrontation, and there wouldn't have been a physical confrontation [in Brooklyn] but for the actions of the marshals. The marshals chose, instead of letting Ray [Levasseur] and Barbara Curzi finish reading their statements, they chose instead to physically assault the defendants. The marshals were spoiling for a fight. All the defendants were trying to do is read a relatively short statement. Later, after Tom Manning was captured, he managed to get stun-gunned as well—since he missed the first one—and he got stun-gunned in the face by the marshals. This was when he got transported. . . . [The marshals] were very candid with me when they talked about it, and their position was, 'Look, we knew these people were tough guys and we knew we were going to have a problem with them sooner or later. So we decided to pick the moment to show them who was in charge. And we picked that moment.' They were very candid with me about it."

But, claims Kuby, his clients' misfortune was more than to be tough guys.

"My experience is that with ODCs, you know, ordinary, decent criminals . . . they [the marshals] are not like that. We had a Hell's Angels trial in Ohio . . . three guys, members of the Hell's Angels, quite frankly a lot tougher than any of the Ohio Seven were, or certainly as tough. They were charged with murder. They machine-gunned a guy to death, the government said. And we never had any trouble with the marshals. The marshals were always friendly, they were polite to the guys, they would joke with them. And, in truth, the marshals and the Hell's Angels had a great deal in common, both in terms of their outlook in the world as well as membership in this quasi-fascist brotherhood. And there were no problems. . . . It actually came to the point when we had one day in court, actually the day Steve was found guilty, he sort of went off. He kicked the chair . . . and I asked the marshals to back off and let me deal with it. And they did. It was a completely different atmosphere. It was relaxed, it was laid back, it was friendly, it was polite. So [the incident in Brooklyn] was absolutely because of the political nature of the crimes."

The crimes, to the political nature of which Kuby refers—the crimes the United Freedom Front, the Ohio Seven, was accused of having committed—included several bombings, numerous armed bank robberies, and the cold-blooded murder of a state trooper, Philip Lamonaco, whose three small children, at home with their mother, were setting his place at the dinner table with Christmas cookies they had helped prepare while he was pulling traffic over on Route 80 in Warren County, New Jersey. And while it may be difficult to understand how such behavior constitutes a form of political expression guaranteed by the Bill of Rights, doing so does not explain away the fact that the group's courtroom statements went unchallenged in Ohio; probably more instructive in evaluating the incident in question is to harken back to the words of Victor Oboyski.

". . . you better bring lunch if you're going to come to Brooklyn and be a tough guy. You better bring lunch and be ready to hang around for dinner."

While the Marshals Service, in pursuit of fugitives, for example, likes to think of itself as proactive, and justifiably so, the agency, overall, by the very nature and the statutory limits of its mission, plays a largely *re*active role in federal law enforcement. The Marshals Service does not bring people *into* the criminal justice system; choking the nation's courts and prisons are people ushered thereto by its investigative agencies and federal prosecutors. (It is the Service's lack of control over the process that makes staffing and annual budgeting such an administrative nightmare.) But though drawn there by forces beyond its control, the Marshals Service nevertheless thrives, prospers just as vigorously as do all the nation's cops, at that bureaucratic trough polluted by the politics of dope.

Civil forfeiture proceedings can be traced through common-law England to the ancient Romans and Greeks. The United States has had provisions for property seizure since the founding of the Republic, since establishment of the Customs Service, which was authorized from the outset to confiscate the ships of smugglers apprehended evading import duties. The U.S. Supreme Court, after the Civil War, upheld the wartime forfeitures of southern-owned property located in the North and reaffirmed the principle during the years of the Volstead Act.

There are currently more than a hundred civil forfeiture statutes in the U.S. Code; they are designed to enforce an array of federal laws ranging from agriculture violations to copyright infringement. But not until the advent of RICO and expansion of the controlled substances laws (the Comprehensive Crime Control Act of 1984 and the Anti-Drug Abuse Acts of 1986 and 1988) did they threaten to distort the focus of criminal prosecution in America.

As the Iron Curtain comes crashing down under an onslaught of democracy, as it gives way under the superb force, the sheer weight of historic inevitability, we witness the sudden growth in the United States of a body of curious case law associated with offenses that smack of crimes against the state.

Today, about a quarter of all federal cases involve offenses that subject defendants to the nation's forfeiture statutes. Not only has civil procedure begun to overshadow criminal prosecution in America, in many cases it has come to replace it. Under its ever-expanding drug and racketeering statutes—legislation is currently pending to broaden the scope of the forfeiture laws even further—the federal government is now seizing the real estate and other private property of its citizens not simply in the absence of an owner's conviction but in the absence of bringing criminal charges.

When seizing real estate—for instance, your home—the government is required only to allege in court that probable cause exists to believe that a crime was committed there, that the property, for example, was used in the possession of drugs, aided in the distribution of them, or was purchased with the proceeds derived therefrom. The probable cause can be the word of an undisclosed informant, say a disgruntled former husband or wife who claims he or she was present when you got loaded with friends on the premises.

The law does not require that drugs be found on the property.

The Drug Enforcement Administration can seize cash and other property, such as cars, boats, and airplanes, with no court proceedings at all. It is the owner's responsibility to bring the proceedings in court and there to prove his innocence. At his own expense—and presumably with borrowed money, since all his assets have been confiscated. That such seizure might violate the Fourth Amendment to the Constitution is irrelevant; the law does not impose the penalty on the owner but, by way of a legal fiction, states that the property itself is guilty and that the property has no constitutional rights.

In civil complaints brought by the government, the burden of proof for upholding a charge rests solely on reasonable suspicion. The evidence introduced need not prove guilt "beyond a reasonable doubt," as it would in a criminal complaint. The property itself, not a criminal defendant, is the object of the government's case, and the standard of proof permits prosecutors to introduce hearsay and other evidence inadmissible in a criminal trial; once the probable-cause showing is made, the burden switches to the property owner to prove by a "preponderance of the evidence" that the allegations against the property are wrong.

In those instances where the civil forfeiture case grows out of a criminal indictment, acquittal on all counts contained therein is insufficient to disprove the presumption of guilt on which the success of the government's case rests. You may beat the rap—

you may be completely innocent—but more often than not you can kiss the property and your bank accounts goodbye.

It is the fear of many Americans, many federal officials among them, that the lure of seized assets is distorting the priorities of the nation's law-enforcement agencies. Increasingly the statutes are being applied to seize very valuable property for very minor offenses. Increasingly, case agents and their supervisors, in deciding what crimes to investigate, are asking themselves, "What can we seize?" Their seduction by the revenue available—asset forfeiture funds come back to the agencies in the form of national drug-war budgeting—not to mention the high visibility that major seizures promise, are clearly skewing the choices authorities make as to what cases to become involved in. The tendency exists to concentrate on relatively safe operations, to pursue the wealthiest criminals, not the most dangerous.

Adding a profit incentive to law enforcement, which up to now has been commonly associated with the corruption of Third World police forces, draws official attention away, it is argued, from securing the safety of the public. Arrests for homicide, rape, robbery, and assault yield dividends that are not negotiable.

Particularly convincing in support of the argument is that the acceleration in application of the nation's forfeiture laws is traceable quite directly to August 1985, following authorization by Congress (in the Comprehensive Crime Control Act of 1984) of "equitable sharing" of seized-assets proceeds with state and local cops. The Act allowed the attorney general to share money forfeited in federal cases with local law-enforcement agencies in proportion to their participation in the investigations. The sudden willingness of the local authorities to devote a significant portion of their time, personnel, and resources to supporting federal drug busts was veritably breathtaking:

The value of assets seized by the federal government skyrocketed from $27 million in 1985 to a projected $700 million for 1991. In 1990 alone the government returned more than $200 million to state and local agencies nationwide, some of them receiving single cash payments in excess of their annual budgets. Equitable-sharing decisions executed by the Department of Justice alone—44,000 of them starting in 1986—have returned a total of $575 million to state and local police.

The Marshals Service administers two key features of the Justice Department's asset seizure initiative: the National Asset

Seizure and Forfeiture Program (NASAF), which manages and disposes of assets; and the Assets Forfeiture Fund, which distributes the proceeds.

The Service is currently managing over $1.4 billion worth of property, half of it real estate. (The figure does not include cash. Managed by the Marshals Service, awaiting final determination of forfeiture in a special Treasury Department account—the Seized Asset Deposit Fund—is another $349 million.) The assets must be secured, inventoried, appraised, stored, and otherwise generally maintained. Much of the work, including the profitable operation of businesses that have been seized, is accomplished through hundreds of property managers and commercial vendors under contract with the Service or through court-appointed trustees.

The Marshals Service hires countless appraisers and auctioneers. It uses brokers, sales agents, and other liquidation services, disposing of property by way of public sale or other commercially feasible means; transfer to federal, state, or local law-enforcement agencies (cars, boats, airplanes, and other crime-fighting equipment more valuable to them than the cash the assets would bring at auction); and salvage, scrap, and destruction.

All forfeited currency and all the money received from the sale of forfeited assets are deposited in the Assets Forfeiture Fund, the primary function of which is to underwrite the expense of carrying out additional seizures. Injected into the fund in fiscal year 1990—in which the Service processed and maintained paper records on 34,000 asset cases, some of which, individually, involved hundreds of seized items—was $460 million. Nearly $56 million of that was used to pay for the program: asset management costs, case-related expenses, and payment of third-party claims. Another $115 million was earmarked for new prison construction. (Since 1986, the first full year of the program, NASAF has coughed up a half-billion dollars to fund the building of prisons.) More than $175 million, through 19,000 equitable-sharing decisions, went to state and local law-enforcement agencies.

A total of $24 million went to informants.

Counter clerks and baggage handlers at airports, bus terminals, and train stations; operators of the X-ray machines at various security checkpoints; and the employees of large package-delivery services thrive on the underground economy that is fueled by asset seizure and forfeiture.

A copyrighted six-day series published by the *Pittsburgh Press* in the summer of 1991 chronicled the results of a ten-month investigation in which reporters for the newspaper reviewed 25,000 seizures made by the DEA, interviewed 1,600 prosecutors, defense lawyers, policemen, federal agents, and victims, and examined court documents from 510 cases.

The investigation, which unearthed an ample number of cases in which the assets of innocent people have been summarily seized by the government, revealed that at all but one of sixteen major airports, private employees are rewarded by drug interdiction teams for drawing their attention to "suspicious activity," the informants typically collecting 10 percent of the value of whatever is confiscated.

Lieutenant Norbert Kowalski, who oversees the joint Allegheny County–Pennsylvania State Police interdiction team at the Greater Pittsburgh International Airport, says his team does not do so and questions the practice, worrying that the system, according to the newspaper, "might encourage unnecessary random searches" and, in Kowalski's words, "may be pushing what's proper law enforcement to the limit."

The newspaper's investigation, bearing out Kowalski, revealed that in 1990 Kowalski's team, checking passengers arriving on 4,230 flights, stopped 527 people and made forty-nine arrests; over the same period a similar team at Denver's Stapleton Airport, where most cases start with informant tips, stopped an estimated 2,000 people. And they made forty-nine arrests.

"As Kowalski sees it," reports the newspaper, "the public vests authority in police with the expectation that they will use it legally and judiciously. The public can't get those same assurances with police designees, like counter clerks, says Kowalski. . . . '[Money as an inducement] can infringe on the rights of innocent travelers. If someone knows [he] can get a good bit of money by turning someone in, then [he] may imagine seeing or hearing things that aren't there. What happens when you get to court?' "

Kowalski's question brings to the topic a kind of ingenuousness that is refreshing, a kind of credulousness that is echoed in his altogether straightforward reference to such legal hallucinations as "the rights of innocent travelers."

The answer to Kowalski's question is that police who work the airports deliberately delay paying informants until a case has been resolved.

"Because we don't want these tipsters to have to testify," Captain Judy Bawcum, commander of the vice division of the Nashville Police Department, is quoted by the newspaper as saying. "If we don't pay them until the case is closed, they don't have to risk going to court."

Where their motivation might be questioned.

(The *Pittsburgh Press* reports that Wackenhut, the company whose personnel man X-ray security checkpoints, refuses to allow Nashville police to use its workers as informants, fearful that the promise of money will prompt employees to look for drugs and cash—watching for "suspicious" shadows—at the expense of scanning for weapons, the more critical activity certainly, and the one to which their mandate is limited.)

Ticket agents alert police to travelers who pay in cash, to those who buy one-way tickets, and to those who dress suspiciously well—blacks, Hispanics, and Asians, for example, who do not appear poverty-stricken. In 121 cases examined by the *Pittsburgh Press,* in which police found no dope, made no arrest, but seized money anyway, 77 percent of the travelers stopped were black, Hispanic, or Asian.

Police affidavits and court testimony in several cities, reports the newspaper, "show clerks for large package handlers, including United Parcel Service and Continental Airlines' Quik Pak, open 'suspicious' packages and alert police to what they find. To do the same thing, police [themselves] would need a search warrant."

Kickbacks to amateur informants, the newspaper's investigation revealed, are dwarfed by those made to professionals; among the best paid of the latter are various convicted drug dealers, more than one of whom is cited as having amassed a fortune in government juice, which can be as high as 25 percent. In a typical case the government is the party offering the dope, aggressively pursuing a buyer, pressing him to make a deal, for the purpose of seizing the cash he ultimately puts together.

In one eighteen-month undercover investigation cited by the newspaper, Arizona state police, acting as drug couriers, actually loosed close to thirteen tons of marijuana onto the streets of Tucson, overestimating their ability to control the distribution (to the gratitude of pot smokers everywhere). John Davis, the former assistant attorney general who supervised the investigation, labeled the operation "a success." It returned $3 million to the state forfeiture fund and resulted in twenty arrests. To Davis's way of thinking—which is no doubt considered enlightened by people who enjoy ready access to dope—that was enough to celebrate success "from a cost-benefit standpoint."

"Neither the decision to seize nor the decision to forfeit," says Ronald Kuby, is the responsibility of the Marshals Service. "Their job is to carry it out; they get their marching orders on how to proceed."

Assets seized over the years by the Service have included cars, trucks, other motor vehicles, boats, ships, and aircraft; residential and commercial real properties such as horse farms, recording studios, golf courses, banks, office buildings, apartment houses, historic mansions, ranches, restaurants, and retail stores; cash, jewelry, coins, gold, silver, other precious metals, financial instruments, art objects, antiques, livestock, electronic equipment, laboratory equipment, chemicals, foodstuffs, and weapons.

There was a brass and aluminum foundry in Wisconsin (operated for a year by the Marshals Service before being sold for $1.9 million); a nursery and flower shop in Massachusetts; a quarter-horse racing stable near Floresville, Texas (the upkeep on which, including feeding, training, and racing the stock—seven of the eighty-eight horses were entered into the racing program at Los Alamitos, California—was $30,000 a month); a championship thoroughbred show horse with stud fees worth $2.5 million; an island off the coast of Florida; a 4,000-tree macadamia nut plantation in Hawaii; a rare 1963 Ferrari 250 GTO, one of only thirty-two in existence, seized in Ridgefield, Connecticut (sold at auction for $1.6 million, of which $144,000 was awarded to the police departments of Portsmouth and Newport, Rhode Island); 21,000 baseball cards in a collection auctioned in Newport; a handmade, 1981 Italian Stutz Diplomatica, one of seven such automobiles manufactured, seized in Portland, Connecticut; five mountain lions seized in Naples, Florida; a herd of cattle in Muskogee, Oklahoma; a reggae bar—The Wild Hare and Singing Armadillo Frog Sanctuary—in Chicago; three fraternity houses at the University of Virginia; a shopping mall and three gas stations in Puerto Rico; two barbecue restaurants named Jilly's Place of Ribs in Atlanta; a card casino in Bell Gardens, California, advertised as the largest in the world (which employs 1,900 people, grosses $100 million annually, contributes $10 million a year in taxes to the city, and shows a profit of more than $1 million a month); a luxury-car dealership in Baltimore; a golf course in Michigan; a recording studio (inevitably christened "Club Fed") in Sausalito, California; a Dairy Queen; a citrus grove; a topless bar in Syracuse, New York; and $2 million worth of rare U.S. gold coins—including a 1933 ten-dollar "Eagle" worth as much as $80,000 and an 1879 four-dollar "Stella" valued at $35,000—which had been buried in five remote locations across the country.

In New York, application of the forfeiture statutes has proved to be an effective law-enforcement tool for shutting down, at least temporarily, certain lucrative drug operations. In raids on numerous crack-and-heroin enterprises there, deputies, to the delight of local residents, have seized apartment buildings by the dozens.

"We took the entire building, a six-story structure," says Bill Hufnagel, a deputy in the Southern District of New York. "We took a hundred and forty city cops, thirty-five U.S. marshals, and five DEA agents—we actually had to have the briefing in a stadium, because there were so many people and so many things involved. We hit it, and while the raids were going on in the various apartments . . . many of the search teams didn't realize it, but they were all being surveilled by the bad guys as the search was going on . . ."

The Marshals Service does not even have a job description for what in other agencies is handled by certain specialists, handled not by investigators or agents but by people commonly referred to as "tech guys." The Marshals Service, underbudgeted and leanly staffed, instead has Huff and Cuff, deputies Bill Hufnagel and John Cuff, a pair of electronics wizards in New York's Southern District who have come by their expertise on the job and solely on their own initiative.

"A wire man," says Tony Perez of Hufnagel, "a magician with that stuff," and Perez is in a position to know. Tony Perez, pursuant to his investigation of escaped bank robbers Conner and Dougherty—their apprehension in 1987 closed a celebrated 15 Most Wanted case—secured the first court-authorized Title III wiretap in the history of the Marshals Service. Perez was required to channel through the FBI the affidavit in request of the surveillance; the Marshals Service did not receive Title III authority, which permits such electronic searches as the live monitoring of telephone communications, until January 1988. It was Conner-Dougherty that provided the precedent and, according to John Cuff, the Marshals Service right now has "the best Title III authority there is." As Hufnagel explains it, "We need very little to get a Title III . . . any escapee, any bail jumper . . . it doesn't take a lot for us. Presumption of innocence isn't as great for an ex-con or somebody who has already been convicted."

In securing Title III wiretaps, good only for thirty days, subject to monthly renewal, agents must prove to the court that all other investigative resources have been exhausted. The burden is on the government to minimize intrusion and agents monitoring the equipment come under the scrutiny of the court.

"Phone taps got to be airtight," Tony Perez insists. "The U.S. attorney will prosecute *you* if you fuck up."

Many federal investigations are conducted in collaboration with local authorities because state wiretaps are easier to procure.

Title III authority is not required to secure court orders for traps or pen registers. A court-ordered trap-and-trace, however, must be conducted by the telephone company, the equipment monitored by its personnel, never by law-enforcement agents. A trap not only logs the date, time, and destination (the telephone number dialed) of all outgoing calls, but logs the date, time, and *source* (the number from which a call is received) of all incoming calls as well. The immediacy of the information—"Your trap just fired"—is controlled by the telephone company.

A pen register, by contrast, can be controlled by the agent himself. More accurately known as a DNR, a dialed-number recorder, and used routinely, for example, by hotels, a pen register is so named for the stylus of the instrument which once rendered the information; detecting dial pulses, it generated what resembled a polygraph readout. A pen register logs everything *but* the source of incoming calls.

Marshals Service personnel, given the agency's recently acquired bugging privileges and given, for example, the sophisticated anti-intrusion equipment used by WITSEC, have developed, as have all cops, a certain familiarity with modern electronics, but when it comes to state-of-the-art knowledge, the Service relies very heavily upon people like Huff and Cuff. If there is an advantage to be derived from the circumstances, it is that, as investigators, such deputies not only take their education from, but exercise it upon, practical application of the equipment in question. Deployed as agents in the field, they *use* the equipment they install. They also see it used against them. And when it comes to the state of the art, they will tell you, the opposition is clearly setting the pace. Dope dealers are, without question, out on the leading edge.

"They had co-ax cable coming up, from an Alert DX12, secreted in the walls," says Hufnagel, "and [they had] over-the-counter transmitting and receiving devices. They had directional antennas six stories up, one in the front of the building and one in the back, [enhanced by a] pulse, so they could get a lot more range out of [the system]. The bad guys would roll around in livery cabs and do two-block grids around the apartment house, and if they spotted any of the under-covers, they would hit the transmitter. The signal would be picked up by the antenna and set off the alarm on the boxes . . . so they would know to start dumping everything, hiding everything. . . . Some of our guys noticed [the equipment] and they didn't know what it was. 'Is this cable TV or what?' They didn't know what they were looking at. We emptied out twenty-something apartments [out of a total of forty-six]. As soon as we hit the place, two and a half kilos of coke came out the window. Two nine-millimeters and $14,000 cash, in a sack, flew out [another] window when we hit the back."

But, as Hufnagel points out, such equipment is available to consumers from any electronics outlet.

"The transmitters and receivers . . . you could use them for anything . . . an alarm system, anything you wanted to turn on remotely . . . say, with a garage door opener. . . . You can buy and sell them [legally]."

What you cannot buy is the eavesdropping equipment.

"They had bugs, actual bugs . . . on an aircraft frequency. . . . They were sitting out in the cars listening to the radio. They were bugging themselves. If they heard something going down . . . a rip-off . . . the strong-arm guys would come in from outside. . . . [The bugs] are controlled equipment. Even the frequency they were operating on, for the manufacturer to use that frequency is illegal. . . . Those are FCC violations, because you're interfering with aircraft. . . . They are not U.S. manufacturers, they're Israeli and German companies. [Those countries] don't have the controls on them that we do. [We have to control entry at the border.] They're usually unmarked devices. The companies don't want [the equipment] coming back on them. You been in the business long enough, and you seen enough of them, you know what's being made where by the circuitry and the way it's designed. . . . Countersurveillance and countermeasure equipment is readily available [to anyone] especially in Europe."

The sophistication of the electronic eavesdropping devices available to the nation's cops (and not unavailable to its criminals), the number of ways the government can get you, is nothing short of stupefying. Much of the technology is classified.

"Most of the warrants are sealed. So a lot of the stuff doesn't come out. And the stuff that does come out doesn't give you the whole picture."

But taking down crack-and-heroin dens is an education in more than one branch of science; in the eyes of the nation's deputy marshals, such property seizures occur where the Space Age in fact meets the Middle Ages, where the modern black market invokes visions of the medieval Black Death.

"We've actually had guys," Frank Devlin confides, "we couldn't put the handcuffs on 'em, their wrists . . . arms, legs . . . are so swollen from drugs. . . . Abscess, infection, sores from shootin' up . . . uncared for. Eventually they lose the limb."

And Devlin reports to work in New York's "Hollywood" district—as Southern is known to those deputies who work the other side of the bridge—so named for the people who have illuminated the many celebrated trials conducted in the U.S. Courthouse at Manhattan's Foley Square: Jackie Kennedy, John Mitchell, Ariel Sharon, Muhammad Ali, Howard Cosell, William Westmoreland, Bess Myerson, Donald Trump, Leona Helmsley, Imelda Marcos, and Michael Milken, to name a few and some of the more recent, and not to mention such illustrious figures in the annals of postwar American crime as Alger Hiss, Whittaker Chambers, and Julius and Ethel Rosenberg.

No man in America has been photographed more often on the arms, completely gratuitously, of more celebrated defendants—descending the seventeen granite steps of the neoclassical courthouse—than Romulo Imundi, who has managed since 1981 to hold the job of U.S. marshal for the Southern District of New York.

If you think of Foley Square as that stretch of Sunset Boulevard that winds through Beverly Hills, you can think of Cadman Plaza East, just across the river, as Front Street on the edge of Dodge.

There, in the headquarters of the Eastern District, the tabloid headline that adorns the door to the office of the Warrants Squad reads: WAR ZONE, BROOKLYN.

"I get more work done," Mike Pizzi says, "between 6 and 9 A.M. than most people do all week."

When, at the end of the day, Pizzi announces into the telephone, "It's total war, no holds barred," he is talking to a reporter and he is talking about his district's preoccupation with drug enforcement.

In support of that preoccupation, Pizzi's crew has developed what amounts to an entire subspecialty in seized real estate.

"Take the door! Take the door!"

Dave O'Flaherty had hollered so many commands through the dilapidated wall of the apartment—he could actually see through it in places—that the occupants beyond it now had no idea what to do. And before the bad guys had time to think, before they got creative and came up with something on their own, O'Flaherty wanted in.

Oboyski hit the door.

Operating openly as a crack factory and a twenty-four-hour drug supermarket, Crack Castle, as it had come to be known, comprised a pair of adjoining, three-story residential buildings, 395 and 397 Westervelt Avenue, in the New Brighton section of Staten Island, New York. To walk-in and drive-up customers, the group occupying the apartment houses had been moving up to 2,500 vials of ten-dollar crack a day. Intimidated neighbors, according to the U.S. Attorney's office, had been complaining "for years," and in the four months before the hit, the two locations had been host to thirty-four drug arrests by city police.

The buildings, located, according to U.S. Marshal Charles Healey, "within walking distance of a public elementary school," had fallen into disrepair; among their numerous escape routes was a hole providing passage through the contiguous stonework separating the two. As Dave O'Flaherty would later concede, the front door had come down easy. And since just before they hit it, O'Flaherty had been hollering.

There was more than one reason to do so.

O'Flaherty says that screaming "lets out [your] anxiety," as much as scares the opposition. But more than that, he is quick to point out, it "lets them know who you are."

Put a tape recorder on a typical hit and you will hear the word "Police!" yelled out more times than you are able to count.

Says one narcotics cop:

"It cuts your chances of getting killed by about 90 percent."

The last thing a cop wants is to be mistaken for a stick-up man.

The first floor had been empty. The stairway had been shaky, it was hanging off the wall. And now O'Flaherty, on the second floor, over the barrel of a shotgun, had totally confused the occupants of the apartment he was about to enter, screaming contradictory commands. He had given maybe a dozen or so, shouting through the holes in the masonry, when Oboyski hit the door.

The door was nothing special, it had not been reinforced, no security gates, nothing like that. A standard steel fire-door, New York City, up to code. But for some reason it resisted the sledge. It was going to go eventually, maybe in several seconds, but that was not quick enough for O'Flaherty.

"Take the fucking wall!" he said.

It was one of those shining moments in the course of human events where a man is invited to accede to a dignity reserved for him by destiny:

Victor Oboyski, exploding plaster, lathing, and structural carpentry, crashing in much as King Kong would, actually entered the apartment through the wall. On any other planet in the universe he would have been allowed to eat the people inside.

Deputies followed him in.

Fifteen people were arrested that day, nine women, six men, and a total of three buildings were seized.

When Pizzi's crew hit the sidewalk, they witnessed a piece of street theater that was like nothing they had seen in their lives. Yet over the months that followed it would be played out again and again for them, set against the ravaged backdrop of an ever-changing urban landscape, and soon it would cease to bewilder them.

The citizens of Staten Island, New York, stood applauding the federal government; they stood there, in force, cheering deputy marshals with repeated cries of "God Bless America."

14.

Too Tough to Die

Irving Berlin's patriotic masterpiece, "God Bless America"—written in 1917, first performed on Armistice Day 1938 by popular radio personality Kate Smith, and finally published a year later, its royalties the property of the Boy and Girl Scouts of America—however unofficially, is by acclamation of the people the national anthem of the United States.

And it is embraced as such for reasons that transcend its own obvious merits.

Chief among those reasons—"America the Beautiful" finishes a very strong second—is that in every way imaginable, in the undisguised opinion of a nation, "The Star Spangled Banner" is a musical disaster.

Written in 1814 and first published under the title "Defense of Fort M'Henry," Francis Scott Key's overvenerated ode, set to the tune of "To Anacreon in Heaven"—no doubt by some sadistic nineteenth-century music teacher—is a song which has busted the musical chops of even its most intrepid performers since well before its adoption by Congress in 1931.

Few are the tasks more thankless, far fewer the spectator sports traditionally more unrewarding, than that adventure which is heralded by a recital of the notes inescapably associated with the words *Oh say, can you see . . .*

"Get him a blazer . . . !"

And today that was only the half of it.

"Is he wearing a necktie . . . ?"

There was a sartorial crisis in the public-affairs office.

Stanley E. Morris, director of the United States Marshals Service, putting a close to the most successful five years of his bureaucratic life, was presiding over the dedication of the most tangible, yet merely the most recent, symbol of that success; having given them back their past, Morris was now tendering to the nation's deputy marshals striking physical evidence of the distinguished future he had engineered for them.

The ribbon-cutting ceremony, in the front courtyard of a modern office tower of bronzed glass and polished granite—new on the Arlington skyline, overlooking the Potomac, within loud-hailing distance of the Pentagon—represented the agency's move of its headquarters from the second floor of a shopping mall in Tyson's Corner, Virginia, out beyond the beltway, out there among the shoe stores, the record shops, the movie theaters, the piped-in music, fast-food tables, the intimate-apparel emporiums, and Nordstrom's . . . "yes, Mr. President, you go down past the Foot Locker . . . ," to the top five floors of a building in the international style from a corner office of which Morris had trained a telescope on the windows of the new Soviet embassy.

The sartorial crisis in question . . . well, history shall record it thus:

On September 26, 1988, just about 4 P.M., Stanley Morris stood facing the Stars and Stripes, his hand held over his heart, presently to introduce Richard L. Thornburgh, the latest in that truly bipartisan line of singularly undistinguished U.S. attorneys general, as the national anthem—yes, that very same "Star Spangled Banner"—was tackled by a hired trumpet player who had shown up for the occasion dressed as if he had been called to work an Allman Brothers gig.

. . . and the home . . . of the . . . brave.

The United States Marshals Service was exactly one year short of 200 years old.

And rock 'n' roll was king.

As Marvin Mack would say:
"What a country."

"Oklahoma is still woolly . . . some youngster would try to put me out because of my reputation. I would be bait for grown-up kids who had fed on dime novels. I would have to kill or be killed. No sense to that. I have taken my guns off, and I don't ever want to put them on again."

Bat Masterson, a former lawman of wide and well-earned reputation, was a national celebrity when in 1905 he declined Theodore Roosevelt's offer to appoint him U.S. marshal for the Oklahoma Territory. Having given up for good the gunfighter's life, earning his living as a newspaper columnist for the *Morning Telegraph* in New York (he would moonlight as a part-time deputy marshal in the Southern District for four years), the man who had tamed Dodge, the toughest cattle town in the West, may have been overplaying his hand a bit when he wrote the twenty-sixth president:

"I am not the man for the job."

Oklahoma may have been woolly in 1905—a fifty-two-year-old gambling man whose eyesight and reflexes were finally beginning to fail him, Masterson, as a former sheriff of Ford County, Kansas, would be in a position to know—but by then the territory and what remained of the frontier could only loosely be considered wild.

The conquest of the Great Plains and subsequent taming of the American West are traced officially through U.S. history to a single twenty-four-hour moment, to February 15, 1876, the day the first patent was issued for the manufacture of barbed wire. But across the frontier of the American imagination, along the trail of the national character, the closing of the wilderness is tracked to another, no less momentous occurrence and a patent issued three years earlier: to development of the first Colt cartridge revolvers, seared in the American spirit by instrument of the .45-caliber, single-action Army Model 1873—marketed alternately and written into folklore as both the Peacemaker and, rechambered for .44-40, the Frontier Six-Shooter—the weapon that mythopoetically *won* the West.

Every soldier, every lawman, and every significant scumbag on the American frontier did at least part of his killing with one of these gate-loaded revolvers, the official cavalry pistol of the

United States Army. From Ben Thompson to Belle Starr, John Wesley Hardin to Tom Horn—they all went about littering the landscape with the help of the late Sam Colt's case-hardened "equalizer."

Wild Bill Hickok, who is famous for having carried a variety of guns, was carrying any number of them—but holding in his hand only aces and eights—when Jack McCall blew the back of his head all over the floor of a Deadwood saloon in 1876, with a Peacemaker. Jesse James was similarly dispatched six years later by the outlaw Bob Ford.

As an expression of the problem in the West and not its solution, the Peacemaker was showcased quite dramatically—there were several of them on hand—in what may be the most celebrated half-minute in American frontier history. That episode, destined to illuminate the annals of the nation's folklore indelibly, was a small-time street fight devoid of all honor, conducted in a dust-blown silver boomtown in the high desert of southeastern Arizona; it is an incident whose lingering association with the United States Marshals Service, while no less indelible, is peripheral at best.

It was in his official capacity as a deputy U.S. marshal that Virgil Earp, accompanied by his brothers Morgan and Wyatt, the latter a Cochise County deputy sheriff, enjoyed his first encounter with Frank McLaury on the morning of July 25, 1880, at McLaury's cattle ranch on the Babocomari Creek outside Tombstone, Arizona. An exchange of greetings right out of *Heart of Darkness*—"I heard the original quarrel arose over a misunderstanding about some hens"—the confrontation followed a misappropriation of government property earlier that month, six U.S. Cavalry mules which had found their way into the cowboy's possession.

It was a showdown the characteristic nature of which revealed itself fifteen months later when, in a matter of seconds, festering personal differences were reconciled on Tombstone's Fremont Street, in a vacant lot between the home of lumber dealer W. A. Harwood and a rooming house owned by photographer Camillus Fly and his wife, a piece of unimproved property situated about ninety feet west of the rear alleyway-exit to Allen Street's O.K. Corral.

On that cold fall afternoon in the American Southwest, on the high plateau, in a town that boasted "a dead man for breakfast every morning"—on October 26, 1881, three months after the death of Billy the Kid some 400 miles to the northeast—when the Earps and a homicidal dentist, the tubercular "Doc" Holliday, dispatched three unfortunate cowboys, Frank and Tom McLaury and the young Billy Clanton (his brother Ike escaped), to Tombstone's flourishing Boot Hill, the frontier lawman, however ignominiously, secured a legitimate lock on American gunfighting legend.

It was in reinforcement of that legend that Heck Thomas entered Indian Territory five years later, scoured it for the following ten, and it is out of the mythology of such events that the deputy marshal rides today. From that overworked saddle tramp wearing out federal horseflesh to an underpaid pair of them putting too many miles on the clock of a low-octane Ford, the deputy marshal exits his second century much as he did his first: setting forth to bring government, however unwelcome, to the vast reaches of a nation one of whose eloquent founders, a full decade after its creation, was moved to declare, "I hold it, that a little rebellion, now and then, is a good thing," to remind each of its citizens that "The tree of liberty must be refreshed from time to time with the blood of patriots and tyrants."

In the years that have passed since Bill Doolin leveled a Winchester in self-serving interpretation of that fluent discourse, since Heck Thomas ranged over a lawless frontier cleaning up after Thomas Jefferson, surprisingly little has changed.

Out of a field office in Moscow, Idaho, a deputy marshal named Denny Scieszinski today patrols terrain stretching from Hells Canyon east to the Bitterroot Mountains, from the Salmon River all the way north to the border of British Columbia, 41,000 square miles of some of the most beautiful and rugged country in North America. And he covers the territory alone. In a four-wheel drive, carrying a radio and a gun—"I have more than one of those"—he serves process and tracks down fugitives, riding the range much as Pat Garrett did in 1881, bringing law and order to a landscape that has changed not at all in 200 years, and, if God and Denny Scieszinski have their way, never will.

Garrett survives in Scieszinski just as he survives in every deputy marshal from Gerri Doody to José López. He survives in deputies like Bill Woolsey, who tracks fugitives today on the squad that some fifteen years ago Tony Perez put together in the Central District of California.

Born in 1951, raised in Arcadia, California, Woolsey, enforcement supervisor in the Los Angeles office, entered the United States Marshals Service in October 1979 after two years of college, a hitch in the U.S. Army, and two and a half years as a local cop in the town of Sierra Madre, a suburban community in the San Gabriel Valley.

To sign on with the government, Woolsey, like deputies before him and after him, took a substantial pay cut, the second time he had done so since acting on the decision to pursue a career in law enforcement—as a bartender in his uncle's Arcadia saloon, the Drinker's Hall of Fame, across from the Santa Anita racetrack, Woolsey, as a civilian, had pulled in up to $200 a day.

In 1982 Woolsey was assigned to warrants. On November 14, 1984, in Seal Beach, California, he and his partner, Phil Martino —who together, working for Tony Perez, averaged 150 fugitive arrests a year—captured wanted Nazi war criminal Andrija Artukovic, who had been living illegally in the United States since 1949. Sought by the government of his native Yugoslavia, Artukovic was charged in the mass murder of over half a million Serbs, Jews, Orthodox Croatians, gypsies, and other "enemies" of the Independent State of Croatia, the puppet regime established there during the Second World War by Nazi Germany.

Pursuant to an extradition order, the two deputies, to a hero's welcome, personally escorted the fugitive back to Zagreb to stand trial.

Woolsey, "five-nine-and-a-half, one-ninety-one, brown and brown," who decided in high school to become a cop—he was working at the time in a drive-through burger joint, where being on the local force was good for a free cup of coffee—is a federal agent who will tell you that police work runs in the family.

You can trace it back four generations, he will tell you, to his maternal grandmother's mother's father, an Alabama-born peace officer who served as a sheriff, a deputy marshal, a Texas Ranger, and a Collector of Customs, a frontier lawman who retired to ranching until, at the age of fifty-seven, he himself died by the gun, at close range, from ambush, shot in the back of the head.

Yes, Deputy U.S. Marshal Bill Woolsey will tell you, "Pat Garrett was my great-great-grandfather."

Epilogue

GERRI DOODY continues to work warrants in the Eastern District of New York. In the year 2000, having put in twenty years hazardous, she will be eligible for retirement, she says. "On the Fourth of July, 2000," she reports, "there's going to be fireworks . . . a big party."

DAVE O'FLAHERTY, in June 1991, replaced Mike Pizzi as the Eastern District's Chief Deputy.

VICTOR OBOYSKI, currently acting Warrants Supervisor in the Eastern District, was elected in 1990—in part, no doubt, on the basis of his angelic refusal to incorporate four-letter words into his vocabulary—to a three-year term as president of the Federal Law Enforcement Officers Association.

MARVIN MACK and BILLY THROWER continue to serve as deputies in Brooklyn.

TONY CROOK left the Marshals Service in 1991 to join the Bureau of Alcohol, Tobacco, and Firearms.

GARNETT LEACOCK has yet to leave Marion.

BUD MCPHERSON retired from the Marshals Service in the fall of 1990. He is president of Donald McPherson and Associates, a security and investigative network in Los Angeles. The thinking man's Philip Marlowe, in the expensive threads and the aviator shades, he is the best-dressed private eye in the business.

JIMMY FRATIANNO continues to serve as the Gloria Swanson of the Witness Security Program. He no longer enjoys the luxury of dealing "only with Bud."

BILL WAGNER left Witness Security in March of 1990, promoted as a supervisor assigned to the District of Colorado.

ALF MCNEIL remains WITSEC chief for Region V, headquartered in the Southern District of New York.

HOWARD SAFIR, failing in an ill-calculated political move to be named Marshals Service director with the 1989 change in presidential administrations, departed the Marshals Service in 1990.

JOHN HAYNES continues as SOG commander.

JOHN TWOMEY, as Deputy Director, admired and respected as the institutional memory of the Service—he has served under all four Marshals Service directors—continues to serve the agency in that capacity.

DUKE SMITH, in October 1990, was named the Marshals Service's number-one cop—he is its Associate Director for Operations. Goin' fishin' is yesterday's news.

FRANK SKROSKI replaced Smith as the Service's Director of Training.

BOB NATZKE, who is credited personally with the survival of deputy marshals in innumerable encounters with deadly force, continues as an instructor at Glynco, one of the few civilians who holds such a position in the Marshals Service.

MIKE THOMPSON, honored for his heroism on that March afternoon in Roanoke, Virginia, received the highest award the Marshals Service bestows, the Robert Forsyth Valor Award, named for the marshal who in 1794 became the first to die in the line of duty. In July 1991 he was invited to share his expertise with the Service's incoming deputies, promoted as an instructor, which carries the rank of inspector, and assigned to the training academy at Glynco.

SHERRY HARRISON, who shared the Forsyth award with Mike Thompson, left the Marshals Service in April 1989 to return to work in local law enforcement.

JOHN BUTLER, in January 1991, was promoted from the El Paso Intelligence Center to Chief of the Air Operations Division of the Marshals Service, headquartered in Oklahoma City. Taking interagency cooperation to what might be considered the limit, he has taken a special agent of the FBI to be his wife.

RALPH BURNSIDE continues as a deputy in Eastern New York. "Young, aggressive, savvy," according to Mike Pizzi, the dedicated Burnside was celebrated for his enthusiasm in the Bicentennial Edition of the Marshals Service magazine, *The Pentacle*, cited for being "highly motivated" when he arrived in Washington, D.C., to participate in a major drug-fugitive sweep, Operation STOP, having brought along from Brooklyn his own battering ram.

MIKE PIZZI, in the fall of 1990, was invited to cross the Brooklyn Bridge, appointed Chief Deputy for the Southern District of New York. Though he loves his new job, he says he misses his Crown Victoria—as Manhattan chief, he is required to drive a seized Mercedes. His retirement from the Marshals Service was scheduled for late 1991.

ROCKY, in December 1990, "just attacked my new couch," Pizzi reported. "When somebody comes to the door and there's no one home, he attacks the nearest thing," Pizzi explained. Shortly before attacking the furniture, Rocky "sent a newspaper boy to the hospital. A Mafia guy's kid . . . I talked to them." By all accounts, Rocky, a.k.a. Doctor Demento, still, more than anything in the world, wants to take that bite out of Vic Oboyski's kielbasa.

BOB LESCHORN, in 1991, was transferred to the Service's Office of Congressional and Public Affairs. The first sworn officer ever to be assigned there, he is charged with coordinating operational activities with that office and with enhancing Marshals

Service visibility within the various news and entertainment media.

ART RODERICK, assigned to headquarters, was promoted in July 1991 to Branch Chief of Domestic Investigations.

CHAD ALLAN is currently Deputy Chief of Training for the Marshals Service.

ALPHONSE "ALLIE BOY" PERSICO, on December 18, 1987, twelve days after his fifty-eighth birthday, in Brooklyn's U.S. District Court, was fined $30,000 and sentenced to twenty-five years in prison on his federal loan-sharking conviction. On Tuesday, September 12, 1989, the sixty-one-year-old Persico died of cancer of the larynx at the medical center for federal prisoners in Springfield, Missouri.

FLIP LORENZONI, replaced by Mike Pizzi as Chief Deputy for Southern New York, in 1990 was dispatched to Philadelphia, appointed by the attorney general to serve as interim U.S. Marshal for the Eastern District of Pennsylvania.

FRANK DEVLIN was promoted in July 1991 to Marshals Service representative to INTERPOL headquarters in Lyons, France.

TONY PEREZ, as field supervisor of Marshals Service personnel in Panama in late 1989 and early 1990, oversaw, among other things, the surrender to the United States of Panamanian general Manuel Noriega. Questions as to whether he is "management material" were officially laid to rest in December 1990 when he was named Chief of the Enforcement Division of the Marshals Service.

LARRY HOMENICK currently serves as EPIC Program Coordinator.

KATO BANKS, a supervisor in the Santa Ana suboffice of the Central District of California, is temporarily assigned as acting Chief Deputy in Los Angeles. And looking good.

GUS, who worked warrants for four years with Tony Perez, died in 1985 in Los Angeles, a year after Perez left for headquarters. On the verge of a new career, he suffered a heart attack during a search and rescue exercise. He was five years old.

JOSÉ LÓPEZ is currently assigned as Marshals Service OCDETF (Organized Crime Drug Enforcement Task Force) representative in Miami.

BILL HUFNAGEL has been promoted to Chief of the Enforcement Division's new Electronic Surveillance Unit at Marshals Service headquarters.

JOHN CUFF, with a merit promotion to Surveillance Technician, is an inspector in the Southern District of New York.

JOHN PASCUCCI was International Branch Chief when, on June 30, 1989, he was arrested by the FBI in Tucson, Arizona. A month later he was indicted by a federal grand jury, along with Kelly Murphy, twenty-eight, a deputy and former girlfriend stationed in Peoria, Illinois, charged with conspiracy and extortion in a plot to blackmail a Kansas businessman with pictures and tapes of a sexual encounter between the businessman and Murphy. Testifying that she had been forced by Pascucci, on twelve separate occasions with a variety of men, to submit to sexual liaisons that Pascucci arranged, watched, and tape-recorded, Murphy was eventually acquitted of the charges against her. The Marshals Service fired her for conduct unbecoming an officer. She has since filed an employment discrimination suit against the attorney general and the director of the Marshals Service. In April 1990, Pascucci, forty-two, was convicted of conspiracy and extortion and sentenced to three years in federal prison.

STANLEY MORRIS, who more than anyone, and quite accurately, is credited with engineering the modern renaissance of the United States Marshals Service—"On the Hill, at DOJ, at the Office of Management and Budget, lobbying for his Service. . . . He is like an octopus with a sword in every hand," Duke Smith once said—was nominated by President George Bush to be Deputy Director (Supply Reduction) of the Office of National Drug Control Policy. His appointment confirmed by the Senate, Morris was assigned to the position in October 1989.

BILLY THE KID was buried in the military cemetery at Fort Sumner, New Mexico, on July 15, 1881.

Author's Note

This book could not have been written without the cooperation of the United States Marshals Service. It *would* not have been written had the Marshals Service not followed through on its agreement to cooperate fully and unconditionally.

After a "limited inquiry" into the author's background by the Service's Office of Internal Security and his satisfaction of a request for fingerprints, the agency opened itself up to complete scrutiny, and not once in the five years following did it attempt to impose any constraints either on the author's investigation or on any of its personnel, whose standing instructions to show him every courtesy were honored for the duration of the project.

Neither did the Marshals Service request, nor did the author grant, agency-approval of the manuscript. The proposition, on both sides, was entered into on the basis of a handshake, and never, from start to finish, did the agency hedge its bet.

Invaluable to the success of the undertaking were the efforts, most significantly of Stephen T. Boyle, the Service's Chief of Congressional and Public Affairs. The initial handshake was with him. The faith he showed at the outset was sustained over several years—his honesty, integrity, his continued support and that of his office are what held the project together.

No less essential to the procedure from the start was the enthusiasm of Marshals Service Director (1983–89) Stanley Morris. It was he who gave the ultimate go-ahead. An uncommonly bold career bureaucrat, he readily unlocked the doors by which the author gained necessary access to the deputy marshals whose story this is.

A successful recapitulation of the two-hundred-year history of the deputy marshal would have been all but unachievable were it not for Marshals Service historian Frederick S. Calhoun, whose recently published book, *The Lawmen*, is the definitive study of the U.S. marshals and their deputies.

Above all, the author is grateful, however, to the deputy marshals themselves, particularly those deputies whose names appear in the body of the book. It was their trust and generosity and that of their colleagues throughout the Service that inevitably enabled the story to be told.

For their support of the project in general, their help in the preparation of the manuscript, or for the research material they provided, the author would like to thank: Bo and Betsy Bryan; Marianne Cacciola; Lorenzo Carcaterra; Bruce C. Fishelman; Sonny Grosso; John Hord; Gael Humphrey; Gregory Katz; John Marshall; Michael Metrinko; Sara Nelson; Joel Parks; Ed Ramey; Dianne Ripley; Kevin Roberts; George Roberts; Anne and Michael Ryan; Kevin Ryan; Bea Sennewald; Jamie Saul; Charles M. Young; and Ira Wood.

For their faith, their perseverance, and for the pure instrumental value of their participation, the author wishes to thank Michael Korda, with whom the idea for the book originated, and Kathy Robbins, whose vision helped bring it to light.

The author wishes to thank his family for their encouragement and personal support and to acknowledge the following two people for their special efforts in his behalf:

Joe Lewis, a source of unconditional friendship and guidance, who was always there when the author found himself ". . . running all over the sea trying to get behind the weather."

And again, and as always, with love, Mary.

New York, 1991

INDEX